Messengers of Healing

Messengers of Healing:

*The Family Constellations of Bert Hellinger
Through the Eyes of a New Generation of Practitioners*

Edited by
J. Edward Lynch
Suzi Tucker

Zeig, Tucker & Theisen, Inc.
Phoenix, Arizona

Messengers of Healing, The Family Constellations of Bert Hellinger Through the Eyes of a New Generation of Practitioners

Edited by J. Edward Lynch and Suzi Tucker

Copyright ©2005 Zeig, Tucker & Thiesen, Inc.

All rights reserved. No part of this publication may be reproduced or transmitted in any form or by any means, electronically or mechanically, including photo copying, recording, or by any information storage or retrieval system, without the prior written permission of the publisher.

ISBN: 0-932462-80-5

Published by
ZEIG, TUCKER & THEISEN, INC.
3614 North 24th Street
Phoenix, Arizona 85016

Cover and chapter illustration by Jack Ryan (www.JackRyanInk.com)
Book design by the The Printed Page (www.theprintedpage.com)

Manufactured in the United States of America
10 9 8 7 6 5 4 3 2 1

Dedication

My dedication is to my wife Barbara Lynch, who has stood beside me in life through deaths, illnesses, and other tragedies — as well as the good times. She is strong, creative, charismatic, and a genius. Everything she puts her hand to becomes more by her touch. Her children, her students, and her friends are gifted by her presence. Her love is boundless and enduring. Her support in my, and our, endeavors is given graciously and with love. Those who have met her remember her well. Raising nine children makes one humble and patient. She is life.

—J.E.L.

To Bart and to Cole, with love.

—S.T.

Acknowledgments

I wish to thank all those who contributed to this book. Their unique approaches have expanded the understanding and the applications of the concepts. They are pioneers in the work, and truly *Messengers of Healing*.

I also wish to acknowledge Wolf Buntig for introducing me to Family Constellations in Montreal, Canada, in what seems like both a long time ago and very recently.

My first constellation by Gabrielle Borkan changed my life dramatically and to her I will be eternally grateful.

To my teachers, Bert Hellinger, Harald Hohnen, Hunter Beaumont, Ursula Franke, Berthold Ulsamer, and Guni Baxa, I give my deep appreciation. To other teachers, who were more my healers, Stephan Hausner, Jakob Schneider, and Albrect Mahr, I bow in respect and honor their gifts.

To my students, who believed and trusted in me when I showed up with this new Family Constellation idea, I say, "thank you." They are: Trish Abad and Paul Rhoda, Beth Bryant, Mike Fontana, Debbie Franklyn, Dan and Mary Gates, Barry and Phyllis Gordon, Anne Johnson, Al Joyell, Bill Mannle, Don and Margaret Opatrny, Don and Chris Paglia, Linda Peterson, Don and Susan Pogue, Norb Spencer, and Barry and Dottie Ten Eyck.

I also want to acknowledge my colleagues at the Family Therapy Clinic at Southern Connecticut State University in New Haven, from, and with, whom I have learned about pain, joy, and love in families.

Finally, it is important to acknowledge my parents with whom I have finally reconnected in love, forgiveness, and pride.

—J.E.L.

This book has roots in many places. I would like to acknowledge just a few: All of the contributors, for their numerous and varied talents. Gabrielle Borkan, Harald Hohnen, Libby Shapiro, and Sophia Leto-Kramer, from the start. Jeffrey Zeig, always. Bert Hellinger, who opened a thousand doors. My uncle, who is in my heart. My brother, Edwin. My father, whom I recall with love. My mother — thank you for everything. I love you.

— S.T.

Appreciation

Some 20 years ago, when I first stumbled on the idea of family constellations, I just thought how interesting it would be to see what comes to light by setting up representatives for the members of a family and placing them in relationship to one another. I was far from understanding the dimensions and the depth to which this experience would lead me and others over the course of time.

When reading the various chapters of this book, I again stood in awe of the breadth and scope of the work. It is clear that the next generation doing family constellations will expand and deepen the work in many surprising ways, whether by connecting family constellations with other proved methods, or by exploring in even greater depth the mysteries of the soul, and of the mental fields in which we are embedded.

I felt in good company here, and as a token of appreciation, I spontaneously offered the editors a short text of my own for inclusion. It is on the spiritual dimensions of this work.

Obviously, family constellations will continue to evolve in a way that will benefit many people, both individuals and groups.

—Bert Hellinger

Contents

Introduction · 1

Part I. Generally Speaking · · · · · · · · · · · · · · · 5

1 The Weight of Words
 Suzi Tucker. 7

2 Insights That Changed My Life: Observations of a Beginner
 Michael Gurevich 22

3 Deep Roots: Musings on the Philosophy of Constellations
 Jane Peterson 40

4 The Role of Energy and Intuition in the Constellation Approach
 Jamy Faust and Peter Faust 58

5 The Stance of the Facilitator
 J. Edward Lynch 83

Part II. Work In Progress · · · · · · · · · · · · · · · 113

6 Begin With the Work: Family Constellations and Larger Systems
 Daniel Booth Cohen 115

7 Some Heretical Thoughts On Organizational Constellations
 Jane Peterson 140

8 A Couple Is More Than Just Two: The Dynamics of Relationships
 J. Edward Lynch and Barbara Lynch 157

9 When Professional Experience Gets Personal: Working One to One
 Daniel P. Gates and Mary M. Gates 182

10 Listening to the Wisdom of the Body
 Dale Schusterman 205

11 Hellinger Meets Shapiro: Constellations and EMDR
 Andrea Stuck 227

12 Hurting for Love: Three Cases of Self-Abuse
   Mark Wolynn 242
13 Spiritual Dimensions of Illness and Health
   Bert Hellinger 269
About the Contributors. 274

Introduction

This book has evolved in a way that has been, for its editors, easy, light, and serious. As students of Bert Hellinger's family constellation work, as facilitators, and as teachers, we wanted to find a way to share some of the contributions being made to its growth right in our own backyards. Almost as soon as the idea was uttered, there was an ensemble of authors to fill it out. We invited people. They all said yes. They made time in their busy schedules to pause and reflect on their particular "particularness" as facilitators, teachers, and students. And then they committed those reflections to paper.

As the editors, we provided general guidelines for the chapters, hoping to find that perfect place between rigidity and chaos so the distinct writing voices might be heard, while, at the same time, the shared understanding of Bert Hellinger's work would come through. Again, each contributor responded with grace and thoughtfulness. What has emerged is a rich and diverse resource for understanding essential aspects of the work itself and for seeing how it might be applied in a variety of environments and circumstances, whether alone or in combination with another paradigm.

Because this work is phenomenological, experiential, and evolving, any book on the topic will offer just a hint of its essence. This is a quality related to the vastness of the work, rather than to any limitations of the books. In this way, our Table of Contents can never be complete. We have selected this group of contributors according to various criteria, and we are proud to be in their company. Each chapter will tell readers something important about both the work and its author. The cumulative effect is like looking into a room through many windows. You can get some idea of the size and shape when you look through one; but when you take the time to peer through all of them, you begin to really grasp its dimensions and possibilities.

Extending the metaphor, one may go to each window in sequence or move back and forth between them. One might begin with Bert Hellinger's "Spiritual Dimensions of Illness and Health" and then return to it again as the last word. Or one might be drawn to Dale Schusterman, who looks at how the work may be used with physical problems, or wish sit with Andy Stuck, as she considers the ways in which constellations and EMDR are compatible. Then again, the reader may turn to Jane Peterson, who tells us about her organizational work, as well as providing a view on the lineage of constellations. Or perhaps Mark Wolynn's discussion of self-abuse will capture your attention, or Michael Gurevich's "Observations of a Beginner," or Jamy and Peter Faust's understanding of the role of energy and intuition. And then there's Barbara Lynch, who writes about working specifically with couples, Dan and Mary Gates, who use the approach with individuals, and Dan Cohen, who explores its use with larger systems. Or maybe you will start with the chapters by the editors simply because it's a place to start. Many windows, many views, one room.

Just as in a constellation, one feels both who is there and who is not, the reader will have this sense either with regard to specific people or to the general topic. Many wonderful practitioners are not included here. Like the work itself, we see this project as evolving. We will look forward to gathering additional voices as time goes on.

Keep in mind too that the Web sites included with the contributors' biographical sketches also contain links to a host of other people teaching and facilitating the work. We leave it to you to discover them for yourselves by investigating their Web sites or picking up the phone to make personal contact. All manner of teaching and learning is available.

To learn more about Bert Hellinger's journey and his current offerings, go to www.hellinger.com, where you will find myriad resources.

Meanwhile, we hope you enjoy reading *Messengers of Healing*. Whether you are a professional or a lay person, you are certain to find someone (or several) who seems to be speaking directly to your area of interest. The title, by the way, alludes to two important themes: the first is that facilitators of the work are conduits rather than initiators of healing. The second is that members of our families, sometimes long dead, are generally willing, even waiting, to step forward to deliver to us essential knowledge from other places in the system. Such knowledge, once revealed, may be key to our gaining courage enough to face what frightens us and enlightens us so that we may turn fully toward life.

Suzi Tucker

Part 1
Generally Speaking

1

The Weight of Words

by Suzi Tucker

When chosen carefully, words linger after a constellation like tiny points of light. They have the power to evoke the deepest feeling, the broadest knowledge, the simplest truths. They may express systemic mantras, reflecting dynamics that took root generations ago that have been passed down like precious heirlooms. They may contain powerful salves to heal family breaches or offer surprising, even shocking, information to wake the sleepiest clients. Yet, even when we know full well the potency of words, it can be a tough assignment not to be careless with them, not to infuse them with ego and reckless narcissism. We, who are endlessly encouraged to speak our minds, may find it difficult to suddenly be cautious.

In family constellations, the role of words, like most other elements, is paradoxical. At once essential and not necessary, they are there for the taking, but it is the facilitator's task to handle them with care, not because they are fragile, because they are not.

When we think about communication, text and subtext, we realize that words can either contain or ignite meaning. In both cases, though, to express in words often takes us away from what is being expressed. If the words contain it well, they reflect the speaker's conscious understanding of what he or she feels, and it is already secondhand. If the words ignite the idea, they touch off an interpretation for the listener that then becomes his or her own. The thing — whatever it is — is stripped of some aspect of its being, whether gently or violently, when we call it by name.

In constellations, the dynamics that come to the surface can be weakened or diverted through verbal expression. Those who have come together in a constellation may be seduced by the wrong words, finding it easier or more pleasant or clearer to follow them. The client, the facilitator, the representatives, the observers — all are susceptible to seduction. After all, it is difficult to tolerate the unhurried gait of unfolding insight, or what Bert Hellinger might call the slow pace of the soul. It is difficult to withstand sadness, illness, or death. It is difficult to remain silent before the fates of others.

Words are in themselves simply tools to help us give shape and form to feelings, events, ideas, or perceptions. They sometimes enable us to craft what we wish for in our child hearts out of what we see and experience as adults; in so doing, they may also hinder the resolutions that truly hold the promise of anchoring a good future. Language can make wishes seem like truth, and allow truth to be obscured with the flick of a tongue. Crowded together, words may offer temporary comfort as white noise against great fear or sorrow. Then again, one word, well placed, may tell us all we really need to know, what lies beneath feelings that seem to ambush us and what might set us free.

Consider this:

L O V E

Drugstore greeting cards try to contain it in verse; but in its tiniest utterance, it contains the universe.

Silence and Sound

As Bert Hellinger has continued in his work, the varied collaborations between client and facilitator often take place in almost total silence. People move — or don't — tears come, embraces happen, smiles spread across the faces of participants, one falls to the floor beside her great grandmother, another reaches toward a young boy he could not have possibly known, a mysterious figure waits patiently. Out of the stuff of collective life, all of our family systems (and beyond them too), there emerges the interstitial reality that cannot be manipulated by narrative. It comes and it shows itself and we know. Words are ancillary, sometimes even detrimental, to this level of movement.

Imagine the fullness of the experience of bowing before the generations that have brought you here. What do words do for that movement? They cannot make it more ... they can only throw a lasso around it to bring it in, make it smaller, with each telling, smaller. And what can a facilitator say as she or he stands witness to this awesome and mundane human expression?

Then when Bert Hellinger asks, "May I leave it here?" he gently closes the curtain. The image remains for a time, maybe for seconds or for years, but the constellation, the part we see, comes to a close. These are careful words. They shift the ultimate responsibility back to the client, allowing Hellinger to turn his attention to the next moment.

Many of us have also seen the work that doesn't take the form of a constellation, at least not the type that manifests in the usual sense. Perhaps Hellinger asks a question or offers a kind of meditation. Two systems, that of the facilitator and that of the client, meet for a moment in a context that is out of normal time and physical location. He engages the attention of the client, but he is really reaching beyond that person and the person is, in turn, responding to a force far larger than one man.

In these instances, especially, the weight of language is clear. He asks, "If you see your life as a ladder, how many rungs do you have left?" Perhaps he answers the client after she has said that she thinks she has many, "No" or "Are you sure?" Perhaps the client says, "Ten," and Hellinger answers "Yes, exactly." Perhaps he extemporaneously begins to speak about a woman's mother or about her addiction. Perhaps he wonders aloud whether a man is ill or dying.

What are these words about? Prognostications from a soothsayer? Bold dramaturgy? Psychotherapeutic challenges? Maybe.

For some of us though, those who have experienced family constellations as clients, as representatives, as engaged observers, or as facilitators, the explanation is different: the words are expressions that arise naturally out of a depth of understanding that is shared among all who are present. Hellinger's clarity and acuity are remarkably pronounced, but everyone has access.

A Small Piece of Work★

> As a woman sits at his side, she hears "Poor lost child." "What do you mean?" she wants to know. "I see the face of a four-year-old child in your face. What happened in your life?" She thinks for a moment, "I can't remember." "Of course, you can't." Hellinger suggests doing a constellation and sets just one person up to start, the representative for the client, who falls to her knees and then to the floor. Hellinger asks the client, "See her anger?" But she shakes her head. He continues, "She never recovered. Because I don't get any information from her, I can't go on." The client offers, "A baby of my grandmother died." Hellinger says, "There's much more. There is a murder." He then allows the representative to sit down and puts the client in. "Do I have permission to go further?" he asks. She doesn't respond, and so he looks to the audience, "It doesn't depend on the client. The system does not allow it. A small step too far is dangerous."

★★★

★Excerpted from the NYC workshop with Bert Hellinger that took place in October 2004.

And the words touch on various levels of understanding. In this example, there is the client's stopping place. The question of what happened when she was four has a literal connotation and an implicit meaning. How does a four-year-old see the world or receive the world? What is missing and what does she yearn for? Who is missing and for whom does she long? For whom does she sacrifice so willingly? Who is affected in her current life? What does she pass on to her children? How can a helpless girl negotiate the world? What would it take for change to occur?

So often we scratch and pick the scabs of life, curious about this and that, acquiring vicarious pleasure or drama or reasons for failure, demanding attention and yet demurring responsibility. If, as in this constellation, the system doesn't give permission for further exploration, what is this "lost child" to do? It is, for her, a question at the very edge of existence.

For the facilitator, for the representatives, and for the client, it takes restraint to not say more than is essential, to not bypass what has emerged from the constellation in order to try to squeeze out something sweet to bring home.

Of course, many times the movement is sweet, and yet it still may be difficult for the mind to stay quiet. Imagine: An old man has carried a grudge against his own father for decades. In the end, he lays his head on his daddy's shoulder, tears in his eyes, heart melted, and never so fully present and strong. How long it has taken to get here.

Can you see it? There is no word that could enhance that image, no writer's pen that might make it something greater.

And yet, Bert Hellinger does speak, and he is often quoted (and misquoted) precisely because he both captures and ignites meaning at the same time. Like the poet, he selects the words that allow us to momentarily grasp indescribable experience. They allude to something we once knew but have lost, something that, if we are lucky, flickers briefly in a constellation.

Being In Tune

The phrase "being in tune" is used often by Hellinger. When I first heard it I thought it a bit corny, but as time goes on, I like it more and more. I think of music and nature and love and God and life. On a practical level, I know the feeling when I am writing. It is fingers flying across the keyboard, thoughts appearing on the page complete, the cursor blinking in time with my heart.

When I sit next to someone, *being in tune* is not as easily described. It is a heightened state of "is ... together." Allowing the breath and the body and the thinking, the story, the experience, the past, the present, the potential, the wish, the life and the death, all to wash over me; that is being in tune with another. Inherent in it is being in tune with the person's system. She is at once very young and very old and just where she is. Behind her, everything. Or he is a boy, a man, a father, a son. Before him, everything.

The thing about being in tune is that it is a seamless state. There is no room for contrivance. The observations that come out of this place are simply that, observations without intention or agenda. As a facilitator, one has the choice to name them or not, and this too comes out of being in tune. From this position one sees, or more accurately, feels what the system can tolerate, and what it will allow.

In New York City in late 2004, Hellinger spoke of three little phrases: Thank you, please, and yes. These words lay at the heart of each of piece of work that was done. Returning to that paradox of essential and not necessary, these words were in the air whether or not they were formed by the lips of the client and whether or not they were understood on a conscious level.

A Little Exercise

I have gone to the mirror and in my face have seen the faces of all who came before. Most immediately, my reflection is a mix of features from my mother and father, all the sorrows and joys imprinted there. I take a moment to slip back to the anger and blaming that I have carried for so many years. It's not hard to do, as these things are still within easy reach. A bitter, fragile woman looks back at me. We are locked in each other's gaze, and I cannot turn away even though I try.

Then, eyes closed, I make an adjustment. As I open them, I allow the words "thank you" to fill me up. It is my mother's straight nose, my father's hazel eyes. Tears come and my shoulders relax. I take a step back as I hear myself say "please." There is love in the word and it hangs in the air without judgment. My chest feels very clear, oxygen beginning to flow. Finally, "yes." Finally.

The woman who looks back now is smiling; her gaze is soft and strong. In its reflection, I am able to turn, I am able.

Being in tune with another requires being in tune with oneself first. And yes, it's just words … until you feel it.

(Re)Frame of Reference

Soul and Conscience

Words have a history. All words do, of course, but a word such as "soul," for example, has been defined and redefined to fit the demands and whimsy of dozens of philosophies across time. It has been stretched and constricted, coveted and sold, used as both weapon and reward. For me such words bring back memories of school chapel and kneeling on hard wood floors. My reference is a kind of religiosity, the nature of which is to separate peoples based on the dictates of one belief system and its supposed superiority over others. The word, therefore, had to be relearned or recast for me to be able to use it. There came a time, however, when nothing else seemed to fit.

But Hellinger speaks of the soul quite often. He has said that the movement of the soul is inclusive. That is the healing movement, one that encompasses what has been lost or denied, and through which we become whole.

As Hellinger conceptualizes it, the distinction between the conscience and the soul is profound, even though most of us grow up learning that these words go hand in hand. We are told: "Follow your conscience" or "Let your conscience be your guide." However, if the purpose of conscience is actually to keep us bound to our group (family of origin, current family, religious community, national identity), then its application becomes confusing early on, a confusion that is especially pronounced as we begin to separate and individuate.

Recall for a moment, perhaps you were in school, and your friends were making fun of a new student. Go back to that time and feel the pull toward the group and the pull away. In your heart, you know that it is hurtful to take part in the behavior and yet you are tempted. After all, you are hesitant to risk membership in this group — a group that is very important at this stage, your "school family." The choice really isn't between being kind and being unkind, but between belonging and being disenfranchised.

Now, this young person in school may decide to stick with the group but feel guilty about the choice. This feeling reflects a conflict between consciences. His or her family, for example, would not be pleased to know about the bullying, and so that membership feels threatened. Often, the peer group is the more central one and at the same time membership has stricter conditions, so it's not hard to see why this group so often wins out, at least in the short term. Extend this example to other groups. Imagine now that the consequences and rewards are greater, and you can envision how extreme actions may be carried out in the name of good conscience.

A good conscience means that we are acting in line with our group. It is a fluid state that changes according to context. Therefore, good conscience has nothing to do with a globally accepted notion of good or bad, an ideal for which we are all striving, or with some definition handed down by a deity, whether in stone, through dreams, or in the voice of a chosen one. If I behave according to the rules and regulations of my group and you to yours, who is to say who is right or wrong? We are both right when considered within the parameters of our peers. We will both feel guilty, perhaps overwhelmingly so, if we stray from the doctrine of that community. The good conscience hasn't room for everyone. It depends on choosing one over another, discriminating between those who belong and those who do not. To open the circle is to allow conscience to dissolve.

The soul, on the other hand, has room for everyone. Membership is not predicated on any special quality or attribute, whether moral, aesthetic, or intellectual. This is a club without "dues" (or don'ts). When we look at our own lives, we can immediately see how complex this adjustment can be. It is a frightening proposition to interrupt a pattern, even if that pattern has been uncomfortable. Such a change may throw into question our sense of safety and even of self. After all, even when our situation is very difficult, at least it is familiar, dependable in a way, and there is consolation in that.

To accept all who came before, including the murderers, the thieves, the traitors, and malingerers, may mean that we break from our group (bad conscience) by revealing what has been secret, acknowledging what has been denied, or loving what has been hated. It takes courage to be guilty in this way. What if we too are disavowed?

But if we can manage to open our hearts to those who were left behind, we actually join with a larger community and at the same time allow that larger community to enter us. When one fights his or her past, yells and screams about the unfairness of it all, that person is gypped out of a portion of his or her own identity. One sees it time and again in constellations: the tough-minded woman, who is brittle as a twig in her anger and despair. Once she is finally able to stand in her place as a child to the mother, a small figure in the midst of the generations, she gains in stature. Then there is the man who has learned to control every facet of his life, or so he thinks. He knows it all and yet every muscle in his body is taut, and there is little room for joy. But when he opens his arms wide to the fates of his ancestors, summoning their strength and bowing to their history, when he becomes one of many, in that moment, he becomes whole.

In this new dictionary, "conscience" and "soul" might be understood as lenses on life, the first being telephoto, the latter wide-angled. We hold onto conscience at the expense of soul. When we embrace soul, we encompass the entire landscape.

Guilt and Innocence

Most of us shape our definitions of guilt and innocence out of the signals received in childhood. We understand that we should feel bad when we are guilty of something and that we should feel good when we are innocent. Guilty: bad. Innocent: good. Further, we generally gauge our guilt and innocence by the acceptance or disappointment of those around us. We learn at a young age — at the youngest, most tender age — to anticipate these reactions based on past reactions and on the overt or covert messages sent by those on whom we depend.

As we head, fast or slow, toward adulthood, these definitions tend to stay with us whether or not they continue to serve their original purposes, and whether or not they still even make sense. For example, imagine a person who understood early on that to express an opinion different from that of her mother was to ask for the cold shoulder (or worse). So, rather than do something that appeared to jeopardize this central relationship, something that might cause her mother to withdraw from her, she immediately learned to keep her ideas to herself and then eventually perhaps to stop forming opinions altogether. Later, this imprinted habit of reserving comment may not have the payoff it had when she was a child, stalling the rejection of the mother, but the pattern is set and she remains enmeshed, no matter the cost.

Now, when we consider the possible reasons behind this woman's ambivalence, we might arrive at a familiar signpost: the one that says "Mother." Stopping in front of it, we will think about how best to help this woman. Should we encourage her to confront or perhaps forgive the mother of the past? Remember, in family constellations, the wide-angled lens is applied; it has no judgment, no agenda, and no preferences. Therefore, neither confrontation nor forgiveness is called upon. Instead, we might simply ask: What will give the daughter strength? The answer can be felt. Thus, even if we arrive at the same signpost, "Mother," the constellation facilitator is not likely to be able to predict what the next step will be — until after it is taken.

Here, the constellation may reveal a child who is loyal to the father who cannot speak up for himself. We might understand the mother as someone who, as a little girl, stepped into her own mother's position to take care of the family when her mom could not. A child who has become an adult in this family, perhaps identifying with the father, must experience what it feels like to stand before her parents as a daughter again, leaving their couple contract to them and accepting the love and strength from them as parents in whatever percentage it is given. After all, it is through them that she has access to the mothers and fathers of all the previous generations. Once she steps into her own place, she can drop whatever anger she may quietly harbor — at her mother for being controlling; at her father for being passive — and gather in all that she needs to move forward.

On the other hand, the constellation may reveal an altogether different and, until this point, untold story. Perhaps several generations back, there was a child of war who had survived an attack on her village by remaining silent and hidden behind the shed. Perhaps making a sound would have killed her. Perhaps the current family member says to her, "I will not speak either; I will remain with you, silently alive."

In both cases, the constellations tell us something beyond what we might conclude through conversation, and in both scenarios guilt and innocence are clearly bound to loyalty. This person will feel guilty if she breaks with the family code by speaking up, by asserting identity. She feels innocent when she doesn't express herself. The cost is high though, and it requires a certain willingness to become guilty, to risk innocence, to become free.

Part of what the constellation allows us to see is that when we take this risk, it isn't only about us. In looking into the mother's eyes and saying, "I love you," in accepting her fully, the child is no longer tethered to the specific behavior; with her gaze looking back, she is now able to turn toward life. In so doing, she makes possible a future that is freer for herself, and beyond that for her children and theirs. She also helps the system to move toward better balance. And her mother, having always loved her daughter, even if her mothering is complicated by other things, is relieved to give her blessing as her daughter says "Yes" to life.

In this light, guilt and innocence are almost opposite of what comes to mind when the words are spoken in other contexts. How different it is to understand innocence as being the servant of conscience and guilt as being in the service of the soul. Put another way, we can see that innocence is small, allowing one to stay connected in a specific way. Preserving one's innocence as an adult requires a great deal of effort; for a dependent child the task is worthwhile.

Guilt is big. Growing up, forming adult ties, loving others outside the group, having opinions that differ — this is all a part of guilt. Hellinger once said that to become an adult, one must go through the door of guilt. Implicit is that the door remains open.

Family Constellations

Many people tell of how they were moved to find out more about this work for reasons they cannot name, that something they read or that someone said touched their hearts in such a way that they felt compelled to find out why. For me, it was what seemed a deep practicality and wide-open accessibility that drew me to it.

When, several years ago, I had the great privilege of working with Hunter Beaumont and Bert Hellinger on *Love's Hidden Symmetry* (1998), Hunter patiently tutored me so that I might begin to grasp at least some of the meaning behind the words. It was a slow process as I was quite attached to a particular concept of the world and to what I considered my place in it.

Also, as an editor in the behavioral sciences for many years, I had read thousands upon thousands of words about helping and healing, and I was perhaps a bit too "well read." After all, there was something important about most of the approaches, always a technique that was clever or a perspective that seemed insightful or a teacher who was especially clear or charismatic. But then *Love's Hidden Symmetry* was published in 1998, and some time after, I had occasion to attend one of Bert Hellinger's workshops. Only then did I realize exactly how much I still didn't know.

Time went on, and I worked on other books and attended other workshops. I also met Harald Hohnen, who had a gift for clarifying and demonstrating concepts. I began to feel a shift in my own thinking—and, yikes, feeling—as the experience of the work piled up on itself and demanded attention. I could see in the eyes of the workshop participants a kind of glimmer of revelation, something that might grow into more in the days and weeks to come. I began to see as well that the work could transcend the messenger so that it held its ground even when the situation was not optimum.

And I began to sense that my mind was beginning to find my heart to be good company, no longer mutually exclusive, no longer subscribing to different processes and following different guides.

Over the years, I have written about the work too. Always there is the search for the right words, the words that carry but don't interpret, that are concise but still leave room for the reader.

The same is true within family constellations. The words used by the facilitator are meant to convey rather than to analyze, to be succinct and yet resonate, to open the heart more than soothe the mind. The words come up through the work, rather than being superimposed on it. The facilitator listens with all senses to the overarching messages from the system, attempting to contain momentarily the fluid place where soul and conscience cross paths, sometimes over and over.

The representatives, too, are messengers from the system. When they are firmly grounded in the constellation, their information may be invaluable. Their communication may be in the form of spoken language or of physical gestures, some sweeping, others subtle, information pushing up through the system to this moment in time. The facilitator will attempt to guide everyone through the constellation, picking up from all available sources and allowing the essential to rise to the top. What is spoken and what is left to other forms of communication is discerned judiciously and intuitively. A constellation, no matter how slowly it unfolds, is a relatively fast process. Once the seed is planted though, it takes its time to grow. If we do not over-water or under-care, it has a better chance. If we step back with love, we demonstrate our respect for the integrity of every client, every system, every fate, every path ... as it is, without judgment or fear or desire.

LOVE

Anyone who is familiar with the literature related to Bert Hellinger's work knows that the word "love" is part of many of the book and videotape titles: *Touching Love, Vols. 1 and 2; Love's Hidden Symmetry; Supporting Love; Love's Own Truths; Holding Love; Healing Love; Blind Love; Enlightened Love; Love at Second Sight*. It is ubiquitous in the literature, as it is in life. The word "love," so well-worn and so often abused, is both the sanctuary of all that lives, as well as the force that is life ongoing.

Love is what unites. You can feel it in any workshop — the room full of strangers is divided on everything that is a matter of choice, but joined in love whether or not it is spoken. We arrive on its heels, each of us seeking in our own way to recall its warmth, and we leave in its care. It is the full and unadulterated truth of our shared vocabulary. The family constellations do not conjure up love; they allow it to be heard no matter who or what has been invested in silencing it; they invite it to be seen no matter how long it has been hidden; they account for it even when the world forbids it; and they remember what the heart sometimes cannot.

References

Hellinger, B. (2001). *Love's Own Truths: Bonding and Balancing in Close Relationships.* Phoenix, AZ: Zeig, Tucker & Theisen.

Hellinger, B. (2003). *Love at Second Sight: Workshop on Couples' Relationships.* Bethesda, MD: Hellinger Institute of DC. [videotape]

Hellinger, B., & Beaumont, H. (1999). *Touching Love, Vols. 1 and 2.* Heidelberg: Carl Auer.

Hellinger, B., & Beaumont, H. (1999). *Blind Love: Enlightened Love.* Phoenix, AZ: Zeig, Tucker & Theisen. [videotape]

Hellinger, B., & Beaumont, H. (2000). *Healing Love: A Teaching Seminar on Love's Hidden Symmetry.* Phoenix, AZ: Zeig, Tucker & Theisen. [videotape]

Hellinger, B., & Beaumont, H. (2000). *Holding Love: A Teaching Seminar on Love's Hidden Symmetry.* Phoenix, AZ: Zeig, Tucker & Theisen. [videotape}

Hellinger, B., Weber, G., & Beaumont, H. (1998). *Love's Hidden Symmetry: What Makes Love Work in Relationships.* Phoenix, AZ: Zeig, Tucker & Theisen.

Neuhauser, J. (Ed.)(2001). *Supporting Love: Bert Hellinger's Work with Couples.* Phoenix, AZ: Zeig, Tucker & Theisen.

2

Insights That Changed My Life: Observations of a Beginner

by Michael Gurevich

Introduction

Three years ago, I wandered into a workshop at the Omega Institute where Dr. Dietrich Klinghardt was discussing Bert Hellinger's work with family constellations. After participating in the workshop, I was convinced: this was something amazing, something I wanted to know more about, to learn to do for myself, and to incorporate into my practice. Now, I have finished the Bert Hellinger Institute USA training, quit doing toxic work on a psychiatric unit, learned Applied Psycho-neurobiology (APN), studied Christine Shenk's intuitive healing and transformed my practice from a holistically oriented one to one that is a completely holistic psychiatry.

Facilitator Harald Hohnen told us after the second weekend of class: "And now go and make all the mistakes you can make." And so I did. A colleague and I began hosting group workshops. However, it was from constellation work one-on-one with my patients, particularly APN, that I learned the most.

The innovative field of family constellations is still in its infancy but is rapidly progressing. We do not even know in which category this method belongs. Should it be considered psychology or psychiatry, spirituality or shamanism? What are the legal requirements for practicing this method in the United States? Do we need to be licensed in a particular field or is it open to anyone? So many questions still remain. Most of us who practice constellation work here are beginners. *Messengers of Healing* will provide an opportunity to benefit from each other's experiences and to further develop our own approaches.

In this work I am truly a beginner. So in this article I would like to share the thoughts, observations, and "discoveries" that helped me to grow and that I have integrated into my work, becoming a better healer in the process.

Adapting the Hellinger Work to My Practice

In class, it was suggested that we use Hellinger's technique primarily in a group setting, as this was thought to be the best and most effective way to do it. However, in my practice, I found this very difficult to implement. Few in my locality know what Hellinger's Systemic Family Constellations are. Explaining took a great deal of effort, and, even though I would try my best, I could not convince many to try the method. In an effort to advertise my workshops, I sent mailings to patients and colleagues but few responded. It was a very frustrating time and I struggled to put seminars together. Actually, after the initial three, I ceased holding seminars for approximately six months. From what I have heard, this is a common experience. Constellation work has established roots in the United States, but the tree is still very feeble.

Is practicing this approach in groups really the best way to start? Indeed, it is extremely dramatic and effective in a group setting. We have all seen it. Masters have performed it with ease, but still issues remain. For example, there is no follow up after a group session and nobody has any idea of how effective the work actually was. Certainly, one constellation cannot solve all of the problems.

On the other hand, doing constellation work in my office with individuals has been fairly easy to adapt into my practice. For me, it was a continuation of the guided imagery approach I had been using. Seeing these patients in an office on a continuing basis allows me to focus on their problems, resolving them, and then evaluating the effectiveness of every intervention. It allows for the overcoming of the fear of practicing constellation work. It teaches us to become more sensitive to energies and prepares us for group workshops. It is much easier to get a single patient to agree to participate than to get 10 or 20 to agree.

A Case Study

Leo, a 50-year-old former businessman, has been on disability for over 10 years. He suffered from chronic pain and was taking large amounts of medication to control the pain and depression. Still, he had no relief, gained weight, and felt confused, resentful, and angry. He was a homosexual who was still in the closet, although he was married with children. Most of his anger was directed at his father. Using chairs as representatives, we worked on healing the relationship between them. There was significant relief after he spent several minutes bowing deeply to his father, who had been dead for several years. I gave him the assignment to write a letter to his father, and this posed a challenge for Leo. It took him two weeks to come in for his next appointment.

His relationship with his mother was more challenging. Leo hated her and perceived her as demanding and manipulative. Once again, chairs were used as representatives. But when it was time to kneel on the floor in front of her, Leo found it difficult to comply. A week after this appointment, he left me a message to the effect that my method was not for him and that he would be looking for another psychiatrist.

It was a disappointment. After four visits, the improvements were obvious. He had started to lose weight, cut the dosages of most of his medications in half, and had even begun to meditate and exercise. He was also contemplating returning to work.

How Much Can One Swallow at One Time?

People differ in their ability to assimilate healing. Thus, the amount of healing given to them has to be proportional to what they can "digest at one time." If the intervention is too aggressive, the patient may end treatment or become angry with the therapist. I am not a proponent of strong purgatives. Having Leo kneel in front of his mother probably was asking too much of him at this point.

Then, three months later, he called me again. He had not seen another psychiatrist. When he returned, I learned that he had stopped taking two of the three medications he was on. He had lost over 50 pounds, was walking straight, quite energetically, and looked much better. But he had again become depressed. This time, I decided to use the constellation method under the guidance of APN work. We began by resolving the toxic memories of his scars, which reminded him of the resentment he felt for his surgeon. He was able to see that the surgeon also was limited as to what he was able to do.

The gall bladder was one of Leo's affected organs. It holds much energy and houses the emotion of resentment. We began to resolve his resentment, layer by layer. The most important layer had been his parents' pressure for him to get married. Homosexuality was not accepted in his nuclear family. There was also resentment toward his wife, who preferred him to be sick, maintaining the pretense of being a "normal family." By our seventh meeting, we had resolved these issues. During treatment, he was able to say to his parents and wife what he had been holding in for almost 25 years. It was powerful and dramatic.

When he came in for his next appointment, he looked very happy. He was able to tell his wife the truth, and discovered that it was something she already knew but pretended not to notice. He decided to work in Manhattan, move out of his house, and begin a new life.

Leo is an example of a man with acute feelings of anger and resentment, but who, at the same time, is very soft and fragile. Even though he often acted in an angry and frustrating way, it usually was directed towards superficial issues. The anger was coming from a deep hidden source of sadness covered by resentment. To touch those issues was a taboo for him. It was particularly difficult because his mother was still alive and a daily source of his anger.

But his loyalty to her was deeper than his resentment. Unable to face these two sides of his feelings squarely, it was easier for him to stop the treatment. He required time to process and assimilate the energy of the information he had gathered.

Another way to watch for how much a client can "swallow" is by providing words to say. After each phrase, it is very important to pause and wait for a reaction. There are signs if the intervention is working. Only if it was effective is there a sense of going on to the next step. It is as if there is a wave that has its own rhythm, vibration, and speed. This wave is what determines the pace of healing. At times, waves take seconds; at other times, they take months.

The Simplest and Most Reliable Intervention

What is the magic of the treatment? It is simple. Ask a patient to look at a representative and ask how he or she feels and would want to say. Then ask the patient to repeat this and say in his own words what he has just said. It is, indeed, simple, but also very effective. Usually, there is a "movement." Ask a patient to observe what I happening. It is fascinating how, after the most hurtful words, resolution suddenly emerges. Some of my patients describe dramatic movie images that are being acted out in their imagination. Remember that the mind has a self-healing mechanism. All that we do as therapists is to stimulate this mechanism. Then the soul knows what to do and can continue. This is the homeopathy of the constellation work.

Homeopathy of Constellations

It was Stephan Hausner who introduced us to how the principles of homeopathy can be applied to constellation work. Another principle of homeopathic treatment is to follow the resolution of a disease: from the inside-out and from the top-down. I frequently ask clients to focus on sensations in their bodies and to follow their movements. I then look to see if a sensation is moving from the inside-out and from the top-down. As a problem moves to resolution, a client frequently notices that initially there is a concentration of sensations in the neck and upper body which then moves to a lower part of the body, and finally culminates in an intense sensation in the toes.

To deepen a resolution, I ask clients to direct their breath down to their bodies, through their feet, to their toes, and outside. You can follow the resolution of a problem by following where the client feels his or her energy. Initially, it may be disorganized, then it may be in the head, then in the upper part of the body, then down, until there are sensations in the toes.

How to Know If the Intervention Is Actually Working

There are several rules I can follow for ascertaining whether an intervention or the word just said was really helpful to the patient.

First I need to get in touch with myself before saying anything. I have to empty my own thoughts and concerns to remove my own ego obstacles. It is like emptying a cup filled with old tea, thus making it available to receive a new one.

I then have to enter the field of energy created by the client and the representative. From this field comes a stream of thoughts and images. There is the feeling that these are not my own and were not in my consciousness before. I am in full control, while being a vessel for the healing of the client. The action plan becomes developed instantly. It is an amalgamation of all of my experience in the constellation work, combined with those thoughts and images that entered my mind just a second ago. I am still in full control. I know what to say and how to say it.

The next step is to observe the reaction of the client and/or representative.

The reaction that touches the soul has distinct characteristics. It may be a client's voice change, a deep breath, a sound, a change in the patient's expression, tears, or strong physical sensations. It is as if some sort of energy begins to flow, releasing stagnant emotions. Wait for this change to appear before making the next move. Something changes inside the client. He or she is not the same person. It may or may not be going in the direction you are looking for. The flow may be sudden, but is usually very slow. Just remind the client: "breathe through your mouth."

If a client repeats your sentence automatically, it may not have reached his or her soul. Ask the client to repeat the sentence several times.

Look for gestures and hand movements. If a client touches a part of his or her body, ask the client to keep his or her hands on that part. It provides energetic resonance, making an intervention more powerful. Stephan Hausner does this all the time. In a one-to-one situation, I often ask the patient to put his or her hands on his or her heart, getting in touch with a heartbeat, deepening the patient's connection to him/herself.

If the reaction is powerful, I wait until it subsides before going on to the next step. For some clients this reaction can be very, very slow. Patience is a key to movement.

Postmortem

It is always gratifying to resolve an enormously complicated issue that nobody could solve before you tackled it. However, what really taught me the most were those cases where I failed to meet my expectations or the patients stopped treatment. In medicine, if a patient dies, we do an autopsy, postmortem, so that we have the chance to learn from the dead. I do postmortems on therapy cases where I failed. A lot of future satisfactory resolutions and improvements come from my failures. However, there is always a fight with my ego and a need to discipline myself. The mind always wants to forget about failures. It is much easier to blame failures on "noncompliant patients" than it is to consider what I could have done better. At times, doing a constellation with your own resistance or with a patient with whom you failed, or writing the case up, or even analyzing it, is very helpful. The worst thing to do is just to forget and move on, pretending that the failure did not happen.

Reasons Why an Intervention Can Fail

1. The healing sentence was too long and complicated. Break it into smaller parts, perhaps just one to three words. It is easier to "swallow" in small pieces.

Insights That Changed My Life: Observations of a Beginner 29

2. You did not mirror the patient's own language and vocabulary. So, in his or her deep emotional state, the patient could not translate what you just said into his or her own soul's language. Change the sentence to match the client's language. It will resonate better.

3. As you say a healing sentence, connect to your own deep source of emotions; from there, you can reflect where the client is at present and connect to his or her energy and vibration.

4. In a case where English is a second language, ask the client to translate the sentence into his or her native tongue.

5. Your intervention was off. It happens all the time. Consider whether you really are connected to the client, or are in your own head, talking about your own issues.

6. The client is much too anxious or preoccupied. No matter how wonderful a job you will do that day, it will be in vain. Before you go any further, help the client to become centered in him/herself. Simple advice, such as to pay attention to his or her breath, to put his or her hands the heart to notice the heartbeat, or to be aware of the sensations in his or her feet, will do wonders.

7. There are people who are poorly connected to their bodies and their own feelings. They live in their own heads. This is an energy that is out of balance. They require more work and patience. I would postpone doing constellation work with them until they notice that they have emotions.

8. Too much talking: too many words diffuse the energy. We all know it from constellations groups. The same issue arises when working one-on-one. Constellation work is not psychotherapy. Too many words distract a client's energy, and, of course, your ability to feel the key issue.

We do not have the microphone that Hellinger always holds and controls so well. But we still have the control to stop a logorrhea (verbal diarrhea).

9. People who are paranoid or argumentative will spoil all of your efforts. Deal with this defensiveness first.

10. People who were adopted are a challenge. Be careful to go very slowly with them. Most have difficulty connecting to their emotions and knowing how they feel. The have blunted emotions. It is much easier for them to act than to feel. One of the factors involved is that in their emotional development, they were not taught how to recognize and name emotions. They need to learn this, but it takes time. Another factor is that a tree whose roots were cut has difficulty putting up new roots. The stress of getting disconnected with parents is one of the most severe stresses in life, no matter how good the adoptive parents are.

11. You are trying too hard or a trying to impress the patient with how great you are.

The Desire to Impress Leads to Failure

In this work, to stay detached from the success or failure of an intervention is critical. I have clearly noticed that the more I try to impress and succeed, the more likely it is that I will fail.

Suppose that while practicing meditation, you were able to achieve a wonderful state of trance; everything is flowing, you can see yourself as truly a part of the universe. Then your mind begins to demand: "I want to stay in this bliss longer." You shift your attention from your breath to the desire to be in the bliss. As soon as you do this, the state of trance is lost. What happened is that your attention no longer was on your breath, or a particular object that brought you into the state of trance, but was now shifted to the need to hold onto it.

If you do constellation work and your goal becomes one of trying to impress somebody, for whatever reason, you are no longer at the service of the forces that can help you to resolve the mystery of the constellation, but are preoccupied with your ego's looking for gratification. Serving your goal takes away the energy and focus needed for the constellation work. Your powerful army is split in two. The efforts to succeed in the constellation are split, making your own ego your biggest obstacle.

I have lost quite a few cases to my ego. Now, whenever it starts to inflate, I know the sign. Then, before proceeding with the constellation, I need to have a talk with myself and to put my ego on notice: "if you continue to inflate, we are going to fail." Usually, paying attention to forces that begin to disrupt is enough to stop the process.

Getting Help in Solving Your Own Problems

Constellation work can be used to solve your own day-to-day problems. All that you need is a couple of chairs and an imagination. I once earned $3,000 by doing a constellation for my own situation.

I rent an office from an interesting landlord. He evidently believes that the building should run by itself, so he does not need to put a penny into its maintenance. A year ago, a building elevator was out of service, a serious issue when you have patients who are not able to climb stairs. I called on the landlord to tell him about the elevator, but nothing changed. After two months I sent him a letter to the effect that I would stop paying rent until the elevator was fixed. That prompted some action, and in another month, the elevator was finally running. By that time, I had withheld over $9,000 in rent. The landlord requested me to send him the money. But I told him that he should compensate me for those months when the elevator was not working. We had a heated exchange. He offered me $1,000, and I told him it was insufficient. He did not speak with me for several months. But then it was time to resolve the conflict.

A few months later, I was still quite upset and knew that if I spoke to him out of anger, nothing good would come of it. So I decided to use my favorite chairs. I set up one for myself and one for my landlord. Initially, there was a lot of anger. I was moving back and forth between the chairs. But gradually we began to resolve the issue. I offered him the solution of paying me $1,000 for every month that the elevator was out of order, or a total of $3,000, and he accepted my proposal. When I called him, I was astonished at how easy it was. After initial threats and my counter-accusations, he asked me what I would consider a fair price.

I gave him my $3,000 and he accepted it. He, then, immediately shared with me that he had had a heart attack two years earlier and decided not to fight as he used to. I gave a bow of respect to my chairs.

Since then, I have used my favorite chairs for every conflict I had difficulty resolving or for something that was stuck in my mind and regurgitated over and over without resolution. So far, the advice I got from the chair has been the best I ever got from anybody. It has become easier to deal with conflicts.

Talking Chairs

My favorite form of doing one-on-one constellations is to use my office chairs. I have sheets of paper with signs: father, mother, wife, etc. When the issue arises I line up the chairs, put the names of the representatives on them, take the patient behind the chairs, briefly explain the rules of the constellation, and we go on.

The usual rules of constellations apply in one-on-one work. The patient is being moved from one chair to another, feeling the energy of each representative. Profound resolutions can be achieved. Of course, there are limitations, particularly when there is a need to get information from those whom the patient did not know personally or no longer is in touch. But most of the situations that involve issues on the same generation level, or one or two generations before or after, can be resolved. It is astonishing how much energy and information becomes available as soon as chairs are placed. Their direction matters as much as does the direction of the representatives. While preparing to be a group leader, you can get excellent training in feeling the energy of representatives, in using healing words, and in achieving resolutions using constellations with chairs.

Constellations and Chronic Pain

A large part of my practice is devoted to working with chronic medical conditions and pain. The work can be very gratifying, but also very challenging.

Most of the time, I do the treatment in the office with only the patient present. Depending on the situation, I use one of several methods. I start with imagery, helping the patient to get in touch with the pain. Pain is a sensation that has many characteristics: shape, size, form, temperature, weight, texture, taste, smell, vibration, spin, and so on. Slowly calling the patient's attention to these characteristics, allowing him or her to see the pain more like something that is changing and moving, rather than as just being there in a rigid position, that alone is often a discovery. The next stage of this process is to show that pain has its own intelligence and has a purpose. I ask the patient to give the pain a name, and then to begin to imagine it as a living being with whom one can communicate and ask questions, such as, "What are you doing in my body?" "What do you have to say?" "What is your message?" The patient is also asked to tell the pain how he or she feels about it.

I give the representative of pain a chair across from the patient. To make pain into a living being, it is important to give it a name that makes it seem real. The patient can look at it, express his or her feelings, and engage it in conversation. Usually, an initial reaction of the patient is anger toward the pain: "Go away," "I hate you," "You are controlling my life." "You are ruining my relationships." "Get lost." The patient has to say this and feel frustration and helplessness for the pain. I would ask the patient to keep his or her eyes closed and would move the patient slowly to a chair where the pain is in position. He or she can then begin to get in touch with how it feels to be the pain. I would provide words to say to him/herself from the pain. Then I take the patient back to his or her seat, let him or her feel what the pain just said, and get back to talking with the pain from his or her point of view. There is a need to do this several times. The pain usually has a very deep and profound message to give the patient, which he needs to hear. Finally, I would ask the patient to ask the pain: "Do you have a message for me? What is it that you are trying to say? I could not hear you." At resolution, a patient usually will thank the pain for the message. He or she begins to see how it can be useful. The level of pain usually begins to change.

You can advance this method and ask the patient: "Who stands behind the pain?" There is usually a person with whom he or she has a significant conflict. It is often the patient's consciousness that feels a need to punish the patient for something that happened in his or her life with that person.

Or you can have a constellation in which there are three representatives: one for the patient, one for the pain, and one for somebody important in his or her life. Very interesting things occur in this type of constellation. Usually, it is not only that there is one important person, but two of them, behind the pain. The interaction and conflict resolution among the three are very helpful.

Working with a Chronic Illness and Getting Free Supervision

Stephan Hausner proposed using the representative of illnesses or symptoms as a "free supervisor." It is done in a group setting. A representative is chosen for an illness and is allowed to move as he or she pleases. The representative is not directly involved. However, as the constellation progresses, he or she will actually show how well we are doing, or how accurate we are. Usually, in the beginning of the constellation, the illness stands very close to the patient, holding and supporting him or her. But if a resolution of a family constellation develops, the illness becomes less interested in a patient and moves out. This becomes a sure sign that we are doing something right: the "supervisor" is telling you how well you have done.

Applied Psychoneuroimmunology (APN)

A unique healing method has been developed by a German-educated physician, Dietrich Klinghardt, M.D. One of Hellinger's students, he has been actively participating in introducing the constellation method in the United Stated. He has developed APN over the last 15-20 years, an amalgamation of several treatment methods and principles: acupuncture, color therapy, the chakra system, eye movements, homeopathy, spirituality, holistic medicine, the use of herbs and supplements, the role of toxins, psychology, family constellation, and kinesiology. In this method, there is a minimal use of equipment or tools. The most important is a healer/client interaction. But the results far exceed anything available in psychiatry, psychology, or pain management.

Dietrich has an amazing ability to process very complex information from all over the world, from both traditional and unconventional medicine. He is an inventor and an incredibly good healer and teacher. Students and patients are coming to see him from all over, and he has a large following in the United States and Europe. I have been using APN for about a year, and have many examples of success with my patients, thanks to APN.

What Are These "Movements of the Soul" and How Do Constellations Work?

I have been asking myself this question since I began doing this work. In medicine, if you cannot explain the mechanism of a disease and its treatment, it cannot work. So, does that mean that if we cannot explain how family constellations work, we should not practice it? To answer this question, I have developed a hypothesis of what happens. The deeper I go into this theory, the more horizons and questions it opens. It has become quite convoluted and complex. So, let me give you a very short version of it.

1. **The principle of a holographic image:** We are all holographic images of something else, something much bigger than we are, and there are holographic images reflecting us. The nature of a hologram is such that it

presents an image that cannot be divided into pieces. If you cut a hologram in half, each half will still hold a whole picture. You can continue to cut a hologram into smaller pieces, but every one on them will contain the full original picture, only with fewer details. The principle of a hologram can be applied to many things. For example, we reflect the whole universe, the whole earth, the whole nation in which we live, the organizations to which we belong, families we came from, and so on. In acupuncture, this principle is utilized quite often; every part of the body reflects the whole body. Detailed charts of the ear, reflecting the whole body, are used in auricular acupuncture; maps of the eye's iris are used in iridology, and the same principle can be invoked in constellation work. Not only does Hellinger apply it to family issues, but he also has been using constellations to reflect nations. We use constellations to reflect organizations, and even organs that are affected by an illness. There are many applications of constellation work because we reflect, and are part of, many things in the universe. Our organs, pains, and illnesses can represent something bigger in our families as well. So, by resolving issues with someone in our family, we have the potential to resolve the pain in our back, or even a cancer.

2. **In constellations, clients and representatives function as receivers and transmitters of information:** Everything around us is energy that carries information. When a patient presents an "issue," he or she becomes a transmitter of information through his or her energy. Members of a group focus on the information, and become receivers and transmitters. To acquire it, they really need to focus. Those who are chosen to be representatives have to become particularly focused on the wave the client transmits. They become a part of the holographic picture. Their function becomes that of balancing the

energy, bringing the holographic picture of the family to an original order. At the time of the constellation, they carry the energy of an original holographic picture of the family. They not only receive signals, but also transmit them. However, as the signals they transmit are very low in power, they cannot go far, and are able to reach just one of the family representatives: the patient. He or she frequently needs to be in very close proximity in order to actually receive the signal. However, the client can then transmit the energy of a repaired family constellation to other family members, who are part of the holographic picture. The direction in which the transmitter/receiver sends signals is very important. That is how the constellation energy can change as we change the direction in which representatives are looking or are positioned.

3. **Movements of energy:** Energy always moves around. Using the power of our thoughts, we can redirect it and change it. All of the energy moves in waves. These waves can be perceived in different ways: heart waves via an electrocardiogram; brain waves by an electroencephalogram. In the body, energy moves through many channels, including the acupuncture meridian, very slowly, just a few inches per minute. We can feel these movements as sensations of heat or as tingling. During constellation work, we also create movements of energy. It also moves very, very slowly. It is visible through authentic movements of representatives and through their emotions, as well as through the emotions and movements of a client. Therefore, every time we employ an intervention, it is important to pause and observe what has moved and how things have changed. On the other hand, if there is a change in the constellation of the family, it can be transmitted almost instantaneously over great distances. Anecdotes abound about how healing takes place for

family members who are on the other side of the world. I know of one such incident from one of my constellations.

4. **Love:** This is the most difficult movement to understand, and also to define. Billions of opinions exist. No matter what one says, one will be wrong. Let me take a shot. Love is an energy that is transmitted by God, whoever He or She is. It is a type of vibration that creates healing and procreation. Love is transmitted on different frequencies. When we connect to those frequencies, miracles happen. Group leaders who are able to connect in this way enjoy positive results. During constellations, we are trying to open the patient or family to those frequencies. When we are able to do so, healing begins to happen.

5. **Every system has a natural tendency toward self-healing:** This is a common principle for many living systems, and one that is utilized in most holistic treatments, naturopathy, homeopathy, and acupuncture. Family is a kind of a system that functions like a living organism. It also has a tendency to self heal. Hence, a group leader has to point out the path to self-healing. His or her skill lies in opening a door for the process and pushing, and then the body or family can find its own way to heal.

6. **Constellations are timeless:** Relationships between family members have no time limit. Children remain the children of their parents. Family constellations are the only method of treatment that helps those who have died, as well as those who are alive.

Conclusion

The Hellinger Systemic Family Constellation work is taking root in the United States. It is growing in popularity and, it is hoped, will become a well-known modality within a few years. So far, we are pioneers in this country. So we need to educate the public and promote self-growth to become really good at it. We need to find our own ways to adopt this work to our practices. We need to develop guidelines as to who should practice this method, who should be considered ready to do it, and who should study further.

If we, as practitioners of the Hellinger approach, expect to grow as a legitimate profession, we should consider research as a necessary tool: not only to show others what this method can do, also to ascertain how effective it is.

Our task is to learn from the masters, and from each other, in improving our skills.

3

Deep Roots: Musings on the Philosophy of Constellations

by Jane Peterson

At my first meeting with Bert Hellinger, he introduced himself not as a psychoanalyst, but as a philosopher. It is both the philosophical roots of his work and its earthy, grounded physicality that continue to attract me, encouraging me to take tentative steps toward the phenomenological explorations of knowing and being pioneered by Husserl, Heidegger, and other philosophers. David Abram (1996), Valerie Bentz (1998), and Barnett Pearce (1989), among others have served as guides to escort me through these deep waters.

The first time I witnessed Bert Hellinger doing constellation work was in April 1998 in Salt Lake City. The vividness and effectiveness of the constellations grabbed my attention, and has never let go. In 1999, I brought Sneh Victoria Schnabel to the United States to offer training in the work here, and I have since had the pleasure of inviting Gunthard Weber, M.D., Albrecht Mahr, M.D., and Ursula Franke, Ph.D., to give workshops in Oregon. These wonderful teachers have all had an influence on my development as a constellation facilitator. In 2001, I began my own training program and this year, 2005, marks our fifth training group. My students have continued to teach me at least as much as I teach them, and I am indebted to them, as well as to Bert Hellinger and the many others who have helped me to follow this path. It is from this perspective of student, facilitator, and trainer that I write.

> *"The young ones are the future of the old ones."*
> — Malidoma Patrice Somé (1993)

Lived Histories

In our post-Enlightenment world, we think of ourselves as autonomous individuals and believe that we can, with sufficient willpower and positive thinking, change our personalities and our destinies. Although there may be some truth in this way of thinking it overlooks important realities: that our lives and our destinies are the result of the lives of our ancestors. Américo Yábar, a mystical teacher from Peru, pointed out that the new grass that emerges from the earth in the spring is feeding off the dead grass matted and composting into the dirt from the season before. Like these new shoots, we grow up out of the soil of our ancestors in a particular place and at a particular time.

Our *lived history* is not the history depicted in school texts or media chronicles. Our *lived history* is the interweaving of the life experiences and destinies of our specific ancestors, the ones who determine the color of our skin, eyes, and hair; whether we are tall or short; what language we speak and what country we live in; what religion we practice; what opportunities are available to us. A child born in Afghanistan in 2005 faces a very different reality than she would if she were born into a middle-class family in the United States. For a young African-American boy in a poor Detroit neighborhood, the nature and quality of his relationships will bear the traces of hundreds of years of chattel slavery and the subsequent segregation that ended only 40 years ago. The context into which we are born and in which our early life unfolds is determined by the complex histories of those who lived before us. We have no influence over this lived history, and we live within the constraints of choices and decisions made well before we took our first breath.

One of my teachers once worked with a Native American tribe in the southwestern United States. The members of this tribe spoke of a person's *long body*[*1]. Unlike our perceptions of, and experience with our bodies in the moment, the *long body* is the body we experience and create over the course of our life. I may not be representing this concept exactly, however the idea speaks to the accumulated consequences of our life experiences. Bert Hellinger's constellations show us how our *long body* is interwoven with the destinies of those who came before and shapes the lives of those who follow.

Two Examples

1. One client of mine was born in East Asia, raised by American missionaries there, and sent to a boarding school at a young age. Although she had lived most of her adult life in the United States and spoke perfect English, she never felt completely at home here. She couldn't abandon her early heritage and felt somewhat unaccepted by her American friends — as if she were a "phony" American. This sense of "not belonging" was passed on to her daughter, who, although she was bright, talented, and attractive, was unable to find friends with whom she could be at ease even though her parents had tried sending her to different schools during her grade-school years.

2. A client whose face seemed etched in a permanent frown actually proved to be very kind and to have a pleasing personality. Although she was deeply involved in the operation of her business and community activities, and was liked and respected, it was difficult for her to make

---

1 * Tom Best. Neuro-linguistic Programming training session in Portland, OR. April 1995.

time for self-nurturing activities, such as exercise or rest, and she was overweight and in danger of working herself into an early grave. And where did the incongruent scowl come from?

As it turned out, at least four generations back, this client's great great-grandmother grown up in grinding poverty. The sentence passed down from mother to daughter was, "You must work very hard and have a better life than me." This sentence exists like a perpetual wave in the client's system. Just as a wave builds up behind a fallen log in a creek, the water molecules change, but the wave remains — the family members change but the sentence remains. The client's frown was the tangible result of this harsh sounding great-grandmother to grand-mother to mother advice, with each admonishing the next to "do better" and to "work harder." From the perspective of a comfortable middle-class background, it would be easy to overlook the legacy of poverty in this client's life.

Anyone with experience in constellation work is aware of the effect that these *lived histories* have on the lives of clients. Most people, however, continue to live as if they had been dropped on the earth by a fairy, their destinies shaped by their positive affirmations, or the potent spell of whatever product television advertising convinces them will change their lives. Unaware of the influence of the *lived histories* that shape their individual lives, they stumble on, searching for magic cures and soothed momentarily by pills.

Malidoma Somé (1993), an initiated shaman for the Dagara of West Africa, described what happened when his father failed to perform the rituals that ensured his family's good relationship with the earth spirits of his homeland. Weakened by the lack of ritual and relationship, resulting from the 10 years of neglect, the earth spirits faltered in their protection. A witch was able to enter the family home and inflict a fatal illness on Somé's stepbrother. Only the grandfather, the *living history* of the father and son, could cause the death of the witch and prevent further harm from befalling the family. As an adult, Somé was finally able to inquire into this mysterious event. He explained: "The death of my stepbrother was symbolic of how spirits 'think,' that is, how they view their relationship with humans on a cosmic scale. The young ones are the future of the old ones. To allow the future to happen, the old ones must work with the Otherworld. When an elder fails to perform his work with respect to the spiritual, the future of this elder is threatened, not the present" (p. 12).

Whether or not one believes in spirits, this story serves as a vivid reminder that we are the future of those who came before us, and that we ignore that connection to our own peril. Many other cultures are aware that we are born into a web of relationships that we did not create, and yet must live within during the course of our lives. In the process, we weave the web that shapes our children's lives. Through the process of constellation work, we have discovered that where one comes from, one's "homeland," is not a trivial issue, and has an important impact on one's life. We can't just "leave home" and pretend that there is no connection to the soil and water and ways of the people who nurtured us through our youth. In Somé's words: "Throwing away one's culture for another is an insult to the dead, and can result, as in the case of Africa, in a lot of unresolved ills" (p. 17). Ironically, constellations show us that the only path to individual freedom lies in honoring and accepting the constraints of the *lived histories* of those who preceded us.

Embodied Knowledge

How do constellations tap into these *lived histories* to reveal the underpinnings of our lives? This is a question that most practitioners grapple with constantly. We can't point to scientific evidence, the currency of present-day "knowledge," to provide measurable data or a cogent theory. Instead, we are tapping into a more ancient stream of knowledge, one that connects us to life itself; that is, embodied knowledge.

Knowledge Beyond Words

Western culture has attempted to banish the body to the realm of medical science, emotions to the laboratory of neuropsychology, and spirit to the realm of physics. There is a form of knowledge in each of these disciplines, but something vital is lost. The body especially, with its primitive dependence on the physical necessity for day-to-day survival and procreation, is connected to the larger dance of Life and thus is in touch with the deeper wisdom that organizes our living planet. The living, breathing body is in a primal relationship with Life, not with the abstractions of the mind.

In *The Web of Life,* (1996) Fritjof Capra says, "The structure of a living system…is constituted by the actual relations among the physical components" (p. 98). Life is relationship. The knowledge of these relationships comes through the body. Being "in the body" means being in relationship. By being present and aware of our bodies, we have access to the larger field of knowledge that comes from our connection to the web of life. Capra goes on to say, "In other words, the web of life consists of networks within networks" (p. 35). By using body awareness, we connect with these interlinking networks and can access information related to a particular organization or a specific family.

Although the process by which representatives in constellations are able to sense the experiences of people they do not know seems mysterious, I believe it is an ancient way of knowing that I call *embodied knowledge,* which allows us to access information about family systems in this way. Placed by the client in specific locations, representatives' bodies spatially recreate the configuration of the individual's constellation. Once they are standing "in relationship," the representatives' bodies can sense information about the persons they represent. To quote Capra again, "There is something else to life, something nonmaterial and irreducible — a pattern of organization" (p. 81).

Pattern is the way that Life encodes information. Whether it is the furl of a new leaf or a fluctuation in the radio frequency of a signal that reaches our antennas, such patterns are what supports life in a complex world. It is these patterns of information that we access with our human bodies when we do constellations. Much like the radio antennas, we use our own bodies to tune into the "knowing field" of human life and to decode the signal that carries information about that person's relationship to other members of his or her system.

One of my students once said, "Space is intelligent" — a seemingly simple remark. Imagine that two people stand near each other. When looking at these two people, we instinctively know whether or not one is within arm's reach of the other. That gap, or space, between the people has meaning for us. It is a very different "felt experience" to see/know that one person can reach another than to see/know that two people are just beyond each other's grasp. The difference in the meaning that we ascribe to these two examples of "spaces between" comes from our experience of living in a human body. This embodied knowledge shows up in the precise placement of representatives in the constellation circle. One can only access this spatial intelligence through the body. We call this the "knowing field."

When training students in this work, I often find that they are out of touch with their own sensory awareness of living in a human body. This shows up, for example, when a student facilitator places a daughter's representative next to the representative of her dead father, who is lying on the ground. This position, with her toes almost touching his arm, produces a very different felt sense and meaning than if the facilitator had placed the daughter's representative six inches away. The intention of the student was to allow the daughter to look at her father. Placing her so close to him, however, enticed the daughter to join her father in death. She was too close to really look at the father, and could only feel him. Our sensitivity to the meaning of body positions in space results only when we maintain an awareness of our own bodies. If we are present in our own bodies, then we instinctively know exactly where to place representatives in a constellation.

Modern Life and Time

Our modern way of life favors mental abstractions of the mind over the embodied, chthonic knowledge of the body. We are cut off from the wisdom of the flesh and from the embodied knowledge of our relationship to our world. This disembodiment leads to many of the illnesses of modern life. Floating free in the imaginal realms of the mind, we are out of relationship with our bodies, our families, our communities, and our planet. We are out of contact with the "knowing field" of our ancestors and unaware of our lived history. No longer in relationship, we have no sense of belonging to something greater, both to the earth and to life itself. Only when we have such a disconnected, unrelated sense of ourselves can we use enriched uranium weapons in the service of "liberating" an "oppressed" people or create an entity that imposes crushing debt on impoverished smaller nations in the guise of "developing" them.

In such a world, to quote from *Women's Ways of Knowing* (Belenky et al., 1986) "Form predominates over content. 'It does not matter,' said one young woman, 'whether you decide to have your baby or abort it. It only matters that you think the decision through thoroughly.'" As any facilitator of constellations knows, the decision to have an abortion has immediate consequences not just for the child, but also for the parents and the future of their relationship. As Hellinger says, "Actions have consequences." Without embodied knowledge, we are cut off from the web of life and the awareness of others that comes with it.

Our heavily noun-based language also works against embodied knowledge and our connection to the "knowing field." To be in contact with the body is to be in the ever-changing currents of the river of life. Nouns freeze the changing existence of phenomena into mental constructs. The word "tree" does not capture the moment-by-moment fluctuating existence of the Douglas fir outside my window, one moment filled with little vireos feasting on its branches, and the next, soaked with a sudden downpour of Northwest rain. Rupert Ross (1996), in his exploration of First

Nations justice systems, discovered that many of the native languages he encountered were verb based, allowing the speaker to maintain a connection with the fluidity of life. He says of the Native view, "All existence is seen as energy or spirit manifesting itself through matter by organizing and reorganizing that matter in ever-changing (but patterned) ways" (p. 115). Opening our body awareness to the present moment takes us into this embodied way of knowing, and into direct contact with the "knowing field."

Another facet of modern life that militates against embodied knowledge is the construct of time. Somé recounts a humorous episode that sheds light on the modern concept of time.

> "One of the elders asked, 'Where do these white people run to every morning?'"
>
> "To their workplaces, of course."
>
> "Why do they have to run to something that is not running away from them?"
>
> "'They do not have time.' I had to say this word in French because there is no equivalent in the local language. The conversation came to a halt when the elder had to ask what this 'time' was."
>
> "Among the Dagara, the absence of 'time' generates a mode of life whose focus is on the state of one's spirit" (p. 16).

As Eckhart Tolle (1999) notes in his book *The Power of Now*, we spend most of our time engaged in mental constructs of the past or the future, and are not really present to the phenomena that are emerging all around us. Many spiritual teachers describe this separation from the present moment as our fall from grace. When we do bring our awareness into the present, a richness of perceptions becomes available to us, including awareness of the knowing field. David Abram (1997) puts it this way, "In the act of perception, in other words, I enter into a sympathetic relation with the perceived, which is possible only because neither my body nor the sensible exists outside the flux of time, and so each has its own dynamism, its own pulsation and style. Perception, in this sense, is an attunement or synchronization between my own rhythms and the rhythms of the things themselves, their own tones and textures" (p. 54).

In the course of my training program, I show students videotapes of constellations unfolding over time. I often replay constellations that students have facilitated during a supervision at three times normal speed. At this rate, the rhythm of a constellation, the synchronized swaying and interlinked movements of the representatives, is immediately visible. Students can see at once whether or not they were able to enter a constellation field in harmony with the rhythm of that constellation, or whether their movements were out of synch with the constellation and created a wake like that of a motorboat darting through still waters. In order to enter a constellation, one must attune one's own rhythm to that of the particular constellation, and that can only be done if the facilitator is aware of both his or her own body and the larger rhythm of the constellation itself.

To access the "knowing field" — this web of life that carries the patterns of information that allow us to access specific information about a specific family — we cannot be running to or from anything. To borrow a phrase from a popular advertisement, we "must be in it to win it."

Phenomenology and Social Construction

I recently did a supervision training with facilitators from a variety of backgrounds and training programs, including mine. During this weeklong training I noticed one of the facilitators performing an interesting little "ritual." To my surprise, this "ritual" was picked up by some of the other students — without a word about it being spoken. The facilitator would sit beside the client for about a minute and a half, and then look up and begin the chair-work part of the constellation. As I watched this performance,

I had the odd sensation of watching the form of a practice without the embodied knowledge. In other words, the facilitator had mistaken the *form* of the practice for its *essence*. I believe that this facilitator was attempting to connect with the client in a phenomenological way, much as described by Hellinger (2003): "If I can open myself, with every fiber of my being, what is essential appears out of the dimness like a flash of lightning. This awareness always exceeds what you could have thought up using logic, or what you might have concluded from the premise or bits of knowledge, but it is never complete. It remains enclosed in that which is inscrutable, just as everything that is is surrounded by what is not. I can, however, grasp the essential aspects in this way" (p. 247).

While pausing for 90 seconds is helpful for allowing one's breathing and physiology to settle down, it does not in itself bring about an inner state of presence, the still, centered awareness of being described so beautifully by Hellinger, Tolle, and other teachers. I never felt that this facilitator completely came into the present moment, left thought behind, and sank into an awareness of his body, nor did he seem to reach a state of inclusive stillness — the "empty center" described by Hellinger that is required for phenomenological work. In short, this facilitator had developed a program, but not presence. Presence doesn't require one to sit quietly for a minute or two, and careful observation of Hellinger's work shows that his presence comes first from a deep contact with his own being. From this inner clarity there is space for the other. Martin Buber (1970), in his book, *I and Thou,* points to the reciprocity that is essential to the phenomenological approach taken by Hellinger. He says, "Relation is reciprocity. My You acts on me as I act on it. Our students teach us, our works form us. The 'wicked' become a revelation when they are touched by the sacred basic word. How we are educated by children, by animals! Inscrutably involved, we live in the currents of universal reciprocity" (p. 67).

In a way, the phenomenological approach necessary for the work is like a hunting cat. She waits by the mouse nest, still, alert, without thought or intention. She's not saying to herself, "What a tasty mouse this will be when I catch it." Nor is she worried about the mice that eluded her sharp claws in the past. She is simply there and available for anything that might happen. Valerie Bentz and Jeremy Shapiro (1998), in their text *Mindful Inquiry*, describe, in the context of advising beginning researchers, a useful attitude for the constellation facilitator: "In mindfulness, the researcher is in a state of care and acceptance. This attitude allows the Beings of the participants of the study to shine forward, to reveal themselves to the inquirer .... Such openness can only be allowed, not forced. In the absence of this kind of openness, all the inquirer can find out is what [he or] she already knows.

"Unmindful (mindless in this sense) inquiry is a form of what Heiddegger calls 'idle curiosity.' This is a form of finding out based on the preconceptions of the inquirer, who simply mirrors this inner, wished-for reality by imposing it on the outer world" (p. 54).

Unless we are doing a *movement of the soul*, social construction also takes place during the constellation. By this I mean the cocreation of an unfolding story that is created among the client; the facilitator, who guides the constellation; the representatives, who stand in the client's constellation; and the group that holds the space. A skilled facilitator will be "following so fast it looks like he or she is leading"; that is, the facilitator will be noticing small body movements, the lifting of a mother's hand towards a child, the change in moisture on the surface of the client's representative's eyes, and following these cues to support the healing movements occurring in the constellation. We *construct* stories with clients whenever we speak to the clients about their states, as in an example from the "Holding Love" series of videos where Hunter Beaumont tells a client, "You are not open." In the act of speaking, we cocreate with our clients or their representatives the story of the constellation. Unless we have had Bert Hellinger's 79 years of experience observing humans, we, as facilitators, need to be very mindful when we are interpreting the movement of the constellation and constructing a client's understanding of what is happening. Likewise in working with representatives, the stories or the representatives' thoughts about what they are experiencing (or think they *should* be experiencing) are very different from gently and nonverbally supporting the movements that already are present in the knowing field. It takes a lot of awareness to know when we are constructing an interpretation of the constellation and when we are supporting the healing movements possible in that constellation. As facilitators we need to be cognizant of the power of our words, and to stay in contact with the client and the knowing field when we choose sentences for representatives or speak to a client about the blind love that might be present in a constellation.

Teaching This Work

Unless we, as trainers, can find a vocabulary for this kind of embodied knowledge, this "practical phenomenology," and a way to teach our "modern" students the ancient art of being present and being in relationship, something essential and precious in the constellation work will be lost. My greatest fear is that the fragile aliveness of presence will become subsumed in the easier-to-achieve dullness of program and prescription. Then what are we doing when we facilitate a constellation? Are we creating a space for the Beings to emerge or are we imposing our own wished-for realities on our clients? How do we communicate this essential aliveness to students steeped in Western ways of thinking and being?

Trusting the Knowing Field to Know

I watched for a few years as my students chose representatives for constellations that seemed to make no sense. For example, a client would present an issue of separation from the mother at birth. The student would set up the client and life, missing the obvious fact that the client got his or her life *through* the body of the mother. It finally dawned on me that my students were setting up the "solutions" to a client's issues instead of the questions. They did not trust the knowing field to respond to their question, or trust their own embodied knowing, nor were they willing to risk simply being present and exposing their inner beings to the client for a few moments (or longer!). They felt that, as facilitators, they had to *do* something for their clients, and were attempting to second-guess the clients' systems and fate and start with the solutions. They thought they could skip the process of interacting with the unknown and jump right to the solution.

It's easy to understand how this response might occur. Combined with the pressure that our school systems put on children to have the "right" answers to questions, the last thing my students would think of would be to let the answer emerge from the knowing field. Instead, the students felt that they had to "solve" the clients' "problems" or they were not being successful. Their focus was on their own roles as "helpers" not on their clients' system or fate. And this was their conclusion in spite of readings, exercises, and discussions about accepting what is and the dangers of helping! It's one thing to read about fearlessly facing whatever unfolds in a constellation, but another to live the experience of it. It takes a special kind of courage to facilitate constellations, and this is difficult to communicate to students. At this point, I realized that a constellation is like a dialogue with a client's system and the lived histories that inform the fate of that system — dialogue in the sense of Martin Buber's dialogue in which the *I* in the exchange is open and affected by the *Thou* of the other.

Metabolic Learning and Spiral Mosaics

As a trainer, I've come to realize that excellence in any field requires both a cognitive understanding of the intellectual landscape — a model or way of describing what is unfolding, and embodied knowledge — the tacit knowing that comes from experience. I can tell immediately if a student has really metabolized Hellinger's concepts of conscience; whether, for example, he or she has a visceral understanding of the balance of give and take needed for love to flow in a family or order to be established in a company. It is this embodied knowing of cognitive principles that is difficult to teach. It takes time, and students often seem to acquire this understanding in what I call a *spiral mosaic* process. As teacher and student, we spiral past the same concepts many times.

Each time the student digests a bit more and his or her mosaic of understanding gains more pieces, the picture becomes clearer. Teaching the inner states of awareness needed for this work is more challenging. Can we teach someone to be present? Can we teach the phenomenological approach? I don't think so, at least not directly. We can provide students with an intellectual framework for moving in the landscape of the constellation, and give them arbitrary orienting maps such as "chair work," the part of the constellation before any representatives are set, and "floor work," the portion of the constellation done with representatives.

In the end, however, it is by providing students with an opportunity to develop a set of reference experiences that we will help them to find their own way to the heart of this work. Try to describe to someone the flavor of rosemary if they have never tasted it. We attempt, in our training, to provide many different ways of experiencing the modes of perception in the hope that one of them will be a match for the student. As a trainer, this can feel a bit like playing roulette; sometimes you strike it rich, and sometimes you go home with empty pockets. Each student is unique. My description of my experience of the empty center might be quite different than the one my student would use. As trainers, we need to assist students in finding their own paths into the constellation work. They will be changed and challenged by the journey. We can provide a safe space for exploration, furnish training in basic perceptual skills, offer a cognitive road map for the trip, and walk with them for a while. Each student will need to find a way to use his or her own body as an instrument of knowing and understanding. I'll never forget the time I worked with a young woman whose primary way of understanding the world was through words and sound. She literally did not see the constellation. All of Hellinger's beautiful descriptions of *seeing* were lost on her. In addition to giving her opportunities to stretch her perceptual skills (and include seeing!), I, as a trainer, had to work with her gifts of hearing and support her in developing a keen ear that allowed her to *listen* carefully to the knowing field.

Staying Awake

Students often come into the work without an understanding of the level of awareness and alertness required to facilitate constellations. It happens at least once in our first supervision sessions that the student facilitator, overwhelmed by maintaining connection with herself, the knowing field, and all the representatives, stands with her back placed squarely in front of the client. The client, the source of the constellation, has temporarily vanished from her awareness. There follows a humorous moment when the client must lean far to one side to get a glimpse of his constellation as it takes place behind the facilitator's back. Too often, students are aware of only one person at a time as they interact with the constellation. Instead of sensing the constellation (and client's system) as a single living organism and noticing, for example, that the sister on the periphery of the constellation responded when the mother's mother was brought in, they zero in on the mother and miss the important movements in the constellation as a whole.

Finally, students must develop a sense of bodies in space. Many students come into constellation training without an awareness that they inhabit a body, unless it hurts! One student who came to me with a rare embodied knowing of the physicality of this work was a hospice nurse. This student literally handled human bodies every day and stood in family groupings throughout the workday. He understood immediately that it means something different if you place the daughter's representative with her toes right beside her dead father's side (who's representative is lying on the floor) than if you position her six inches away. Students often do not realize that two representatives in conflict cannot make eye contact until they are the right distance apart. This work cannot be done as a mental exercise. Facilitators must be in contact with their own bodies and must be alert to the subtle physical responses of the representatives' bodies when they make a movement or a change in the constellation.

Students in the work sometimes think that information comes from some mysterious ethers during the chair-work portion of the constellation session. Meanwhile, the client's body is talking continuously to them, but they are busy thinking and miss completely the nonverbal part of the conversation. In short, their energy is focused *inside* on their own processes, not outside where the client is. This does not mean, however, that facilitators should abandon awareness of their own felt sense of themselves. Quite the contrary, a good facilitator is in touch with *both*. If the facilitator is at home within herself and her field of awareness is open to the other, the facilitator will know if she is in sufficient harmony with the client to proceed with the work. This is not magic, this is skill. I think that, in some ways, the work suffers when we relegate it to the realms of mystery and magic. If we cannot teach this way of working, this alive awareness of the present moment, then its essential nature will perish. The challenge to us as trainers and teachers is to find ways to build on Hellinger's vocabulary and to communicate the core skills, states of being, awareness, and attitudes needed to allow the magic of constellations to occur.

Two Final Questions

In this chapter we've discussed *lived histories*, the "presence of the past" in our lives, to borrow the title of Rupert Sheldrake's book on morphic resonance fields. We've talked about how embodied knowledge plays an important role in our ability to access knowledge outside of our normal cognitive processes. We've dipped briefly into the deep wells of phenomenology and social construction, and looked at the many challenges facing teachers of this work. As a final thought, I would like to leave you with two questions that I often ask my students toward the end of a training program. The answers are always varied, and sometimes surprising. I invite you to explore your answers to these questions in conversation with others, as well as in the privacy of your own being.

- ❖ What *is* a constellation?
- ❖ What are we *doing* (or *not* doing) when we "facilitate" a constellation?

References

Abram, D. (1997). *The Spell of the Sensuous*. New York: Random House.

Belenky, M. F., et al. (1986). *Women's Ways of Knowing*. New York: Basic Books.

Bentz, V. M., & Shaprior, J. J. (1998). *Mindful Inquiry*. Thousand Oaks, CA: Sage.

Buber, M. (1970). *I and Thou* (trans. by Walter Kaufmann). New York: Charles Scribner's Sons.

Capra, F. (1996). *The Web of Life*. New York: Doubleday.

Hellinger, B. (1998). *Love's Hidden Symmetry*. Phoenix, AZ: Zeig, Tucker, & Theisen.

Hellinger, B. (2003). *To the Heart of the Matter: Brief Therapies*. (Trans. by Colleen Beaumont). Heidelberg: Carl-Auer.

Pearce, W. B. (1989). *Communication and the Human Condition*. Carbondale and Edwardsville, IL: Southern Illinois University Press.

Pearce, W. B., & Pearce, K. A. (2000). Combining passions and abilities: toward dialogic virtuosity. *Southern Communication Journal, 65*.

Ross, R. (1996). *Returning to the Teachings*. Canada: Penguin.

Sheldrake, R. (1999). *The Presence of the Past; Morphic Resonance and the Habits of Nature*. New York: HarperCollins.

Somé, M. P. (1993). *Ritual: Power, Healing, and Community*. Swan. Republished (1997) by Penguin Arkana.

Tolle, E. (1999). *The Power of Now*. Novato, CA: New World Library.

4

The Role of Energy and Intuition in the Constellation Approach

by Jamy Faust and Peter Faust

This chapter gives an overview of the constellation approach from the perspective of energy awareness and utilization of intuition. A framework for recognizing the subtle energetic nuances that happen for the facilitator, client and representatives is presented.

Introduction

When we first saw Bert Hellinger, we became very interested in the way he worked with each client as they approached, sat with him, and explained their reasons for being there. We noticed his manner of what we call, body reading, energetically scanning, or opening his third eye to gain an intuitive sense of knowing to deeply connect with the client. As he proceeded further to query or to sit in silence, we recognized that his method engaged many of the ways that we also work with clients on an energetic and intuitive level. We waited patiently for Bert to explain what he was doing, to describe, to postulate. But as each constellation progressed, he continued to work in ways that one may expect a shaman or healer to resolve the meaningful issues that were presented to him, with little or no description. We have studied many forms of energy healing and realized quickly that Hellinger was presenting yet another approach.

In traditional Hawaiian Huna Healing, for example, a form of family therapy called *ho'oponopono* has been practiced since ancient times by the Kahuna, similar to the shaman. An opening prayer is recited, an issue is presented and it is the Kahuna's job to assist the family in releasing old and stuck belief systems, or *hilina'i*, that keep the family or one of its members ill. *Hilina'i* can be literally translated as "a knotted braid, net, spider web or thicket" that is not only physical; the issue can also be psychological or spiritual. Once the entanglement is consciously recognized and healed, the issue is settled, and *mana* (life force) and *aloha* (love) flow again. *Ho'omalu* (peace) is declared within the soul of the family; the subject is closed for good and not raised again (King, 1983).

The constellation approach presents a unique way to understand how systems work together. If we are able to refrain from our usual desire to understand intellectually what is wrong with the client, and allow the complexity to present itself, we can untangle the places where love, energy, or life force has stopped. Like Huna Healing, constellation work can be used to not only become intimately familiar with the entanglements that keep us blocked, but also to unravel how our individual energy system along with that of our family energy system is hindered from allowing our life force to flow.

Congenital Essence

Modern medicine teaches that we have genetic predispositions for certain illnesses and diseases if our forbearers had these conditions. Prescreening based on our family's health history is accepted protocol in our current Western healthcare model. In fact, it would be considered negligent if this history was not included by a physician when determining a patient's physical and mental health care planning. This seems like a perfectly modern approach to thorough health care, yet in Eastern Medicine this concept was well understood for over 2500 years.

Congenital Essence is considered to be all the energetic qualities that are inherited from one's parents (Mociocia, 1994). Each parent has his or her own congenital essence which they inherited from their parents and incorporate into their being. It is said that who we are is merely an extension of our parents and ancestors. This Congenital Essence becomes the basis for our individual qi, or energy signature. In Eastern medicine it is believed that one can not change their inherited congenital essence. However, with wisdom and understanding, a person can utilize their inherited congenital essence to foster strengths and limit the effects of lesser qualities. Everyone receives aspects that are considered more or less desirable but it is always up to the individual to accept fully what they inherited in order to know how to best cultivate their Congenital Essence. In the constellation approach, similar to Eastern medical philosophy, we move towards acceptance of what life has presented.

Defining Energy and Fields

Energy has a multitude of meanings in our fast paced 21st century world. Advertisers tell us we can get more of it through what we eat, drink or how we exercise. The word exists in Chinese as *qi (chi)*, Japanese as *ki*, Hindu as *prana* and Hawaiian as *mana*. We know that all matter - solid, liquid and gas - is composed of vibrating particles. In a solid, the particles vibrate so closely together that we can only perceive a solid form. Gas particles, however, pulsate much further apart so that we actually see their energetic movement. We, along with everything in our world, are made up of vibrating energy and in fact, the entire universe is a network of interconnecting energy frequencies. When people interact, energy frequencies are emitted that can be felt, seen and even heard by a trained individual. Vibratory frequencies create energy fields and most importantly, these fields contain consciousness. In our work, we tune in to these fields to help us sense and interpret what we perceive.

The Morphic Field

Through scientific study and experimentation, the contemporary biologist and philosopher Rupert Sheldrake describes the idea of a morphic field, also referred to as a morphogenetic field.

"Morphogenetic" meaning a kind of developmental form-shaping that exists within and around living organisms that includes both structure (morphic) and creation (genetic). He observes that these morphic fields are organizing and evolving fields that create patterns, have a built in memory bank, and also influence behavior and create habit. A series of fields can exist within other fields and through "morphic resonance" or the "influence of like upon like" they connect one another. Therefore, our heredity is not only influenced by DNA, but as Sheldrake postulates our existence is also shaped by both morphic resonance and morphic fields. (Sheldrake, 2005)

In family systems, we feel our sense of belonging through this morphic field. Its resonance tells us who we are; it links us. We respond to it without words, without being taught how. Sheldrake describes a "social bond" as part of a social field that can deeply influence and affect an organism's way of being in the world. As constellation facilitators, we call this morphic field the Family Energy Field.

The Family Energy Field

We begin to notice the Family Energy Field immediately as a constellation is set up. As the client commences to choose representatives and slowly shifts them into their places, the Family Energy Field emerges. We see the bonds of energetic alignment, distortion, resistance and alliance within moments.

The Family Energy Field resonates, is felt and sensed by the others within it, mostly on an unconscious level that exists chiefly beyond the scope of the rational or conscious mind. It exists as a magnetic pull. It draws in as well as retracts outward. This energetic force is how one may experience the pull of loyalty and love that happens in all family systems. An individual can feel a deep sense of belonging or a feeling of being excluded.

In working with constellations that involve issues other than that of the family, such as those that are personal, organizational or regard illness and disease, we use the term constellation Energy

The Individual Energy Field

Everyone has an Individual Energy Field, which is a type of organizing field that guides the molecules and atoms of our physical, emotional, mental and spiritual bodies into place. Known as the aura by healers, it is personal, individual and uniquely one's own. Most importantly, this emanating field contains our consciousness. We interconnect, merge, and bond our Individual Energy Field with others every day throughout our lives.

Although the Individual Energy Field is shaped via the process of physical development, it is also influenced by the Family Energy Field. The Individual Energy Field and its formation, gives us a map to determine the client's journey and whether life force is restrained, pushed forward or stopped. This is an adaptation created in relation to the family system, to adjust for the ebb and flow of love.

By cultivating the senses in heightened form and by tapping into the manner through which energy is already perceived, the constellation facilitator can gain clearer insight into the deeper meaning of the client's issues. The facilitator practices his/her skills of reading the client's body language, listening for subtle nuances in their speech and observing the energetic relationships of the representatives. The Individual Energy Field is perceived through our senses of sight, sound, feeling, and knowing.

In our view, the constellation approach coalesces the concepts of energy and consciousness, Congenital Essence, and morphic resonance to help us understand the fields of all constellations as well as the individuals within.

Intuition and the Chakras

When we learn to expand our awareness in all directions, the wave frequencies of our Individual Energy Field travels outward and information can be received, much like an antenna. This expansion allows us to find solutions because all information already exists in the Universal Consciousness.

For thousands of years, Eastern spiritual belief has told us that we are all One. The scientist and explorer of consciousness, Itzak Bentov took into account that when time and space intersect, this intersection point is the "now." If we allow the wave frequencies of our energy field to expand across time and space and hold that all is one, then we can know everything we need to in the present moment. The universe is in constant communication and can be known "instantly by consciousnesses whose interest or business it is to know these things." (Bentov, 1997) This is what we term, intuition.

Sitting with our friend Barb one night as we described what the word intuition meant to us, she ventured, "Intuition is really just the way we process data." Clearly Barb is right! When we slow down enough and open ourselves up, we can indeed garner ways for intuition/data to come.

From our experience, we find that intuition can be innate or cultivated. Using techniques to develop auditory, visual and kinesthetic awareness, the constellation facilitator can begin to utilize skills that already exist within him or herself. All of us are born with a heightened ability to perceive, however it is often shut down, or not given space to emerge.

There are myriad ways in which we "process data." Intuition comes as a 6th sense, a gut feeling or a warning. Sometimes it is a deep inner voice, as in words or guidance, heard in an important dream. Many experience intuition as a physical sensation or emotion. And last but certainly not least, a symbol or sign manifests just when we need it.

In our work as constellation facilitators and teachers, we take intuition very seriously. We teach our students to understand first how they process information through their own Individual Energy Field. We ask them to inquire for themselves how they've learned to intuit their home environment, or Family Energy Field, for this is where our intuitional abilities began. For example, were they kinesthetic, knowing and through a gut feeling or felt sense, when their parents were happy or sad? Or was it possible that they were visual, recognizing a frequency of light or color between their siblings as loving or contrary? Did they hear a voice that guided them to follow a certain path?

The Chakras

Within the Individual Energy Field, there are vortices of energy that correspond to major nerve plexuses of the body, located in the pelvis, the solar plexus, the heart, the throat, and the head. These vortices called chakras appear as wheels of light and create a frequency of light, color and sound. They expand from the top of the head and base of the torso as well as from the front and back of the body. The chakras are a complex system of sensation through which energy and information come into and flow out of the body. When we understand what the chakras are and how they function we can, as constellation facilitators, start to incorporate this information within our methodology. Intuition, or the way we process data, begins with allowing energy to flow in and out of the chakras.

Through studying and teaching healing with one of the world's foremost holistic healers, Barbara Brennan, we learned to intricately intuit the subtle nuances of the chakras, the emanating aura that is created by the chakras, and the physical, emotional, mental and spiritual layers of the energy field. Brennan observed that the chakras receive and process energy as information, in addition to enabling the expression and healthy functioning of the individual's own consciousness, psychological characteristics and physical well-being.

Although most chakras have front and rear aspects through which energy moves, only the first and the seventh chakra have one aspect, moving upward and downward. The first or "root" chakra located between the legs at the perineum - *muladhara* in Sanskrit - gives us the ability to be grounded and present. When this chakra is open it brings energy into the feet, legs, and bottom of the pelvis contributing to our state of awareness, patience and presence in the unfolding moment.

Moving upward from the base of the body the second chakra, *svadhisthana*, is located above the pubic bone in the front and at the sacrum in back. This chakra, often associated with sexual energy, works together with our first chakra to assist in furthering our centeredness by allowing life force energy to flow throughout our being.

The third chakra, *manipura*, is in front of the body between the solar plexus and navel and in the rear at the adrenals. This is the chakra of clairsentience or kinesthetic intuition. It gives us the sensation of the gut reaction. We are able to completely sense a situation through this chakra, and often that sensation travels to other parts of the body. In families, we learn to sense our environment through this chakra.

With most of us, the fourth or heart chakra, *anahata*, is our relational chakra, the "you and me" chakra. This is the chakra of compassion and love of the other. It opens in the front at the heart and between the shoulder blades in back. Facilitators must have a sense of opening in this chakra, not to create a specific type of relationship with the client, nor to take care of them, but more importantly to open a relational field between one another. This opening may be called the 'allowing field' and it is the place in which two people connect in order for healing to occur.

The fifth or throat chakra, *vishuddha*, helps us to take in, to receive energy and to bring the voice and inner feelings forth. This chakra allows us to open to clairaudient sound, or auditory intuition. Facilitators, standing directly in the constellation Energy Field may hear a specific word or sentence which is often used in this approach. After standing in the energy field of thousands of constellations over the years, Hellinger has developed more than a hundred particular sentences or "statements of empowerment." Auditory intuition leads us to the right sentence.

Moving upward to the head, the sixth chakra or third eye, *anja*, opens from the brow in the front and the occipital in the back, and leads to the center of the brain, the pituitary and pineal glands. This chakra is associated with clairvoyance or visual intuition. "Seeing" is perceived in the "mind's eye." Often a complete vignette unfolds, or symbols familiar in meaning to the facilitator appear in the mind. Individual facilitators cultivate the reception of data through visual intuition by practice and patience.

Using the Tantric model of seven chakras, the seventh, *sahasrana,* is at the top of the head, corresponding to the crown. This chakra opens up to what is called "Universal Consciousness," which allows "direct knowing" to occur. In energy-healing terms, when the facilitator is grounded and present in the root charka, as well as in relation with the client through the heart chakra, the crown chakra opens. In this way, the wave frequencies of the facilitator's individual energy field resonate to receive information that is available within the constellation energy field. Direct knowing is not emotional or sensual; it is clear and concise guidance that emerges spontaneously without conscious thought or action.

By working with energetic and intuitive awareness, the facilitators come to discover "how they know what they know" from their own responses to the environment. This is more than a learned or cultivated path; it is a personal and individual process that the facilitator decides to follow. Ultimately, it is a path of self discovery and opening of consciousness through the facilitation of constellations.

Application of Energy and Intuition in the Constellation

Visual Intuition

Visual observation of the client and representatives is the first and probably most relied upon form of intuition that is utilized in the constellation approach. Author Malcolm Gladwell (2005) explains that in the first few seconds of interaction with another person, the mind picks up an astonishing amount of data that is processed unconsciously and helps with decision making. This "adaptive unconscious," as he calls it, allows us to make surprisingly clear judgments with very little information. Because the constellation approach limits the verbal story, we too can rely on this type of an unconscious process which can help determine the direction that healing that needs to take. This is not the same as a snap judgment, but rather a clear intention to allow our internal unconscious mind to process information and then tap into that knowledge to help to direct us. Our visual intuition then becomes a combination of our conscious and unconscious mind, literally giving us abundant deciphering ability.

Facial Emotions

As a facilitator, the first place we bring our visual awareness to is the client's face. After studying facial expressions for over forty years, Paul Ekman (2004) professor of psychology at the University of California has discovered that there are a set of voluntary and involuntary muscles that control facial expressions. A person cannot control the involuntary muscles through will. "Whenever we experience a basic emotion, the emotion is automatically expressed by the muscles of the face. That emotional response may linger on the face for only a fraction of a second, but it is always there." After the initial involuntary muscle response the client's voluntary muscles take over and express the emotion that the client wants us to see. By knowing this difference and trusting in what we first perceive in these micro-expressions, a clearer understanding of healing is often revealed. With clear intent, we look with our visual intuition and feel with our kinesthetic intuition to find that information can not be suppressed and is consistently there to inform us.

Body Language

Observing the faces of the representatives in a constellation can be helpful, but their overall body language and Individual Energy Field allows us a much larger field of information with which to work. Using not only our physical eye to perceive the obvious, but also our third eye, we can engage our visual intuition for clairvoyance. Sitting with the client on the outside of the constellation Energy Field allows a unique perspective. We notice by starting at the head, the direction to which the representatives' eyes are drawn, who they are watching and who they are trying to avoid. The stance of the representatives informs us if they are strong or weak, aggressive or passive. Their hands will unconsciously curl into fists if there is anger present. After a few minutes in their positions the representatives will often unconsciously shift their feet in the direction they wish to move. Frequently a representative's upper torso will be twisted slightly in a different direction than the lower half of their body. The legs will be supportive and firm or begin to weaken and buckle depending on their life circumstances. By observing the body language of each representative in the constellation, their general energetic pattern is revealed within the larger energy system of the constellation Energy Field.

Lines of Energy

The constellation Energy Field offers a host of information in the form of energy connections and energetic groupings of representatives within the constellation. The lines of energy are similar to "ley" lines on the earth. They can distinctly be felt and with careful awareness, seen. Using visual intuition to observe the floor of the constellation energy field, we get a sense of clear pathways and where barriers are held.

The amount of space between representatives is an indication of the degree of closeness or separation. There are times a person is placed in a constellation but their proximity is a strong signal that they are not truly part of the issue or solution. Representatives that are fully facing one another indicate strong connection. Inversely, the opposite can be true.

A classic energetic grouping is the triangle of three representatives in which two people have a strong connection and one will not, but is still intimately involved. Grouping of representatives helps to explain the feelings of exclusion and belonging so often experienced by the client. By observing how representatives are grouped together and then reading the lines of energy between them, an entire energetic picture is presented to us for interpretation.

Kinesthetic Intuition

Our body's own chakra system can be used as a sounding board to get a sense of what the client or individual representatives are feeling. Again, we need to allow our unconscious mind to be active and to permit space to recognize when our body is feeding us information. Just as it is common for representatives to have body sensations for the person they are representing, we as facilitators can pick up feelings in our own bodies when we are in tune with a person.

Unlike visual intuition which can be done from across the room, to utilize kinesthetic intuition, it is essential to be within the energy field of the person. This requires the facilitator to actively move into the constellation Energy Field among the representatives. By quieting the mind and allowing stillness, we can tune into our bodies and internally ask "what am I feeling?" This somatic feedback will inform us.

With visual intuition we use our eyes to take in information. With kinesthetic intuition, we are using our third chakra and through it, bodily sensation. The facilitator not only relies on the eyes and sixth chakra, but notices his or her entire body with clairsentience. This is a comprehensive system of gathering information about the energy of a constellation and needs to be approached with clarity, intention and conscious awareness.

Sensing the Chakras

By combining visual and kinesthetic intuition, we can move beyond reading physical body language and observe the representatives' chakras for additional information. For example, tuning into the heart chakra of a representative will help us determine their feelings for another representative in the constellation. Often what is expressed on the face of the representative is different from the emotional feeling coming from their heart center. The throat chakra will inform us if a representative has something important to say. On the physical level the chin will become slightly raised; energetically the throat chakra will appear open and the representative will seem to be on the verge of speaking.

As facilitators, we continually scan the physical and energetic bodies of the representatives to gather information that our unconscious mind processes and then feeds back to us in order to guide the constellation towards solution. The key is to not rush this process. It is vital to allow time for both the conscious and unconscious mind to work in unison to gather a complete picture of the representatives in relation to each other.

Auditory Intuition

It is possible to allow a deeper unconscious level of listening, auditory intuition, to open when facilitating constellations. This hearing intuition involves our fifth chakra which controls listening. Like kinesthetic intuition, the facilitator needs to be standing in the energy field of the client or representative in order for this deeper level of hearing to open. As with all intuition, it is important to be still long enough to listen beyond our conscious range to an internal, not external, form of hearing.

Although there are many standard solution sentences that are appropriate for various constellation situations, knowing which one to use often comes in the form of clairaudience, auditory intuition. The conscious mind may have an idea of what is appropriate for a representative to say, but it is the facilitator's patience to wait long enough until they hear the sentence internally, that will most directly lead to the truest sentences for resolution.

Direct Knowing

When a solution sentence hits the mark, everyone who is in tune with the constellation can energetically feel the rightness of it. This is an example of opening the seventh chakra for "direct knowing." Direct knowing is the facilitator being in harmony with the "knowing field" and allowing it to direct them along the path of healing. It is the culmination of intuition, and outwardly appears as if the constellation is guided from beginning to end. When facilitating a constellation, direct knowing experiences can happen from the first moment a client raises their hand through to when you absolutely know it is time to end the constellation. There does not need to be anything more added in that moment; it is a felt sense of knowing.

Energy Shift Awareness

When perceiving the client and the constellation Energy Field, we become aware of the subtle energy shifts that constantly happen throughout the constellation. It is these energy shifts that lead the constellation step by step from the initial issue to the solution. Awareness of these energy shifts happen in many forms and it is important that our intuition be attuned to them. A change in facial expression, a deep breath taken by a representative, the feeling of sadness when a client turns towards a representative, or a sense of the tension in the room just released are all simple examples of when energy shifts in a constellation.

Once an energy shift happens, it is important to be calm and wait for the next direct knowing experience to lead the constellation further along. It always comes; we must merely be patient enough to allow ourselves to be lead by the gentle shifts that are steering the work.

Larger Perspectives of the Approach

Circles of Energy

There are several circles of energy constantly present in a constellation workshop which can offer a valuable tool for assessment and information gathering. The primary circle of energy is that of the client and the facilitator. The client's own energy field, as described earlier, is what we try to get 'in tune' with when the client sits with us and presents their issue. It is imperative that the facilitator be aware of how they primarily run their own Individual Energy Field so they can modify their energy pattern to match that of the client. In this way, the process of becoming aligned with the client happens more quickly. By being still and not getting too analytical, it allows the energy of both the client and facilitator to drop from the traditional attempt of mental understanding of an issue into the underlying "knowing field" of what the client is actually trying to heal. When the facilitator softens and matches their energy to that of the client, a resonance begins to happen between them and a trust begins to take root for the client. Often at this point the client may begin to have feelings.

In the constellation approach, there is not a great deal of emphasis put on hearing the extensive 'story'. When there is excess information discussed, it automatically keeps the facilitator and the client on the mental level, which in turn makes it difficult for the facilitator to soften their energy field and come into deeper contact with the energy field of the client. Once resonance between the client and the facilitator occurs, it is likely that the facilitator will begin receiving information from the client's field in the form of images, feelings and language. This resonance begins to inform the facilitator at a subconscious level and can be intuitively viewed as two partially overlapping circles of energy, blending and vibrating at similar rates. Without this resonance, it is difficult to begin the constellation and move into the next circle of energy. Connection with the client is the foundation for attunement with the constellation Energy Field.

This constellation Energy Field has a distinct boundary. It includes all those within the constellation and extends a few feet outward from the outside edge of the representatives. The constellation Energy Field and what is happening energetically between the representatives can be observed by the participants, client and facilitator. Observing the constellation Energy Field is the first step in energy awareness for the facilitator and client together. Often it is enough for the facilitator to point out "what is" happening between representatives for the client to get an important insight into their issue. Further, it is equally important to give ample time for the representatives to connect with the energy they are representing. Only after it is clear that all the representatives have settled into the constellation should the facilitator point out what they observe or enter into the constellation Energy Field.

Once the facilitator leaves his/her seat and enters into the constellation Field a whole new set of insights is possible. Often we will get insights about the client or their issue by merely standing among the representatives. The facilitator, when standing next to a representative must modulate their energy in a non-invasive, non-threatening and supportive way so the representatives can relax and the facilitator can pick up any insights at the level of the unconscious. Participants will often ask, "How did you know that?" Our answer is, by slowing down the mind along with listening and feeling with our whole body to the constellation Field.

The outer circle of energy which supports and ultimately holds the work is the energy field created by the participants in the workshop. When conducting a workshop we prefer to work in a circle whenever possible. An auditorium situation with large numbers of people offers a unique situation but generally the first two rows in the auditorium, along with those on stage, represents the circle of energy holding the work. Of course, in our view there is another circle of energy, which is present yet unseen, that of the ancestors of each participant in the workshop

The Participants Energy Field will vary in strength and support throughout the day and during particularly powerful or seemingly subtle constellations. Because this is a field that supports the facilitator as well as the work, it is important that the facilitator pay attention to the fluctuations in the Participant Energy Field. Rarely will all of the participants be equally engaged in what is happening in any one particular constellation. It is imperative that enough of the group is energetically present in the constellation or the facilitator will become tired. If the Participant Energy Field is particularly low, it is usually a good sign that the constellation is not moving in the direction of healing, has been going on too long or the group needs a break. When another representative is needed to be brought in, it is important to notice if that participant is energetically connected with the constellation. One's energetic presence can be evaluated by observing the eyes and body language of the participant and their attunement with the facilitator.

The circles of energy are concentric; the largest is that of the ancestors, then the circle of participants. Within these two circles are the constellation Energy Field and finally the blending of the client and facilitator's energy field into one unified field working toward healing.

Journey of a Workshop

In a workshop setting we visualize this journey as a type of spiral from the outside to the inside, from above to below, from the conscious to the unconscious. Whether facilitating an individual constellation in a private setting or conducting an entire day long workshop in the constellation approach the process is similar. There is a direct intention by the facilitator to move from the conscious understanding of the issue to the unconscious realm of a fuller wisdom. We utilize the process of going from the mental into emotional awareness and finally what we consider the spiritual dimension, allowing a larger perspective to emerge for comprehending the issues.

By giving an overview of the work or highlighting a particular theme in the constellation approach, we engage the participants on the mental level of understanding. This helps to start the creation of a "holding container" for the group by establishing our intention and focusing the energy for the day as the leaders. It also allows us to move about the room and connect energetically with the participants. After our overview, we shift the energy to the participants by asking them to introduce themselves and to state their issue, if they wish. This process of shifting from leader to listener balances the relational energy of the group. It has two additional effects; as the participants introduce themselves, they automatically become more present and the energetic holding circle becomes more solidified. The process of spiraling inward and downward for the group has begun.

Something profound happens for a person when they openly share what they have come to try to heal. A noticeable emotional response is evoked among the participants as they take in and receive each other and their heart centers begin to open. Empathy and compassion play an important part in the process.

After the participants have shared and the energy circle has traveled back to us, we lead them into a meditation. The meditation is intended to move the group out of their individual consciousness into connection with a larger one. This is the consciousness of the family of origin. The journey from the mental to the spiritual, from conscious understanding inward to the edge of the larger field of the unconscious, is where we begin the first constellation.

As the day moves on and the constellations unfold, there often seems to be an uncanny similarity among participants in what they needed to heal. We are constantly in awe at the synchronicity that happens for and between the participants. It is one of those amazing circumstances that could not have possibly been orchestrated. Continually we see how this work is guided by larger forces than ourselves.

Meditation

Opening Meditation:

Close your eyes, bring your feet flat onto the floor, take a few deep breaths. Allow yourself to think about your morning, all that it took for you to get here, to bring yourself to your seat in this group.

Become aware of the person on either side of you, become aware of your place in the circle of people here today. Become aware of the space in front of you, of this space in which we will do this sacred work today. The working area is held by our circle and by our intention to be honest and truthful and our intention to travel from the conscious to the unconscious so we may find answers to the questions we have brought here today. We are not alone in holding this circle, if we allow ourselves we can also feel the circle of ancestors that are standing with us today and everyday.

Imagine standing behind you, on your right side is your father, and standing behind you on your left side is your mother. Regardless of your personal relationship with your parents just allow their energy to be there with you, standing behind you. Take a deep breath in, and a deep breath out. Now imagine standing behind your father, his mother and father, your paternal grandparents, even if you did not know them, allow their energetic form to take shape behind your father. Now imagine standing behind your mother, her mother and father, your maternal grandparents, even if you did not know them. Allow their energetic shapes to take form, in this way beginning to see and feel where you have come from, where your life has originated. Now imagine standing behind your grandparents and your two sets of great grandparents. Allow yourself to see and feel this pyramid of energy that you are merely the tip of at this time. Life has traveled down to you from before your great grandparents to them, then through them to your grandparents, to your parents and finally to you. All that life has come before you to bring you here today, to your place in this circle. This is the line of energy that is uniquely yours. Just as there is no one else like you, there is no other family like yours. This is your family's energy signature in the universe from which you have come from.

In your mind's eye, imagine that you stand up and turn around, looking at your parents, grandparents and those who have come before you. Ask them for their support and permission to do this work, to do your own work. Take a deep breath in, and a deep breath out, allow yourself to soften, allow yourself to be humble. Notice what you feel and hear from your parents and grandparents. Take a few deep breaths. Now imagine yourself slowly turning around and sitting back down in your chair, with your parents and grandparents still standing behind you. Come back to your breath, taking a breath in and a breath out.

Become aware once again of your place in the circle, of the person on either side of you, of the working area in front of you. Notice your feet on the floor, notice any body sensation you have and then slowly and with a soft gaze begin opening your eyes taking in the floor in front of you and then slowly the rest of the room.

Closing Meditation:
Close your eyes, bring your feet onto the floor, take a few deep breaths and allow the process of letting go of the day to begin for you. Become aware of the person on either side of you, of our sacred working area and of your place in the circle. Know that your presence was needed here today. Know that you were part of a sacred circle that allowed for this journey into the unconscious to unfold so healing could occur. Take a deep breath in and a deep breath out.

Imagine in the working area, standing in front of you are the various people you represented today, and the various people you were of service to. Take a deep breath in and a deep breath out. Take a slight bow in respect to all these people. With your next breath, begin allowing these images to start to dissolve. Like fog disappearing, like leaves blowing across a patio, like clouds breaking up. Allow these people to go, trust their fate and begin returning more fully to yourself. Take a deep breath in and a deep breath out.

Start to become aware of your line of ancestors standing behind you. Imagine once again your father standing behind you on the right side and your mother standing behind you on your left side. Breathe them in and breathe them out. Imagine once again your two sets of grandparents standing behind your parents, your mother's parents and your father's parents. Even if you did not know your grandparents, allow their energy to be present behind your parents. Now begin to imagine your great grandparents, a man and a woman standing behind your grandfather and a man and a woman standing behind your grandmother. Allow yourself to feel this pyramid of energy that has traveled down through the generations to you, your unique family heritage and ancestry and all that has transpired before you in your family lineage. Breathe in deeply and allow a deep breath out.

In your mind's eye see yourself standing up from your chair and slowly turn around to face your parents, grandparents, great grandparents and all those who came before your great grandparents in your family line. Feel yourself standing tall and looking in the eyes of your ancestors. Notice what you feel and hear coming from them, notice what you feel in your own body. Take a few breaths. Now slowly take a gentle bow with your head, acknowledging this line of energy from which you came and from which you are uniquely a part. Now see yourself standing tall again and slowly turning around and sitting back in your chair. Feel your feet on the floor, become aware of the person on either side of you, feel your place in the circle and of the sacred working area in front of you. Take a deep breath in and on your exhale begin to slowly open your eyes softly and see in the floor, your feet and gradually the circle of people of which you have been a part. Know that your presence was needed here today.

A form of these meditations was originally taught to us by Harold Hohnen.

Case Study

Client: Katherine is 55 years old, originally from Ireland is married to an American and has lived in the United States for the past 25 years. She has two daughters age 23 and 25.

Issue: Her eldest daughter does not want to have anything to do with Ireland or mother's family of origin. No clear reason is given, and Katherine has had a difficult relationship with this daughter most of her life.

Additional notes: I invited her husband of 25 years to sit beside Katherine both as witness and support. In this way, a healing could also possibly happen for the husband.

Sitting with Katherine, I gathered the above information and then became quiet in order to get in tune energetically and to find the resonance that would best serve her. After a few moments of quiet, Katherine began to tear. The kinesthetic feeling and direct knowing of missing her family came to me, and I stated, "You miss your family." Katherine began to cry deeper, from her heart center.

The Role of Energy and Intuition in the Constellation Approach   79

The energy was right to begin the constellation, no more talking was necessary. The spiral inward had occurred from the mental, (story/issue) into the emotional realm of feeling deeply held emotions. I asked Katherine to place representatives for her immediate family in Ireland, herself and her two daughters into the space before her.

Katherine set up two distinct groups. On one side of the working area were the eldest daughter, herself and the younger daughter in that order, standing fairly close to one another facing the opposite group. On the other side of the working area were two sisters, the father and mother in that order from left to right. Katherine's younger daughter was looking towards the mother's sisters very relaxed. The elder daughter was facing the grandmother. The elder daughter's body language was rigid and tense with an angry glare. The representative for Katherine appeared frozen and scared. It seemed that she was avoiding her mother who was looking directly at her. There was a large floor space between the groups. The energy lines and grouping indicated that there was something between the two groups that needed to be resolved, but Katherine had no idea what it could be.

By moving into the constellation Energy Field, standing beside the elder daughter, and moving from visual intuition to kinesthetic intuition, I suddenly got the sense that there was someone missing. I asked Katherine if there was someone excluded in her family. A wave of emotions came over her and she said her mother's brother committed suicide. He was ostracized for being a homosexual. It was never spoken about in the family. I asked if her daughters knew about their great uncle and she said no.

At that moment, there was an energetic shift in the constellation Energy Field as all the representatives relaxed and a sense of greater space could be felt in the room. There was a feeling that everyone could stop holding their breath. The tenseness in the elder daughter softened and she took a slight step away from her mother. The representative for Katherine lifted her head and began to look directly at her mother for the first time. The shift in energy was a clear indication that the constellation was headed in the proper direction of healing. The elder daughter was carrying the anger of exclusion for her uncle. The secret needed to come out, the truth told so the chasm could be bridged from Ireland to America, from one generation to another. Exclusion needed to transform into acceptance. Her representative sat down and Katherine took her own place in the constellation.

A representative for the uncle was brought into the constellation and placed near the grandmother. Immediately, the representative for the grandmother began to cry as did Katherine who was now watching her mother and uncle. After a few moments the grandmother and her brother began looking at each other with fondness. Another energy shift happened and it became clear that it was time to move into auditory intuition and solution sentences.

By standing in the field of the grandmother and uncle, I heard these words in my head and asked the representative for the grandmother to say to her brother, "I've missed you. "You are a part of this family."(It was only later that I realized that in the beginning when Katherine first sat with me that she "missed" her family.) The representative for the uncle, after hearing these words began to stand a little taller, took a deep breath, started to smile and slightly turn his body towards the elder daughter and Katherine. The shift in energy indicated that the constellation needed to move to the next phase. I had the grandmother say to Katherine, "This is my brother, your uncle, please accept him fully as I now do." Katherine began to smile, her body visibly relaxed and the feeling of her heart center opening became evident.

Bringing my attention back to the original issue of the elder daughter not accepting her mother's family, the next step was between Katherine and her daughter. By standing in their energy fields, I could determine when the right solution sentence was felt by the daughter and when the constellation would be complete for Katherine. I had her say to her elder daughter, "this is my uncle, your great uncle who was excluded, his death was not talked about, but who is now accepted." After a pause to let the energy shift between the daughter and Katherine, I had her say to her daughter, "please accept my family as they are."

I heard these words in my mind, "with all their secrets", and then had Katherine say that to her daughter. A big smile came over Katherine as she said it, and there was suddenly warmth between the elder daughter and Katherine with the elder daughter also smiling broadly. The energetic sense of completion was overwhelming at this point, so we agreed to end the constellation. When Katherine sat down she was still smiling happily. She commented that there were a lot more family secrets and that she knew it was now time to be more open with her daughters. Her husband nodded in agreement.

Summary

Awareness of the energetic level enables us to have a broader perspective and gives a roadmap to help comprehend the seemingly mysterious progression that occurs in a constellation. The Individual and constellation Energy Field is rich with useful data that can guide the course of action if we know how to read and gather the information. It is our hope that by explaining the process of intuition and highlighting some of the energetic components of a constellation, the reader will have a keener sense of the work and another lens in which to view the Approach.

References:

Bentov, Itzak. (1977). *Stalking the Wild Pendulum: On the Mechanics of Consciousness*. Rochester: Destiny Books.

Brennan, Barbara Ann. (1989).*Hands of Light: Healing the Human Energy Field*. New York: Bantam Books.

Ekman, Paul. (2004). *Emotions Revealed: Recognizing Faces and Feelings to Improve Communication and Emotional Life*. New York: Holt.

Gladwell, Malcolm. (2005) .*Blink: The Power of Thinking Without Thinking*. Boston: Little, Brown.

Hellinger, Bert. (1998). *Love's Hidden Symmetry: What Makes Love Work in Relationships*. Phoenix, AZ: Zeig, Tucker & Theisen.

Hoffman, Enid. (1976). *Huna: A Beginner's Guide*. Atglen: Schiffer Publication.

King, Serge. (1983). *Kahuna Healing: Holistic Health and Healing Practices of Polynesia*. Wheaton: Theosophical Publishing.

Leadbeater, Charles W. (1974). *The Chakras*. Wheaton: Quest Books

Mociocia, Giovanni. (1994). *The Practice of Chinese Medicine: The Treatment of Diseases with Acupuncture and Chinese Herbs*. New York: Churchill Livingstone

Robinson, Lynn. (2003). *Compass of the Soul: 52 Ways Intuition Can Guide You to the Life of Your Dreams*. Kansas City: Andrews McMeel

Sheldrake, Rupert. (2005). *Morphic Fields and Morphic Resonance: An Introduction*. Retrieved February 20, 2005 from http://www.sheldrake.org/papers/Morphic/morphic_into.html

Ulsamer, Bertold. (2003). *The Art and Practice of Family constellations: Leading Family constellations as Developed by Bert Hellinger*. Heidelberg: Carl-Auer.

5

The Stance of the Facilitator

by J. Edward Lynch

Introduction

This chapter provides guidelines for establishing the attributes, traits, and ideas that enable the therapist or facilitator to provide for effective and successful family constellations where the movements of the soul can be realized. The belief system from personal and professional viewpoints make up the stance of the facilitator or therapist and are considered herein as each affects functioning in this role. Characteristic aspects of the individual who is successful with soul work are examined with a constructive critical eye. A case study focusing on the differing points of view of the therapist and the client serves to illustrate the position taken by the therapist and its impact on the work.

The author is indebted to Berthold Ulsamer, author of *The Art and Practice of Family Constellations* (2001), for his descriptive and comprehensive coverage of the family constellation process.

Background

Role-playing family members was first introduced in the 1930s when Jacob Moreno developed psychodrama and later in the 1950s when Virginia Satir began her work with families. Throughout subsequent decades, therapists have continued to use psychodynamic concepts to view the role players and as a direct consequence have made significant contributions to human growth and development. In order to be effective and credible to their fellow colleagues, therapists had to be familiar with the leading theories of the times and to be trained in the use of accepted intervention strategies. The stance of the therapist was of interpersonal distance. The mode of conduct was interpretational and nonrelational. There was an expectation that the therapist would not engage in revealing personal thoughts, ideas, or feelings. The common position was one of neutrality. Therapists usually were seen as having all the answers and as being very insightful. Often this was probably true, but it was not a result of the role itself, but rather as a consequence of the therapist having knowledge that others did not have. This imbibed the therapist with an aura of mystery and glamour.

As the profession evolved, the therapist generally began to be viewed as more of a "real person" and there began to be a tolerance for, and even expectation of, more self-revelation forthcoming from the therapist. In family constellations, the thoughts that are occurring to the facilitator during the time of working with the client can be shared with the client and representatives. This position of bringing the process of family constellations to the awareness of the clients, representatives, and the group allows what could be the covert dynamics to become visible and available for comment and question.

Attributes of a Family Constellation Therapist

The family constellations method and process developed by Bert Hellinger is new and old at the same time. Hellinger took the concept of phenomenology and used this way of viewing the process to work with the family constellations. The method required a different kind of therapist from one of the Moreno/Satir style, one who could be open and touched by life and death issues, be courageous in the face of despair and trauma, could trust the unknown, and remain engaged and present while waiting for a resolution to emerge for the client.

Conducting a family constellation demands extreme attention, suspension, courage, and receptivity on the part of the facilitator. Each of these attributes must be more than a "natural" state; they must be honed, mastered, and used judiciously. Ulsamer (op.cit. page 12) quotes Hellinger's response to Hohnen's question about whether he thought that family constellation work could be learned: "You can learn certain things. Having the appropriate attitude alone won't insure that people can lead [f]amily [c]onstellations. There is a certain knowledge needed and then if someone is truly observant they can learn."

Attention, from the French attendre, means to be present to and be there for the actual persons and situation. Attending and being present for a person means giving the individual the sum total of concentrated interest, time, and compassion. The result must be that the client has a felt experience of being seen, heard, and held in a way that fosters an openness to the situation and the growth possibilities in the self.

Suspension, to hold oneself in animated belief, is an important psychological posture for a facilitator. By allowing personal thoughts, feelings, beliefs, and behaviors to remain in the background a new experience can be cocreated by the facilitator and the client, and the facilitator can be alert to what emerges in the field of the constellation. By suspending preconceptions, the facilitator is open to the field and can be more easily in tune and directed by it. Relegating (well learned and understood) theory to background, and allowing for the emergence of the integrated therapeutic self is a more than an important skill; it is the hallmark of a facilitator who conducts effective and meaningful family constellations.

Courage is the adhesive that binds the therapist attributes and allows the facilitator to proceed with faith. Coeur, the French word for heart, is at the core of this work. The facilitator must be fearless in the ability to initiate a family constellation, even when there appears to be little discernable data for this entry into the realm of healing. Remaining with the process in the face of uncertainty, without being deflected from the chosen course of action, and then knowing when to exit from the family constellation requires the valor that may appear, to the uninitiated, as audacious. This ability does, however, emerge from an inner place in the facilitator who has examined self and is unafraid of drawing on *informed* faith. The work of the family constellation therapist involves meeting head-on the human issues of life, death, pain, suffering, loss, and intense grief. "Certainly in order to lead constellations you need to have the courage to listen to your own inner voice, even if it leads you into uncharted territory with no signposts and many surprises"(Ulsamer, op. Cit pg. 11). The therapist must have emotional stamina and must be able to withstand the intensity of emotions without closing off any emerging emotional possibilities. The facilitator must have "heart." This concept of "heart," as compared with the physiological heart, having four chambers, can be thought of as needing four associated qualities; lion heartedness, open heartedness, warm heartedness, and big heartedness. Recognition of these as the foundation of working, and intentionality in actualizing them, helps to ease the facilitator into a space where work emerges from the most effective stance; a place of love.

Love is not an abstract position. It is both learned and studied, yet once recognized and integrated, it flows naturally. It involves the ability to love the excluded, and the children, the humanness of *both the* victims and the perpetrators, and it enables the therapist to have support from a deep emotional wellspring. The therapist must be able to recognize and depend on support from personal family ancestors and this is paramount to ensuring his or her successful entry into this work.

Receptivity to the family constellation morphogenetic field, sometimes referred to as "the knowing field," is an additional requirement for the therapist. This unique field is the area or region within which the soul exerts an influence at every point. Within this field, barriers to being open to and affected by all forces — seen, felt, or intuited — need to be eliminated. Allowing mind, heart, body, and soul to be touched facilitates deep and accurate awareness and fosters the ability to access the knowing field. "The force for change comes from contact with the present. Only our sensory awareness brings us into direct contact with what is" (Ulsamer, op. cit pg. 37).

Active Processes

Boundary setting in family constellation work must be a calculated and planned action on the part of the facilitator. Creating parameters may be perceived as controlling, however, this procedure is necessary in order to allow the work to unfold in a safe and trusting environment. Such limits ensure the freedom to facilitate the process. Sometimes, informing a client, in the presence of a group, that the intended work may not proceed at this time constitutes establishing a boundary that is necessary. Defining the workshop day is another form of limit setting. This action, where the facilitator maintains a stance of caring control, and is clear about the expectations and format of the day, fosters trust and security for the group, and demonstrates to the group that the therapist is a benevolent leader in charge of the process.

A facilitator needs to be supportive. However, there are instances where this stance creates dependency or regression on the part of the client. The facilitator must be alert to this possibility in the work, and be attentive to reinforcing the client's ability to remain strong and present to the work that is unfolding. Both the therapist and client must maintain this stance to allow for the next level of constellation work to emerge. When either the client or the therapist is unable or unwilling to stay strong, the client may resort to resources of internal pictures and vignettes, the realm of the familiar. The facilitator must take care that this does not occur since it will move the client away from the forming constellation picture. "Just enough but not too much," is the phrase that most beginning surgeons hear when they make their first incision into a patient. Facilitators of family constellations must also know when to do "just enough but not too much." They learn to initiate, guide, and be guided by subtle cues from the client.

The facilitator must have metaphorical permission from personal family ancestors. There is an inherent strength that emerges when there is backing by the awareness gained from investigations of the generations that have gone before. This permission is a natural consequence of working on personal family constellations and reclaiming the lineage of power and intrinsic life sustenance that emanates from past generations. A facilitator, who does not have the permission of ancestors to do the work, will produce superficial, analytic, and psychodynamic-oriented constellations. These constellations represent fragments of the potential for development and awareness that are possible when the work is allowed its full power.

In addition to attending to all other factors, the facilitator must be sensitive to both physical and psychological place in the F. By the therapist assuming the correct physical place, the client and the representatives will be able to take optimal positions. The correct place for the therapist to take is to the left of the client. The position to the right of the client is one of preeminence. The therapist on the right has prominence, assuming the "first" position in the natural order. Once the family constellation is set up, the facilitator should be on the left side when asking questions of the representatives. It is also better in the process of facilitating the family constellation if the therapist avoids moving through the field of the family constellation because it disturbs the energy flow.

The therapist is frequently in close proximity to the constellation of the client. However, it is also important to get a perspective from a distance, to stand back to take in the whole constellation and to walk around the constellation to see it from many positions. In this manner, the therapist gains information from several points of view, thereby enlarging the possibilities, and exploring all "angles."

Psychological place relative to the constellation and the client can be a significant factor in determining the maximum benefit to be gained from a family constellation. The therapist must be able to allow the psychological boundaries between self and client to be permeable while at the same time keeping in contact with self and the environment. The therapist needs to be in a "place" of receptivity to all the nuances that emerge from *both* the client and the soul. The therapist who maintains a place of accessible awareness will be in synchrony with what is necessary and be able to aid the process of the constellation on a deep level.

Respect for the individual client, the representatives, and the process is a crucial factor in healing constellations. Respect involves an awareness of the visibility of the individual and a valuing of what is seen. The facilitator has to convey respect for the client, the representatives, and the group, all at the same time and in a seamless manner. The group should have a felt experience of respect from the moment the facilitator begins the workshop. This is a natural manifestation of the manner in which questions, comments, and responses are handled. No interaction is too trivial or too mundane in the process of conveying respect. A climate in which disrespect is present leads to fractious interactions, group splitting, and splintering. This results in the collapse of the "holding position" so necessary for the unfolding of the constellations. Each facilitator must be brutally frank about his or her ability or inability to manage group process as well as to manage the "mechanics" of a family constellation.

Respect for a person has additional meanings, including the provision of a psychological mirror where the client is visible in a way that there is recognition of the self and the behaviors and actions that have led to the current pain. Disrespect is connected to a contaminated, therapist-constructed view, an interpretation of reality. If it is decided that the client is not ready to work, the facilitator needs to convey this respectfully to the client. When the client experiences being seen and heard in the process of presenting, and receives, through feedback, what was close to the description that was forthcoming, respect is the outcome. The facilitator mirrors the client, the representatives, and the group in a respectful context so that everyone present can take in what is possible from the work. Respecting the process involves yielding to the power of the unfolding field and work. When the facilitator's words and impact are informed by the moment-to-moment, part-to-part, person-to-person, and event-to-event development, and each aspect is held as valid and informing, the result is a powerful experience of respect.

Acceptance of what is emerging in the constellation, whatever data is revealed, however the phenomena unfold, can be a decisive factor in achieving maximum benefit for the client. Facilitators need to be able to recognize and accept the family of the client as separate from their own. If the facilitator cannot do this, there is the risk of transference in which feelings about his or her own family are projected onto the client family, a subliminal process that inevitably contaminates the constellation. The therapist must also have the ability to accept fate and the client's destiny, even when it is not in agreement with the therapist's personal values, hopes, or expectations. The facilitator must not interfere with a client's fate. Maintaining a stance of neutrality in the face of an unfinished, incomplete constellation may be contrary to customary practices and comfort level, but acceptance of this possibility is a hallmark of respect for the process and the client. The therapist must not be attached to the outcome of the constellation in the process of acceptance. Inherent in this stance is the acceptance of the idea that at this time and in this place there are limits to what can be accomplished.

Intense emotions arise in the process of family constellations and facilitators need inner strength to be able to tolerate them. This ability only develops as a result of working through personal issues in constellations as well as in other forms of therapy. The results of therapeutic learning for the facilitator allows for the ability to be touched and yet remain strong, and be overwhelmed by them. The therapeutic process undertaken by the facilitator opens one up to the tolerance of tragic and traumatic events. For example, hearing that a client's mother was murdered can be heart wrenching. However, the facilitator needs to be able to hear it with compassion and still move within the work. When asked if she had any abortions, one client said, "Yes, thirty-five." This could be horrifying to a facilitator, a jolt to his or her belief system and values and be difficult to assimilate. Or a client might say, "My son killed three of his friends, then killed himself." Such a statement might be hard to grasp. Yet the sharing of these types of events in clients' lives is not uncommon in a family constellations workshop. The facilitator needs to stay present and strong so disabilities, trauma, and life and death issues can be held and effectively contained in the constellation. "The closer we are to the moment the easier it is to feel our way into the unknown" (Ulsamer, p. 38).

Systemic Factors

Facilitators with extensive knowledge of family systems and the dynamics of interaction taking place in the family have a greater wealth of possibilities in conducting family constellations than those who do not. A thorough understanding of hierarchy and boundaries assists the facilitator in recognizing order and how the soul has been affected by the system's dysfunction.

Symptoms are viewed by systemic theorists as manifestations of a dysfunction in the family dynamics. These symptoms, which come out of love, are the soul's way of calling out for help. The symptom bearer is often the most caring member of the system, reaching out for assistance for the family but, not knowing the words to use, doing so in other ways. Often this person's actions or behaviors, including physical maladies, have the effect of temporarily adjusting the system in a manner that somewhat resembles health. However, this is short-lived, and in time, the symptom becomes *the problem*.

Decisions

In the process of conducting family constellations, the facilitator is confronted with many decisions that determine the course and depth of the constellation. The facilitator must be able to determine if a brief, one- person constellation would be sufficient, or if a full constellation is needed. A brief constellation would entail perhaps a single representative, or doing the work internally in fantasy. A full constellation would be working with the family of origin, the family of procreation, or extended family members. The choice is established by the clarity of the issue as elicited from the client, and through a process involving both the client and the facilitator. Trusting the process requires that facilitator and client yield to the unknown.

The facilitator needs to be aware that it is counterproductive to work harder than the client. If the client seems to be involved with only 80% of his or her energy, then the therapist should match that amount. If the client is giving 80%, and the facilitator is giving 100%, it is likely the therapist is leading and doing analytic constellations and not working from the phenomenological perspective. In this situation the therapist is not being guided but is leading and planning.

The following is a list of informed decisions that the facilitator must consider in the process of doing the family constellation:

- ❖ Defining the issue
- ❖ Choosing the approach, such as working internally or with a full family constellation
- ❖ Attending to the nonverbals of the representatives
- ❖ Collecting, through observation, the spatial relationships
- ❖ Utilizing theoretical foundations for working
- ❖ Listening to the field for stem sentences
- ❖ Trusting the movements of the soul
- ❖ Following the unfolding developments in the family constellation
- ❖ Discerning when there is a good reason to stop the constellation

The general task of the therapist is to be able to follow the movements from the beginning problem picture as it is presented by the client, and then find the healing steps within the unfolding images from the constellation picture to the resolution picture. This skill requires constantly checking in with oneself and the phenomenological emergence of the constellation. The facilitator's vision must be clean, clear, and precise in order to follow the salient and resolution-producing movements.

In general, there needs to be a resonance between the therapist and client. In this stance the therapist facilitates for the client a feeling of being honored. Additionally, the client needs and wants the therapist to be in synch. At the same time the therapist must be alert to the similarities of personal and client issues to avoid the over-identification that can lead to a contaminated constellation. As a therapist exposes himself or herself to the whole system there emerges an experience of where the work needs to be done. Knowledge of who is excluded and with whom to connect becomes evident.

The therapist must be acutely aware of the movement from the problem picture into a transformational picture, which then ends in the resolution picture. The therapist has a firm belief that the soul wishes for this resolution and completeness and from that foundation is mindful of the transitions that occur in the flow from problem to resolution.

The factors that guide the facilitator in making decisions will emerge from his or her own soul and from new resolution pictures of his own situation that lead forward. In order to build this foundation for decision-making relative to a client's constellation, the therapist must have completed the major pieces of constellation work personally. This allows free access to the unknown with thoughtful abandon, guiding emotion, and open heart and soul. It could be said that the facilitator's ancestors greet the ancestors of the client. In this meeting between ancestors, the facilitator's ancestors looking at the client's ancestors creates a mirror, an echo into the greater soul from where shared healing, love, and growth occur. The ability to acknowledge the ancestors makes the facilitator's work easier. There is confidence in being helped by the ancestors and knowing that, in this realm, the unknown is understood.

The family constellation leader will be taking risks, showing strength, power, and presence in order to provide the ground upon which the constellations will develop. A prepared facilitator will have an impact on the group through the "ground" that emerges, and the participants will respond accordingly. If there is a fragmented leader, the group and the constellations will reflect it. An unprepared or superficial leader will foster a group that responds in kind. Although group process is not the focus of the family constellation work, the group is the container in which the work occurs and therefore conscientious leaders need to know how to appropriately handle group dynamics.

For example, what happens when group members enter and leave the room at will? How should the facilitator respond? The facilitator must have a way to deal with inappropriate side talking or laughter. Each of these situations requires knowledge of group processes so that they may be handled in a manner that takes into consideration the best interests of the client, representatives, and the group as a whole. The leader must have a stance to deal with the free unsolicited movements and spontaneous talking by representatives as well as the client talking aloud in the family constellation. The facilitator must have the confidence and clarity to be able to manage the emotional climate of the day. The facilitator must be governed by principle and theory rather than by desires. Being in ultimate control, as well as being responsible to self and others, has to be predicated on sound data. The group is moved into preparedness for the family constellation work from the very beginning of the day.

Some facilitators discuss the following guidelines at the beginning of the workshop:

❖ What is expected from the client.

❖ What representatives are supposed to do.

❖ What is the function of the group.

❖ What are the behavioral limits for the group, with respect to talking, moving, and the like.

Covering these basic expectations guides participants as to what to do, and it has the added advantage of relieving some anxiety for them.

There is no one set of "rules" to be followed in family constellation work. For example, some facilitators can work with free movement and talking in the constellation because they see it through a broader lens. No matter how it is done, the facilitator must contain the collected centeredness of the group in order to allow work to proceed in a safe and respectful manner.

It has been found that on occasion a group member, who is not in the constellation, can sometimes be enlisted to assist the process. When the constellation seems to be blocked, he or she will go around to each member and ask for his or her observation. This can free the flow of energy and begin the deepening process for the client in the constellation.

The facilitator must be prepared to confront the possibility of making mistakes. The initial decision, beginning the constellation process or not, presents the first opportunity to make a mistake. Frequently, in the enthusiasm to engage in the constellation process, a novice facilitator may initiate a constellation when there is insufficient energy, an unclear issue, or lack of focus on the client's part. Along with a lack of experience, it may be that the facilitator is not in tune with the process, or may feel hurried or pressured by the group. Sometimes the ego needs of the facilitator may lead to the idea that constellations can be "performed" without help from internal or external sources and that it can be done with anyone at anytime. Facilitators should heed the examples of family constellation masters, recognizing that at times a constellation should not be done.

Once the decision to begin a constellation is deemed correct, the next decision to be made is the number of representatives to include. Choosing to have too many or too few representatives is a common error. This error usually signifies facilitator confusion, non-attending, or decisions being made on an analytical basis rather than an intuitive one. Other mistakes include the representatives being moved into ineffective places or what they say being trusted too much or too little. When the facilitator moves the representatives into the wrong places, it is usually because there is a preconceived plan, perhaps following a previous constellation. Another possibility is that there is a lack of attentiveness to the nonverbal responses of the representatives. At the core of these mistakes is the facilitator's inability to listen to all of the emotional information that emerges from his or her own heart and soul.

The therapist needs to have an inner attitude of plenitude for the work to progress in a deep, meaningful way. The therapist needs to respect and follow the client when the client makes it evident that the work can go no further. The client needs support in leaving or ending the work. Continually being in touch with the client's needs is requisite practice for the therapist. Clients' movements emerge from a deep love and need to be held in high regard. The therapist could become angry with the client if the client does not or cannot withstand the solution. If this happens, it is a sign that the idea of the work is more important to the therapist than the feelings and process of the client.

The facilitator may seem to be rude in not answering a client or when interrupting the client, because she or he has enough information. In reality, therapy is not social conversation and the rules of politeness are suspended. Issues need to be contained to allow the therapist to do the most effective work.

The level of trust in the representatives varies from facilitator to facilitator. Some have said they don't trust the representatives at all. Others report that they trust only representatives' body and feeling responses. A few facilitators trust whatever is said as being a manifestation of the one represented. The facilitator needs to know what is and what is not useful in moving the soul. Failing to discern what is and what is not relevant can lead to disorientation, confusion, and chaotic movements that end in a poorly done constellation and frustration for clients, representatives, and the group.

Another area in which mistakes may be made is the choice of stem sentences. The facilitator may decide to use stem sentences that intellectually ring true but fail to have an impact on the client or which are hollow to the representatives. The facilitator is more likely to be accurate in selecting sentences when the locus of his or her decisions arises in the soul, emerging as a result of self-trust, an outcome of having done extensive personal work.

The issue is not avoiding mistakes; if that were the goal, the constellation work would become stilted and unnatural. If handled correctly, mistakes can provide valuable feedback. The first step is to acknowledge them. All mistakes must be accepted as a function of the facilitator's humanness. The next step is to take responsibility for them with humbleness, not with guilt or remorse.

A significant mistake that has broad impact arises from an unaware position, which is the basic stance of the facilitator who is on a power trip. This can be harmful to all involved. The facilitator can guard against this eventuality by first acknowledging that it can happen. Further assurance is gained through talking about the work with other facilitators and, more important, receiving supervision from an experienced, well-trained leader who has a long history of doing constellations. Supervision can be a humbling process, one that renders the facilitator and the process more effective. Some individuals are drawn to leading constellations because of a need for power and control over others and to be admired and praised. When the choice to be a constellation facilitator is motivated by a self-serving intention, the benefits of the model will not be forthcoming. Basically the order of seniority is not being respected in that the soul and the family come before the facilitator. The facilitator must also engage in a self-check process to determine if motivations emerge from a state of humbleness, which serves the approach, or one of arrogance, which ultimately interferes with the process.

Disturbances in the Process

Facilitator disturbances to contact may lead to misreading nonverbal signals and to mistakes that will be detrimental to the client, the representatives, and the group. For example, a therapist who projects will be hampered by not seeing clearly what is actually occurring. The idea that everyone can see phenomenologically is faulty, since (especially meagerly trained) facilitators are prone to projection and retroflection. Retroflection is manifest through a holding-back process, in which the facilitator hesitates to say something. An example of this is the therapist who upon seeing or hearing something, thinks about saying it but then stops short. This energy to speak, originally stimulated from the outside, remains inside or held back. Such retroflection can rob the constellation of potentially important information.

Introjecting is another significant potential disturbance to being in touch with the client and the constellation process. It involves taking the information, attitudes, and beliefs of the client into consideration, without critically thinking about them. This can lead to overdependence on the content or being so organized by the client's story that the constellation can become chaotic and unproductive.

Being confluent with the client is still another disturbance to contact. In this stance there is an unaware assumption that there are no differences between client and facilitator. Such an assumption leads to confusion, blending of feelings without clarity, simultaneity of thought as if the client and therapist are one, which in turn may develop into a complicity between client and therapist, or an agreement to not "rock the boat," and a covert shared decision to avoid looking at the difficult issues.

Egotism and overdevelopment of the ego inhibits new information being available to the therapist from the client. The client who has this kind of therapist will be restricted. The therapist will hear just a little and then do a preplanned or preprogrammed constellation based solely on personal choice, excluding the client's wishes and needs. This, along with the previously mentioned disturbances, inhibits the therapist from being in good contact with the client and being able to do the work.

The therapist's relation to time and rhythm is important to the constellation as well. At the beginning of the constellation, there is more therapist activity and presence. Choices are made, senses are acute, thoughts are figural, and the facilitator attends and meets the client at the contact boundary. The facilitator is most alert to the forming of the possibility of the client's presenting picture for the constellation. In the middle phase of the constellation the facilitator is less active, as there is a cocreation and codevelopment of the constellation, with the representatives, along with more emerging information from the client and the field. This middle phase of the work is moving from the problem picture through numerous new pictures to the resolution picture. During this time the therapist is more intuitive, open to field information, in tune with energy movements, aware of spatial situations, and attentive to the useful information from representatives. This is the teamwork phase of the constellation in which everyone is open and willing to move into a satisfactory direction for the client's best interest. Although the representatives don't know how to get to resolution, they help the facilitator to process the work.

In the ending phase or resolution picture, the facilitator can move to the background as active work is done and the client is left to see, drink in, and integrate the new resolution picture. The therapist may make minor adjustments, for example, moving the client into a more appropriate position or one that allows for the expression and reception of affection. Not disturbing this resolution picture when the constellation is finished allows it time to become assimilated and eventually integrated into the client's being.

The knowledge of the time phase and the differences in each one helps the therapist learn how to relate more to the ongoing process. The art of timing is so important in therapy in general and it is especially so in family constellations.

Foundations That Sustain the Facilitator

Bert Hellinger, the creator of the Systemic Phenomenological Approach, knew of the power of the ancestors from his work with the Zulus in South Africa. It is likely that he also felt the powers of the ancestors of the priesthood and of his own family. Each facilitator has a career ancestry as well. For example, some could enter the psychotherapy field with professional ancestors harking back to Sigmund Freud. Others may come to the profession from literary roots with ancestors that go back to the first writers. Still others may have career or personal ancestors who were early historians. Each facilitator has both family ancestry and career ancestry that inform and sustain the work being done. It can be assumed that all these forebears are benevolent, helpful, and harbingers of success. They are the facilitator's backbone and foundation of strength and courage. As the therapist taps into them, there are connections to the wisdom of the ages. There is no substitute for the cornerstones of historical knowledge that informs decisions made in the process of constellation work.

This leads to the importance of the theoretical grounding of the work through reading and training. As Kurt Goldstein (1939) says, "There is nothing like a good theory." These mental constructs support thinking, making and eliminating options, decision-making and the informing belief systems relative to the work. Theory needs to be foreground when learning is complemented with ample examples to clarify, demonstrate, and solidify salient points. The development of the therapist needs to include the experience of the theoretical dynamics in order to have a clear mind and to be in tune with body and soul while doing a family constellation.

Theory naturally becomes background in the actual work, but still remains a support for the phenomenological vision from which one draws. This background position must be close to the foreground in order to supply the group with appropriate explanations, discussions, and answers to questions.

Competence in the work is also developed by personal participation in three additional ways: receiving, representing, and leading. Receiving, or participating in personal family constellation work to resolve issues, is both personally and professionally useful and rewarding. The method that Freud inadvertently created whereby the analysand became the analyst seems to be valid in family constellation work as well. To know the work in oneself through having experienced it a number of times makes for a unique form of personal integration that results in an understanding, knowledge, and trust in the process. As facilitator there is vicarious knowledge of the client's experience in the constellation process. This results in a unique knowledge of oneself that has professional value as well as personal. The process of the facilitator coming face to face with personal life and death issues is humbling, moving, and humanizing. This experience can foster deep genuine compassion and empathy.

Representing is another means of developing expertise through which a person can deepen his or her understanding of the human condition and its many manifestations. For example, to represent a murderer and to feel a basic humanity, to stand in the place of a holocaust survivor, or an aborted child, are all opportunities that allow for personal learning as well as learning about others. Representing leads to a profound awareness of one's humanity. It also fosters clarity about and around the boundaries of what is the facilitator's issue and what is not. Because of the "surprises" that are possible in each representation, a trust in the process and a willingness to be open to the informing field is promoted. To feel the movements of the soul on a personal level is enlightening, exhilarating, and essential to becoming an effective facilitator.

When facilitators have had training or grounding in trauma work, their understanding may be enhanced. Peter Levine's work, Somatic Experiencing, blends effectively with the family constellation work, and many facilitators have profited by learning this approach.

The matter of career ancestry gives rise to the question of facilitator education and training. Does the facilitator need to be a trained therapist with an advanced degree? This argument has historical precedence in other therapies as well. Psychoanalysis, when developed by Freud, was a humanistic approach to working with the soul, but American doctors wanted it to be scientific and therefore it became tied into the medical profession. This effectively excluded laypersons from practicing the art and also changed it into a more restricted practice model.

Gestalt therapy was learned by both trained therapists and by laypersons. This led to a broadening of the applications to the work of organizations and other systems. In some instances, unskilled, untrained individuals seemed to be enamored of the power of the work. They were motivated by a desire to help others, and so became therapists. This led to a misunderstanding of Gestalt therapy. In many instances untrained individuals had successes and were revered by clients. However, in the eyes of more rigorous professionals in the field of psychology and psychiatry, this work was dismissed as foolishness and successes were determined to be a matter of "luck."

The family constellation field faces the same dilemma today. Facilitators may be from several different career backgrounds. In their move into family constellations they bring significant gifts to the work. Their innate creativity and sensitivity allows them to transfer the talents of their primary careers to the field of constellations. On the other hand, there are other individuals who are excited by the possibilities of constellation work who proceed, well meaning but blindly without the knowledge of family systems, phenomenology, or psychopathology.

The acceptance of family constellation work in the field of psychotherapy will follow in the footsteps of other fields. A uniformity of training will lend credence to the stance of the facilitator. This is a common practice in all professions and leads to professional recognition. Other fields have met this challenge by forming professional associations that have the function of being a governing body. The establishment of guidelines will support *any* facilitator who wishes to do family constellations and will lead to the field having more respect and integrity. In addition, consumers will have greater confidence in choosing a facilitator, knowing at least that he or she has been fully "educated" in the work.

Putting It All Together — A Case Study from Two Points of View

The author engaged in discussions with a client, (circumstances changed to preserve anonymity) following a constellation. The client consented to sharing the thoughts and feelings together with the impact of the therapist's direction. As a result, the inner workings of a family constellation are exposed. This case study highlights the decision-making processes of the therapist and the thoughts and ideas that accompany the constellation.

The Client

It seems like an interminable walk from my seat to the facilitator and the vacant chair beside him. I wonder how many walks like this I've made before? Of course, some, but this one seems different as if the possibility exists that this one offers great healing on the other side. I so desperately want something! Please God, let me be transparent and grant that he sees me and can help me. My anxiety is sky high as I come to arrive at the designated chair. "What can I do for you?" he asks me.

I tell him, "My heart is broken since my wife died in a terrible car accident three months ago."

I begin to cry and the facilitator calmly and gently pulls me toward him. He holds me, and this comfort and safety opens a release valve in me. Maybe this is my obligation at this workshop.

He lets me go and I straighten myself in the chair and look at him. Very loving eyes look back at me. I feel open, and real, and present. I am moved when this facilitator says, "What can I do for you?" I believe he has already done a lot just allowing me to experience what happened, and I answer, "Death seems to be following me all the time. My brother died two years ago, and my mother three years ago, and my father five years before that, and my wife … " My voice trails off.

The Facilitator

I am watching this person come forth. What a heavyhearted walk this young man seems to have. I notice this as he comes toward the chair designated as the place to sit to begin to work. His eyes are downcast; he exhibits all the signs of a grief-stricken person. I wonder what his losses might be? I briefly question my perception and at the same time I recognize that I must keep the possibilities open. He glimpses me but does not see. I allow my hearing to add to what I see as he comes closer, and now I both hear and see him as he sits beside me. I am tuning up all my receptors to be available for him.

"What can I do for you?" I ask.

As he tells me his story I feel my heart open wide and I turn inward, going deeply and expansively inside. So many deaths. I gently put my arm around him, and without words, suggest that he lean into me. He folds into me in a profound and tearful way. He weeps from his soul. I recollect, in these quiet moments, some of the losses I have sustained and how I look at them differently since I have been doing the family constellation work. After a brief time the young man straightens up in the chair and looks at me. I feel a deep love for this fellow sojourner. I see him being human. Feeling as though there was a loving soul movement already happening, I ask him "What can I do for you?"

He begins to tell me about more losses he has experienced, and then he comes to a quiet place and I follow him there. I sense a strong pull in him toward death and to all those who had gone before. I feel guided to set up the constellation with all the dead ones present. He chooses representatives for his father, mother, brother, and his wife. I ask him to pay attention to his breathing and to move slowly in the process, as I want him to remain strong in the face of the enormity of death. He then puts them into position.

The Client

I feel at a loss as to what more to say. The facilitator slowly and calmly tells me to pick representatives for my dead relatives. I think I might become unstable again, but then I feel an unusual strength in myself, and, I am able to do it. I put the representatives in place in the room and come back to my seat next to the facilitator. He does not tell me to pick someone to represent me, I wonder why ... next, we watch. As if in slow motion, the representatives begin to move, guided seemingly by an unseen force. My father and mother move toward each other in a loving way and are joined by my brother. Viewing this scene, I feel a deep, profound compassion well up in me, full of love, gratitude, and peace, for the gifts that they gave to me. I can see the love and feel it in the room. This picture will be indelibly painted in my mind, now, forever, I am sure of this.

The Facilitator

Now, to watch and see what movements develop in the representatives and what the observation through the phenomenological approach will reveal. I look to see that the client is also observing, and he seems to be engrossed in the constellation as it unfolds. I notice that the father, who had been situated facing the mother about 10 feet away, moves toward the mother with some slight hesitation, and she is quite clearly open to him. At the same time, the mother moves toward her husband. All ambivalence dissolves as they meet and hold each other. The brother who had been facing the client, turns toward the parents and after a time moves next to the parents, who then invite him into a warm embrace. The deceased wife did not move during this time, but rather, stood still as if watching life unfold in death. She had been placed toward the outer edge of the circle, and slightly turned to the side. She begins to turn toward the trio in the middle of the room although she does not approach. More recently dead, I wonder if she does not know how to fit into that realm. I want to feel the "field" a bit more so I get up and move around the constellation. I feel the love among the dead ones, flowing well. The client is very attentive and looks as if he is holding the constellation and himself at the same time, very strongly. The observers show signs that they are all being moved during this work and all seem to be in a place of love and peace. I return to my seat.

The Client

I watch this scene in front of me and I see my wife looking at the three members of my family. She knew them for a short time and she loved them. At this moment I remember that she once said she wished they were around longer so she could get to love them even more.

The representative of my wife next looks at me and I feel as if my wife in some way is really here. My heart opens more. She approaches me where I sit in the chair, slowly, and with love in her eyes. Truly, I don't know what to do, how to be, or what to say, or feel. She stops about five feet in front of me and looks at me. I am full of feeling, strong in a new way. I am fully aware of my power, and depth. I barely notice that the facilitator has left the seat beside me. Now he returns at about the same time my wife comes to be in front of me.

The Facilitator

I observe his wife moving in his direction and I feel it to be a correct and "field/soul guided" movement. As I sit down in the chair, I see how much love there was for this young man and I realize how terrible it must be for him to lose her. I feel moved again. The representative's hands begin to turn upward and she uses a universal gesture signaling him to come to her. There is no mistaking her outstretched arms. More loudly than words they tell him to go to her. I ask my client if he has a movement and he replies that he wants to move toward her as she stands in front of him. I suggest he follow the movement and he slowly gets up and walks the steps into his wife's arms. He cries deeply and it sounds strong, not weak. As he straightens himself, I tell the representative to say to her husband, "It was my destiny, it was my fate." She then continues without any instructions from me: "I am with family members and those deceased of my own family, too."

The client seems to receive these words well. I give him a sentence to say, "I will always have a place in my heart and you will always be my first wife." The representative begins to cry and so does the client. This work, so important, real, and deep is about to come to a close. I recognize that the soul is moving and will do what is necessary to complete the work. It might take a year or more for the client to integrate and find himself anew, but his work will continue. It will unfold for him beneficially in his life. I will check with him in about three months to see what has happened as a follow up to this piece of constellation work.

The Client

I look at the representative for my wife and I cannot believe the resemblance. It is so clear. This is uncanny. I feel the love emanating from her in a very deep way. Next, she opens her arms in a welcoming gesture, inviting me to come to her. This is something my wife would frequently do and it all seems so familiar to me.

The facilitator suggests I do what my body wants to do. There is only one place for me to go and that is to her. I slowly get up from the chair and walk the few feet to my wife/representative. When I hug her, more tears come. She feels like her, and different at the same time. The facilitator has me say some important sentences to her, and I experience the words as true and they resonate from my heart and soul. After a time, the facilitator asks me if he can stop the work at this point, and I say Yes.

I return to the chair and the facilitator is quiet for a while. Next, he tells me that I need to recollect this resolution a few times every week until I feel it thoroughly belonging to me in my innermost being and I agree.

The Facilitator

This is a powerful unfolding of the love, pain and humanness of us all. This young man, whose fate it was to have had these losses, will go on in life in a very different way. His path, I suspect, can now be one of deeper understanding of life and death. He also can have more awareness of the tenderness of people and human relationships.

I sit quietly savoring the work that has been done. I am reminded again how the healings that flow from the family constellation work continue to help those in need. The completeness of the process comes to mind. I review the beauty and the power of the movements of the soul, of the spirit. I am filled with the knowledge of how this process moves with the love of God, and the great gift of life that has been passed on to us from our ancestors and parents. I marvel that what we pass on is a mystery and a blessing blended.

Summary

The stance of the facilitator in the field of Family Constellations is solidified in the process of answering penetrating questions in an informed and genuinely honest manner. The following questions are presented as possibilities to be considered by any individual contemplating leading family constellations.

- ❖ As facilitator, what is the inner source of the work — the self and the outer-unknowing field?
- ❖ How does personal constellation work and psychotherapy contribute to effectiveness?
- ❖ How can a facilitator avoid working from an inner child state?
- ❖ Is there a sound grounding in theory that can then be "forgotten" while working so that the soul can be the guiding force?
- ❖ Are the orders of love an intricate part of functioning?
- ❖ Is there a thorough understanding of the three consciences?
- ❖ How thoroughly do the dynamics of family constellations and the movements of the soul order the work?
- ❖ How is the heart and soul of this work integrated so that the process emerges from an integrated self within?

Answering these questions in self-examination can lead to a functional attitude from which to perform constellations. In turn, this process advances the ability to gain radical insights, and fosters openness to the phenomenological approach. The result of this introspection will lead to a therapeutic stance that allows for personal growth of the facilitator as well as clients who are fortunate enough to choose family constellations as a means of problem resolution.

The stance of the therapist needs to include the concept of authority — benevolent versus restrictive. Authority that is benevolent can be nurturing, caring, disciplining, and kind in many ways that are fruitful for the therapist, client, and the group. The feeling of assuredness, confidence, and trustworthiness emanates from the leader in such a way as to open, deepen, and clarify the processes of the family constellation work. Being nurturing, warm, and caring establishes a climate where, if there are storms, they are handled easily. If there is sunshine, it is welcome, and if there is snow, it is warmed.

Being disciplined in a healthy, authoritative manner means that the therapist may have to say "No" to a client. A representative may have to be replaced or anxious group energy may need to be redirected.

Restrictive authority, which is often fear based, has no place in a family constellation group. Restrictive discipline can lead to anarchy in the group, confusion in the representatives, and regression in the client. Constellations can be overwhelming, and as a consequence, facilitators control more intensely out of their own fright in the face of the field and its unfolding. Nonsupport, non-nurturing, or other manifestations of aware or unaware restrictions are usually a signal that the facilitator has areas of personal or professional development that need attention. The following list represents examples where restrictive authority might be employed. When, upon reflection, the facilitator realizes that any of the following has occurred more than once, extensive supervision is needed:

- ❖ Group is covertly inattentive and unruly;
- ❖ Group is overtly challenging of the resolutions and the leader;
- ❖ Representatives seem confused and lack precision;
- ❖ Client keeps changing issue and rejects facilitator suggestion;
- ❖ Therapist becomes blocked in two or more constellations by shortcomings or knowledge gaps;
- ❖ Therapist feels overwhelmed rather than moved by deep issues;
- ❖ Therapist sees the same 3-5 dynamics and applies them to all constellations.

Facilitators need to become competent in representing and leading. Experience as a representative has been discussed in another section. Leading, as previously mentioned, under the guidance of an experienced trainer, builds the confidence, trust, and strength necessary in order to become an effective constellation therapist. Constructive criticism, seldom welcomed, can be very helpful to highlight underdeveloped, untapped, and unknown areas. Acknowledging shortcomings becomes an invitation to broaden skill levels, and it supports continuous growth and development.

When supervision is not readily available, a viable and temporary substitute can be found in writing. Writing case studies, experiences as a representative, as a client, as a leader, and as a group member has the potential for insightful learning. Including in the writing new ways of looking and hearing allows the work to have the potential for informed creativity.

Sensitivity to self, other, and group, is another vital attribute of the family constellation facilitator. Sensitivity is codeveloped while being a client, representative, a leader, and group member. To become sensitive means to come into tune with seeing, hearing, smelling, tasting, and touching; using the five senses that interact with others and the environment. Sensitivity is more than vulnerability; it is an active rather that a passive process. Without active intent, sensitivity becomes receptivity to being overwhelmed emotionally. The active process involves reaching out to perceive the world as it is. It is the phenomenological method.

The facilitator recognizes two forms of presence: provocative and evocative. Presence is important in the stance of the therapist, as it is basically what is required of the client, representatives, and group. The facilitator needs to be able to "hold" all who come to be present, which is not an easy task. Developing presence is important. It involves feeling and experiencing self-depth, breadth, resonance, ancestors, capacities, humanness, and flaws. All of which are occurring in the moment. It is spiritual in scope because when the facilitator is present, the presence of the eternal god seems to enter the constellation.

This chapter has examined and discussed the stance of the facilitator. The author recommends that potential facilitators seek out the knowledge and learning offered by the authors of the other chapters in this book and also read the excellent books written on the subject of family constellations. Experiencing the power, grace, dignity, and spiritual qualities of the constellation work is strongly recommended. There are possibilities to do this in many major cities in the United States. To experience the work is the gift of the work, and in the experience very deep healing occurs.

In conclusion, it is imperative for the facilitator to have integrated, or at least have a working knowledge of the foregoing factors to be able to stand up to the power of the constellation work and its revelations. This necessary stance is one that cannot be taken by everyone. The psychological, spiritual, and mental stamina required is only for those willing to go to the depths of the soul where life and death, pain and love, sacredness and surrender, lightness and darkness, and all the facets of human living and being operate in a real, truthful, and profound way.

References

Benner, D. G. (1993). *Care of Souls; Revisioning Christian Nurture and Counsel.* Grand Rapids, MI: Baker Books.

Budman, S. H., & Gurnam, A. S. (1988). *Theory and Practice of Brief Therapy.* New York: Guilford Press.

Goldstein, K. (1939). *The Organism, A Holistic Approach to Biology.* New York: The American Book Company.

Hellinger, B. (1996). *Touching Love, Bert Hellinger at Work with Family systems.* Heidelberg: Carl-Auer.

Hellinger, B., & Beaumont, H. (1999). *Touching Love, Volume 2.* Heidelberg: Carl-Auer.

Hellinger, B. (2003). *Peace Begins in the Soul: Family Constellations in the Service of Reconciliation.* Heidelberg: Carl-Auer.

Levine, P. A. (1997). *Waking the Tiger, Healing Trauma.* Berkeley, CA: North Atlantic Books.

Moreno, J. (1990). *Who Shall Survive? Foundations of Sociometry, Group Theory, and Sociodrama.* (3rd edition) New York and London: Routledge.

Nerin, W. F. (1986). *Family Reconstruction, Long Day's Journey into Light.* New York: W. W. Norton.

O'Hanlon, W. H., & Weiner-Davis, M. (1989). *In Search of Solutions, A New Direction in Psychotherapy.* New York: W. W. Norton.

Satir, V. (1988). *The New Perspective.* Palo Alto, CA: Science and Behavior Books.

Schutzenberger, A. A. (1989). *The Ancestor Syndrome, Transgenerational Psychotherapy and the Hidden Links in the Family Tree.* New York & London: Routledge.

Ulsamer, B. (2003). *The Art and Practice of Family Constellations as Developed by Bert Helllinger.* Heidelberg: Carl-Auer.

Part II
Work In Progress

6

Begin With the Work: Family Constellations and Larger Systems

by Daniel Booth Cohen

When a facilitator begins with a group that is not familiar with constellations, the reasonable way to start is with an introduction that explains the history, key concepts, and basic mechanics of the method. I have given such introductions many times, and find that they are invariably wasted. Since constellations are conducted in near silence and stillness, their impact and power cannot be conveyed into lecture form. No matter how I approach the introduction, the message the audience hears is, "Blah blah blah constellations yada yada yada."

A professor of psychology at the State University of New York recently invited me to present constellation work in three successive undergraduate classes on one day. Before the start of the second class, as students were drifting in and my host was getting some fresh air, a student blurted out:

> You're a psychologist; can you answer my question? I'm 21 years old and I have been diagnosed with clinical depression for 13 years. When I see my therapist, all she wants me to do is talk. So I talk and talk and talk, and it doesn't do me any good. The therapist never offers any advice, except that I

should be on anti-depressants. How is psychology supposed to help people?

Hmmm. Where to begin? I asked if she wanted to see how I approached the issue of depression. When the professor returned to begin the class, the student was sitting on my right and I was preparing her for a constellation. After a brief interview and orientation, I asked her to set up representatives for herself and her "depression."

The client's depression had begun when she was 8 years old and her beloved grandmother died. The two of them shared the most affectionate and caring kind of love. The girl made a solemn vow that because she loved her grandmother so much, she would never allow herself get over her death. And she never did.

What the constellation revealed was that the grandmother had made the same solemn vow years before. We could not tell who the lost love one was, or even whether it had begun with her; it was unimportant. The grandmother was carrying a burden of undying grief and the granddaughter took it over from her, out of love.

The healing solution was for her to perceive how sad this immature loyalty made the older woman. The grandmother told her, "Go live!"

The constellation both unraveled the riddle of her depression and answered her original question within a single 50-minute hour.

It's too soon to evaluate whether the new image of the grandmother's love will take hold. A woman with whom I worked two years earlier on a similar issue, and with whom I had not been in contact in the interim, sent me a message out of the blue that revealed the possibilities of this simple way of facing problems. She wrote, "I was actually thinking about you the other day because I think that I finally know what it is to be in love."

Nothing I could have said in an introduction could have made clear the power of this work or left a lasting impression on the students. By beginning with the work itself, all of us, including myself, were privileged to receive an insight of deep wisdom.

Constellations in the Context of the Jewish-Palestinian Conflict

Some weeks later, I was scheduled to lead a workshop entitled, "Peace Begins in the Soul: Ethnic Conflict, Trauma and Reconciliation" at the 2005 national conference of Brit Tzedek v'Shalom, the Jewish Alliance for Justice and Peace in New York City. There was no way to anticipate who might attend my session or how many people would be there. However, I assumed that few of them would know anything about constellations or Bert Hellinger.

Again, the common sense approach would be to begin with an introductory lecture. I had 90 minutes with a group of people who had no knowledge or experience of constellation work, and who had registered for a political and policy oriented conference. I thought I might follow the lecture with an experiential demonstration, such as a closed-eye visualization or movements of the soul using generic representatives.

Unfortunately, as I discovered, such lecture/demonstrations fall far short of imparting the energy and meaning that are present in an actual constellation. As I turned over ideas for how to proceed, the guiding message that recurred was, "Begin with the work."

To begin with the work, I needed to prearrange for a client. I made some inquiries and a woman to whom I was referred agreed to work on her personal issue in front of the group.

This woman met three criteria: (1) she had a direct familial connection to either the Holocaust or the Israeli-Palestinian conflict; (2) she had a serious personal issue that was deeply troubling to her and that she would be willing to shift; and (3) she was willing to work on her personal issue in front of the group.

The woman had lived in Israel. Her ex-husband was the son of Holocaust survivors. One of their children was filled with rage.

There was a heavy snowstorm on the morning of the workshop and the client was unable to get there, putting me in the unenviable position of a choreographer who steps in front of the curtain on opening night to ask: "Who brought toe shoes?"

But unlike the choreographer's audience, mine didn't even know what to expect from me.

My offer to demonstrate an obscure therapeutic intervention that would point to a solution to one person's most serious personal issue *and* cast light on the insoluble issue of peace for the Jews seemed to be being met with subtle, and not-so-subtle, resistance.

The room itself seemed to be rebelling against this proposition. The windows were opened to let in air, but with the air came the drowning loud rat-a-tat-tat of a nearby jackhammer. People drifted in late; others stood up, gathered their belongings, and walked out.

It all seemed like a fitting background metaphor. The Israeli-Palestinian conflict is messy, chaotic and confusing. Even with the comings and goings, the seats remained occupied. We all know the existing tools are woefully insufficient. There's a dawning awareness that, in the words of Sun Ra, "Once you've done everything that's possible, there's nothing left but the impossible."

I asked if anyone in the circle satisfied the three criteria mentioned earlier. A woman volunteered that her grandparents had immediate relatives who had died in the Holocaust; she had a serious relationship problem with her adopted daughter; and she was willing to serve as a client. So, we began with the work.

The interview revealed that she and her husband had adopted a young girl from Russia who was now 21. From the start, their relationship had been strained, often combative. The client was clearly distraught over the enmity that characterized the relationship and anxious about the young woman's prospects for having a relatively healthy and content adult life. "She's the angriest person I know. I'm frightened to be with her a lot of the time."

The client's mother had had a successful career and had given the job of child-rearing to an African-African housemaid (here called V). The client and V remained close. V had gone on to become prominent in her church and a respected community leader. The client had married and had two miscarriages before deciding to adopt. The marriage endured.

I asked her what she would most want to change in her relationship with her adopted daughter, if she could. She answered, "I would just like us to be friends."

I told the group that while the issue was serious in terms of the parent-child relationship, I was uncertain as to how it related to the topic of the Brit Tzedek conference and our purpose to shed light on the role of American Jews in the Israeli-Palestinian conflict. In any event, having begun this way, my focus was to serve the client's system. The client responded, "I see the connection. It's like I'm living with a terrorist in my midst. I actually say that sometimes."

After sitting with the issue in silence, I asked her to select two representatives from the group: one for herself and the other for her daughter. I then showed her how to set up a constellation and gave the representatives instructions on what to do.

The two representatives were set up back-to-back, about three feet apart. The representative for the daughter disclosed that she was uncomfortable with participating; I replaced her. After several minutes, the representatives became tuned into the emergent information field.

Clearly, the two were estranged. Their attention was elsewhere. How was the adopted daughter feeling? She said she felt very sad and alone. And the adopted mother's representative? She reported feeling pained at trying to love someone who could not receive. She wanted to care, but could not reach out. The client confirmed with a nod that the portrayal of her and her daughter was accurate.

I brought in a woman to stand facing the adopted daughter and two other women to stand facing the adoptive mother. The daughter and client's representatives felt relieved.

What emerged was that the daughter was greatly burdened by the circumstances of her birth, her abandonment by her parents, and some events that had caused enormous suffering in her family of origin. We did not know anything of the details of the young woman's family background, and could not speculate. However, our knowledge of Russian history tells us that 40 million Russians died as a result of the Communist-forced collectivism the two World Wars, and Stalin's reign of terror and its aftermath. Such a burden was too much to bear, and the daughter expressed these wounds in her hostile and disturbed behavior.

The adoptive mother had taken on the responsibility of caring for a child whose own mother could not do so. The task proved much more demanding than she had imagined, and besides she, too, was drawn to some distant source of suffering. The exact facts and circumstances were not important, and I did not inquire about them. What was evident was that the daughter's burdens were too great and the adoptive mother's resources were too little. They could not hold on to each other in love. Instead, their meetings were collisions between "too much" and "too little." The result was a hostile state of enmity, with each person turned away toward the original source of her strength.

In observing this scene the client seemed deeply moved. I was careful not to interfere with her processing of the information by offering too much interpretation or soliciting her comments. It was enough to see the expression on her face and her body language to know that something had touched her deeply.

The constellation changed at this point from being very still and silent to becoming slightly more active and verbal. My role as facilitator is to read the field using a combination of intuition and experience. Between each of the actions described below, there was a long period of time, several minutes in some cases. The movements of the soul are always slow. Constellations allow time for the images to be perceived and absorbed.

I told the representative for the daughter that the woman I had placed in front of her was her mother, her Russian birth mother. They faced each other, connecting deeply with love, grief, and pain. Tears welled.

Representatives in a constellation repeat words suggested to them by the facilitator. This is not role playing or psychodrama. The words are meant to verbalize reality, for example, "You died and I lived." The words are used in two stages: first, to cement the image of the current reality, and second, to offer another image that represents healing within the system and the possibility of a future existence on a different footing than in the past.

The (birth) mother said to the daughter, "I couldn't hold on to you. It was too hard for me. I lost everything."

The daughter told her, "I missed you so much. There was no one to love me."

I brought in a representative for the Russian father to stand beside the mother.

The daughter said, "I see you now. You will always be my mother and father."

The mother volunteered that she wanted to touch her daughter, but felt she had lost the right to do so. Nevertheless, they faced each other with love.

I told the representative for the client that the two women standing before her were her mother and V.

I observed that V must have also carried a deep burden of suffering from her family's experience of American slavery. Imagine how much was lost, how the family was torn apart and scattered. How many died? And yet, when that impoverished Black woman working as a servant in an affluent White family's house was handed that baby, she just loved her. Through all her pain, she loved the baby and took care of her as best she could. What a great gift! When the client had been unable to have children of her own, she decided to take good care of another mother's child. But what she took on was overwhelmingly difficult.

The client's representative said to her mother, "Thank you for giving me life. I will do something good with it." And to V, "Thank you for loving me and taking such good care of me."

She bowed deeply to them both and they embraced.

The client's representative went to the daughter and her parents. She told the parents, "I see you now. I see how much you suffered. Thank you for your daughter. I will always love her and take care of her as best I can." The parents accepted the acknowledgment and indicated their approval, thanking the client for taking care of their child.

With the daughter reconciled with her parents and the adopted mother cognizant of the larger systemic forces that weighed on the girl, I brought the client herself into the constellation. Once she had tuned into the field, her representative sat down. The client repeated seeing, acknowledging, and honoring the parents.

The client brought the daughter to meet her mother and V. She said, "This is my mother. This is V. She is my best friend."

The daughter expressed feeling strong, loved, and supported. The client saw that her role was as caregiver. She was not her daughter's mother, even if she was the only mother she had. Warmth flowed between them and they embraced for a long time.

I said, "Let's leave it here."

When we sat down, the room was still and the group hushed. Even the jackhammer was silent, although no one recalled its stopping. Tissues came out. Once again, in the stillness and silence of a constellation, deep emotions were felt and profound truths seen. It was a lot to absorb, even for me.

Relating an Individual Constellation to Larger-Group Conflicts

As our attention was released from the field of the client and her adopted daughter, we as a group were left with questions of how to integrate what we had just seen. Now what? Is it possible to extrapolate meaningful messages from a single constellation to large social issues and national conflicts that involve millions of individuals?

Each constellation can be seen as a spontaneous, living novella that encompasses both unique individual experiences and universal principles. If we proceed with humility and openness, we can respect the sanctity of the individual and perceive how each person's story is a part of our shared common humanity. Done with care and respect, it is appropriate to draw lines from the specific to the general. We can use the information that comes through the field to expand our understanding of larger social and political issues.

Those of us who have witnessed numerous constellations become accustomed to being awed and moved to tears by the information that comes to light. We are surprised and *not* surprised to see that ideas that are universally accepted are often manifestations of collective fantasies or illusions.

In this case, the adoptive mother did not respect, or even see, the suffering and loss felt by the birth mother. She mentioned afterward that this is common in many adoptive families and the organizations that support them. Birth parents disappear from the family portrait. In a constellation involving adoption, the biological mother and father are always given a place. It is to them that children owe their existence, regardless of the circumstances of birth. One of the foundational principles in constellations is that excluding a person who belongs to the system creates suffering and that restoring his or her rightful place brings relief.

Thus, there exists a great gulf between commonly held views in the public discourse and the inner movements and motivations that reveal themselves in the constellation field. This gulf represents both an obstacle to taking the work forward and an urgent call to expand the use of constellations.

In relation to the Jewish-American community and its influence on the Israeli-Palestinian conflict, there are three overarching themes that sit on opposites sides of this gulf between a common culture and the will of the soul. In constellations, we see their validity confirmed again and again, but in public discussion, we hear them just as frequently dismissed and denied. The first theme is the relative worth of feeling justified in one's actions. The second is how the living can best honor the dead. The third theme is how we view the perpetrators of genocide.

The Limits of Innocence

There is a nearly universally embraced precept that persons, groups or nations can justify their actions by weighing the good against the bad. A typical example comes from the Anti-Defamation League (ADL). When the Oslo Peace Process fell apart in early 2001, the ADL published an article entitled, "Advocating for Israel: An Activist's Guide" (2001). Its purpose was to "present facts and talking points on the history of the Israeli-Palestinian conflict and information for reaching out to elected officials and the media" (p. 1).

I read the article to see how it presented good versus bad as determinants to bolster support for the Israeli government. The number of times the word "violence" appears: 20. The number of these 20 references that refer specifically to Palestinian violence against Jews and Israel: 20. The number of times the word "peace" appears in the document: 19. The number of these 19 references that refer to Israel's desire for peace or Palestinian's rejection of peace: 19. The number of times the word "terrorist" is used: 19. The number of these 19 references where the word terrorist is conjoined with the word Palestinian: 18.

This approach to argument and advocacy is mirrored in many pro-Palestinian sites. The following table contains excerpts from the ADL document and an article, "Understanding the Palestinian-Israeli Conflict," published by the Trans-Arab Research Institute (Bennis, 2002). Claims of innocence and guilt are employed in the service of shaping public opinion.

Anti-Defamation League	Trans-Arab Research Institute
The Israel Defense Forces have shown the greatest possible restraint.	Violence is central to maintaining Israel's military occupation.
Prime Minister Sharon is maintaining the policy of restraint.	Israel has increasingly escalated the weapons it deploys against the Palestinians.
The targeting of known Palestinian terrorists by Israeli agents is a policy of self-defense.	Palestinian violence is the violence of resistance.
Israeli policies toward the Palestinians are dictated solely by Israel's need to defend its population.	Shoot-to-kill curfews were imposed on Palestinian cities, imprisoning people in their homes.

Anti-Defamation League	Trans-Arab Research Institute
There is no systematic Israeli plan to persecute, exterminate, or expel the Palestinian population.	Palestinians were forcibly expelled.
Israeli Arab citizens enjoy the same rights as their Jewish neighbors.	"Nationality rights" favor Jews over non-Jews in social services, access to bank loans, and education.
Palestinians seek out and provoke Israeli soldiers and civilians.	The second intifada was the response to lost hopes and deteriorated lives.
The Palestinians have demonstrated that they are not willing or able to make the serious decisions necessary for peace.	In an enormous compromise, the Palestinian National Council voted to accept a two-state solution.
Palestinians have rejected negotiations and used violence and terrorism.	The "generous offer" was a myth.
…unceasing Palestinian violence.	Brutal occupation.
Palestinians…turn to violence.	Israel's occupation became increasingly harsh.

The point is not to argue the facts on merits, but to illustrate that the practice of assigning innocence to ourselves and guilt to our enemies is the rhetorical device favored by advocates of all stripes.

This style of advocacy is a function of the workings of conscience. Conscience whispers that we are the innocent ones, our actions are justified and righteous, our beliefs are merited, and our opponents are misguided, or even evil. We believe our conscience because we understand it to be a mechanism for distinguishing the good from the bad, even though it invariably determines that our people are the good ones and our enemies the bad ones. Even when we do bad things, these actions can be justified by good reasons.

What comes through in constellations time and again is that opposing parties cannot reach reconciliation by maintaining a good conscience. Instead, we see that healing and acceptance come from embracing what we viscerally reject and acknowledging and honoring what we would reflexively exclude. Yet this is the very opposite of what commonsense tells us.

In Jewish and Christian theology, and Western philosophy more generally, conscience is seen as a regulator of ethical values and behavior. We are taught that a good conscience acts on the soul to encourage righteousness. Conversely, a bad or guilty conscience is the product of thoughts and deeds that are against God's beneficence. If not atoned for, confessed, or absolved, the corrosive effects of a bad conscience lead to eternal damnation or shame.

In scientific psychology, conscience serves a similar purpose, to regulate in favor of behaviors that support mutual survival and to make taboo those behaviors that society and culture have determined to be destructive or evil. With or without a soul, conscience is seen as an internal driver that praises what is good and discourages what is bad.

Bert Hellinger (1998) has written extensively on this topic.

> Whenever conscience acting in the service of belonging binds us to one another in a group, it also drives us to exclude those who are different and to deny them the right to the membership we claim for ourselves. ...
>
> Conscience inhibits evil within the group, but lifts this inhibition in regard to those outside the group. We then do to others in good conscience what is forbidden within our own group. In the context of religious, racial, and national conflicts, suspending the inhibitions on evil allows members of one group to commit, in good conscience, atrocities and murder against others....
>
> Thus guilt and innocence are not the same as good and evil. We do destructive and evil things with a clear conscience when they serve the groups that are necessary for our survival, and we take constructive action with a guilty conscience (p. 10).

Reconciliation cannot emerge out of a game of one-upmanship that competes as to who is more innocent or aggrieved. Yet the players persist in framing arguments in these terms because appealing to the good conscience of group members is an effective way for leaders to maintain power and control.

Entanglements Between the Living and the Dead

In looking for solutions to pressing personal problems, constellations turn to one's ancestors. Boszormenyi-Nagy (1973) introduced the hidden loyalties that connect the problems of those living with traumas of the dead to the field of family systems therapy. He observed, "The structuring of relationships, especially within families, is an extremely complex and essentially unknown 'mechanism.' Empirically, such structuring can be inferred from the lawful regularity and predictability of certain repetitious events in families" (Boszormenyi-Nagy & Spark, 1973, p.1). Hellinger made a similar observation in a different context. He lived for 16 years with the Zulus in South Africa and became immersed in their tribal form of ancestor worship.

The Zulu people live and act in a religious world in which one's ancestors are the central focal point. "The ancestral spirits are of fundamental significance for the Zulu. They are the departed souls of the deceased. Although they are regarded as having gone to abide in the earth, they continue to have a relationship with those still living" (Lawson, 1985, pp. 24-25). Their ancestors are regarded as positive, constructive, and creative presences. Failure to show them proper respect invites misfortune; proper veneration ensures benefit. When a family member suffers the consequences of incurring an ancestor's wrath, the punishment is not regarded as destructive. Rather, it is viewed as a legitimate expression of the failure of the individual to uphold his or her duty to the family unit.

Hellinger (2001) explains his therapeutic stance toward ancestors this way:

> What I have been looking for in my work is actually the Alpha, the source from which everything

emerges, from which everything springs. Therefore, in my individual work, and in my work with others, I always look to see, "Where is the beginning and where is the original strength?"

All therapy, as I understand it, has to go to the source. For each one of us, the source is, first of all, our parents. If we are connected to our parents, we are connected to our source. A person who is separated from his or her parents is separated from his or her source. Whoever the parents are, however they behaved, they are the source of life for us. So the main thing is that we connect to them in such a way that what comes from them can flow freely to us, and through us, to those who follow.

In constellations involving Jewish families, we frequently see that the connection between clients and their parents has become a transmission line carrying victim-and-perpetrator energy. This is not always perceived in conscious awareness, but it emerges when clients set themselves and their parents up in a constellation.

What comes to light is that the presently configured collective Jewish-American psyche is resistant to efforts aimed at conciliation between Israelis and Palestinians. Our community recoils from such efforts. We equate being Jewish with having enemies who want to kill us; we cannot see a way to give up one without giving up the other. It is not felt this way, of course. What is felt is that we are Jewish *and* we have enemies. It is the weight of generations of trauma, persecution, and genocide that is burdening upon us.

Loyalty to the dead defines Jewish identity, beginning with Abraham. In Genesis 12, the Lord says, "Unto thy seed will I give this land." It is in this declaration that the root of the current conflict is clearly stated.

Jewish history is a series of stories about the descendents of Abraham being tested: whether to assimilate into the indigenous population or remain apart. Each holiday presents another lesson in sacrifice and perseverance. We honor those who keep the covenants and erase our memories of those who forsake them. Holding allegiance to the lineage of Jewish martyrs becomes the highest principle of existence.

The Nazi Holocaust pushed the keeping of this covenant, despite all costs, beyond the breaking point. The murder of six million European Jews in seven years took an enormous toll on the collective Jewish psyche. The grief was unbearable. Time has not healed these wounds, only redirected them.

Jewish children born after 1945 are taught that Judaism is like an exquisite, precious crystalline sphere that was created by God, given to Abraham, Isaac, and Jacob; and then passed down to each successive generation. Today's post-Holocaust Jews are its custodians, commanded to protect it, above all else. But this exquisite, precious crystalline sphere contains a dark secret. It's unspoken, but the soul knows.

Vegh (1979), cited in Schützenberger (1998), collected oral histories from children who had not been told the truth about their parents' deportation and subsequent death in concentration camps. She presents the case of Robert, a 14-year-old Jewish child, who recalled:

> When my father was deported, he cried out as he left, "Robert, don't forget you are Jewish and must remain Jewish!" These were his last words; I can hear them as if it were yesterday. He didn't say, "I love you, don't be afraid, take care of yourself," but just that one sentence. I hold it against them, don't you understand? Yes, I hold it against the dead who paid for my life with theirs. It's unbearable (pp. 50-51).

Robert's anguish may be considered aberrant, the result of the trauma he suffered. However, he is vocalizing a feeling that surfaces in many constellations. Schützenberger (1998), commenting on this story, writes:

> It is better to know a truth, even if it is difficult, shameful or tragic, rather than to hide it, because what we hide, others pick up on or guess and this secret, this unspoken truth, becomes a more serious trauma in the long run (p. 52).

The secret is that for Jews whose relatives died or were terrorized in the Holocaust, and this includes the majority of American Jews whose immigrant ancestors left family behind, that exquisite, precious, crystalline sphere is also a piercing shard of the Kristallnacht in their hearts.

Robert's loss was too immediate and personal to overcome. His grief and anguish were unbearable. In the souls of American Jews, this unbearable grief is present, but suppressed. As in the case of the adopted Russian girl, when unbearable grief is suppressed, it returns in a later generation as aggression.

Reconciliation at the Expense of Innocence and Loyalty

Constellations reveal that reconciliation with our enemies comes at the expense of a measure of innocence and loyalty. The insistence that we are the good ones and our enemies are the bad ones interferes with the movement toward peace. It is painful and uncomfortable to expand the circle of our conscience to include those we oppose.

Sara Roy, whose mother and father survived Auschwitz, is a senior research scholar at the Center for Middle Eastern Studies at Harvard. In her Holocaust remembrance talk, *Living with the Holocaust: The Journey of a Child of Holocaust Survivors* (2002), she claims license, by virtue of her family's past, to acknowledge how the descendants of the victims of one generation's genocide become the aggressors when given the opportunity and means:

> In the post-Holocaust world, Jewish memory has faltered — even failed — in one critical respect: it has excluded the reality of Palestinian suffering and Jewish culpability therein. As a people, we

have been unable to link the creation of Israel with the displacement of the Palestinians. We have been unwilling to see, let alone remember, that finding our place meant the loss of theirs.

Very few Jewish Americans are willing to take on the guilt that comes with this recognition. The internal dialogue says, "Yes, what a shame." Then it restores its equilibrium and life goes on as before. A message I received from a friend captures this response, "Of course, Sharon has a history, and quite probably a ruthless one, but right now, today, he's doing the best he can to keep schoolchildren from being hurt, that's his job" (Eskin, personal communication).

Sara Roy ends her speech with a quote from Irena Kepfisz, whose father died in the Warsaw uprising:

> I have concluded that one way to pay tribute to those we loved who struggled, resisted and died is to hold on to their vision and their fierce outrage at the destruction of the ordinary life of their people. It is this outrage we need to keep alive in our daily life and apply it to all situations, whether they involve Jews or non-Jews.... At those moments of recognition, we remember the past, feel the outrage that inspired the Jews of the Warsaw Ghetto and allow it to guide us in present struggles.

I agree with Sara Roy that the fierce outrage we feel for the destruction of the ordinary life is connected to our relatives who were murdered by the Nazis. There is strength in this outrage if it lifts us above resignation and despair. If we connect with the outrage that inspired the Jew of the Warsaw Ghetto and allow it to guide us in present struggles, perhaps we can do something constructive to end the continuing cycle of killing and revenge.

Yet, this also exposes the limitation of outrage as a source of healing. For what is the bulldozing of houses and fields except an expression of outrage in response to the destruction of ordinary life? What is a terrorist attack? All the combatants are connecting in some way to a family member who was murdered or subjected to injustice. Outrage fuels it all. Irena Klepfisz's call to distinguish between "good outrage" that defends ordinary life and "bad outrage" that perpetuates the cycle of atrocity and retribution creates a standard that is hopelessly muddled.

Here's an alternative ending that paraphrases Hellinger: One way to pay tribute to those we loved who struggled, resisted, and died, is to look them in the eye and say, "I see the terrible price you paid that I may live. I accept life and I will make something good out of it. Rest in peace, knowing that I will live so that your loss is not in vain." Love at a higher level demands that we relinquish the belief that outrage changes the fate of the dead for the better. Doing so transforms the blind love that creates and perpetuates suffering into a love that heals.

The Dignity of the Perpetrator

Still this is not enough. There is one more step required to give strength to peace-building efforts. It is the most challenging part.

On the last afternoon of sessions at the 2003 International Congress on Family and Systems Constellations in Würzburg, Germany, I was undecided as to which program to attend. I wasn't able to choose between Sami Adwan and Dan Bar-On on facilitating dialogue between Israelis and Palestinians and Albrecht Mahr on methods of using family constellations in political and conflict resolution situations.

Over lunch, I discussed my choices with Karin Cramer, a German friend from our membership in One-by-One, a dialogue group for the children of victims and perpetrators of the Holocaust. Like many members of One-by-One, Karin is skeptical about the constellation process, but came to Würzburg to learn more. She recommended a workshop I had not even considered, led by Eva Madelung on the topic of Perpetrators, Victims, and Resistance. There's an Arab saying: "When you must decide between two difficult choices, always pick the third."

Karin sat beside me and whispered a contemporaneous translation as the session began with a round of introductions. It quickly became clear that this was no ordinary group. Nearly every participant said that one or both of his or her parents were Nazis, many of them of high rank. As I listened, my imagination went back one generation to the war period. I, as a Jew, might have been killed by them immediately. And I might have killed them in combat, as a soldier in the U.S. Army that defeated Germany.

As the only one requiring an English translation, the only one from a Jewish family, I felt threatened as a *Juden*, an *Auslander*. Yet, I also felt that I was a welcome guest. The children of Nazi murderers ordinarily do not gather together like members of an astronomy club. Their meeting in this private setting to confess, confront, and heal embedded wounds was extraordinary in itself. Within the context of the Würzburg conference, they were expressly making an opening for me to join.

The first constellation was for a woman whose father was a high-ranking SS officer. Her issue was suicidal depression. She set up her father, mother, and herself in a family constellation. After some time, Eva Madelung added some other representatives to the system. Then, after several more minutes, she came to me and, without a word, placed me directly behind the father.

Although I was aware of my personal feelings at being placed in this situation, I was also aware that the constellation was in service of the client, and that my willingness to be in the room carried with it a responsibility to respect the process.

My initial feeling was of a fear to which I would never admit. The representative of the father appeared to be strong and dangerous, and my response was to be stronger and more dangerous. I expressed this by standing erect, immobile, and by looking directly, and only, at him, without expression.

After some more time, Madelung came to the father and turned him around to face me, saying to him, "This is Hitler." There was a communal gasp in the room. My feeling of fear that I would never reveal, and also of solid, impenetrable, immobile, expressionless strength, heightened. It was comparable, perhaps, to the way that Death may appear in a constellation.

The father reported that he loved Hitler as a small boy loves his father, completely, devotedly, unconditionally. He would do whatever Hitler wished, without question or guilt, out of love. The solution appeared when the daughter was able to see the human quality that lay beneath her father's extreme behavior. Without absolving him of guilt or excusing his actions, she was able to take in his strength and dignity.

For Jewish-American families, the perpetrators of murders against Jews also belong to the system. It cannot be justified intellectually or explained. When the perpetrator is not acknowledged and given a place in the system, someone in a subsequent generation becomes a perpetrator. Despising the perpetrators fuels perpetrator energy in the family system.

The rage held by the grandson of Holocaust survivors could be inherited unconsciously according to "the lawful regularity and predictability of certain repetitive events in families" (Boszormenyi-Nagy & Spark, 1973, p. 1). Since the protagonists of the historic event are now dead, the rage is expressed against anyone who represents them. This is how the descendants of the victims in one generation become perpetrators in the next. As the novelist Shirley Hazzard (1980) puts it, "Of those who had endured the worst, not all behaved nobly or consistently. But all, involuntarily, became part of some deeper assertion of life" (p. 171).

Including and acknowledging the perpetrators does not mean forgiving them or excusing their crimes. On the contrary, their guilt cannot be reduced, absolved, or washed away. What such acknowledgment means is seeing the perpetrators as human beings; full human beings, who had parents, lovers, and children.

They, like their victims, were caught up in something greater than themselves. They suffered too.

By saying, "I see you. I respect your guilt. I leave it with you," the outrage — unconsciously taken on by the families of victims — is returned to the perpetrators. The dignity of the perpetrators resides in their guilt. The victim leaves the perpetrators with their dignity, and leaves it to them to face their guilt.

Thus, there are three emergent themes that promote reconciliation. The first is to acknowledge that acting in good conscience is not the same as doing good. In fact, peacemakers must be willing to bear the cost of being disloyal to their own group to reach out to members of opposing groups.

The second theme is that the memory of the dead is not served by perpetuating suffering in the living. This is true whether it is our suffering, as in the case of the granddaughter who was willing to mourn forever, or the suffering of others, such as when children seek to avenge the violence and injustice perpetrated against their parents and ancestors.

The third is that when murder occurs in a family, the killers (or victims) become members of the family system and must be given their rightful places. As Madelung (2001) states, at the deepest level of common humanity, "everybody is equal, facing something greater, and each fate has its own dignity. For the child of a perpetrator or for the child of a victim the inner stance that facilitates resolution is a stance that integrates both parts. This stance pays equal respect both for the fate of the victim and for the fate of the perpetrator."

These themes are not substitutes or replacements for conventional approaches, such as negotiations, dialogue, political advocacy, or shared empathy. The insights from constellations augment the ways of achieving reconciliation.

Influencing Others Versus Healing Oneself

Systemic constellations could be used in the service of healing the wounds of the Holocaust that remain alive in the American descendents of European Jews. These wounds, which can be expressed as emotional, physical, and relationship difficulties on a personal level, also express themselves in the political realm. I envisioned constellation work as a means of bridging between the personal and political spheres. However, despite considerable effort in these past five years, my attempts have been slow to gain traction. The workshop at the Brit Tzedek conference represented one more effort to place the insights of constellations onto the canvas of public debate and discourse.

The need for such insight was revealed once again before I even stepped into the building. On Saturday evening, at the start of the conference, a well-dressed man in his 50s stood on the sidewalk handing flyers to the participants. I was not surprised when I read the opening paragraph, "Doesn't trying to appease a group like the PLO, who are Arab Nazis whose goal is still to try and murder every Jew in Israel, make them see Jews as weak and easy targets?" This confusion over Nazi and Arab, victim and perpetrator, the guilty and the innocent, the weak easy target and the most virulent armed force on the planet, becomes alarmingly apparent in the information field of a constellation.

The constellation process is designed to reveal these dynamics. But those who are most likely to be entangled in this way are the least likely to be willing to participate in the process. As one hawkish member of a synagogue dialogue group told me, "I will gladly do your constellation process, but only if you can assure me beforehand that it will reinforce, not overturn, my preexisting beliefs."

This type of reaction is to be expected. What has been more difficult to address is that the peace activists are almost as reluctant as the hawks to join a constellation circle. I have done my best to introduce constellation work to various grassroots groups working on Israel-Palestine issues, but with a glaring lack of success. The response has been a uniform, "No, thank you."

One workshop participant explained her reluctance this way: "If I come to a meeting about politics and policy, I do not want to end up doing personal therapy. And if I choose to do personal therapy, I don't want my being exposed in front of people coming to a politically oriented meeting."

Otto Rank (1998) spelled out this dichotomy between the desire to influence others and the reluctance to change one's own opinions through a process of personal growth. He wrote:

> We must distinguish between two facets of psychology: that of self knowledge and that of knowledge of others. The first is psychology of self-awareness, and the second is psychology as a means, tool or "technique" to control others. Deep down, we don't want to observe ourselves and increase self-knowledge. First of all, the search for self-knowledge is not an original part of our nature; second, it is painful, and finally, it doesn't always help but often is disturbing. Knowledge of others can be put to use; too often, self-knowledge proves a hindrance (p. 5).

This dichotomy is proving to be a formidable obstacle to bringing constellations into the discourse. Nevertheless, I persist. Slowly the work is taking hold. As Rank warned, constellations are often painful and disturbing. However, the feedback suggests that they do help, often quite a lot. In beginning with the work, we are, if nothing else, helping to heal one person and his or her family. Maybe that is enough.

Conclusion

When the terrorist in our midst is a Palestinian suicide bomber, we can deploy the armed forces to destroy his or her family's house or an entire village. We can invade other countries. We can construct a security fence to wall ourselves off from the danger. We can install a ruthless warrior as the prime minister of the Jewish state and then call him "Our best hope for peace."

When the terrorist in our midst is our child, lover, or even an aspect of ourselves, the Israeli Defense Forces won't defend us. Some people fight to the end. Others look for peaceful solutions.

Jews can live as Jews without having enemies who want to kill them when they acknowledge and accept that Palestinians have the same dignity, the same honor, and the same rights as the Israelis. A Palestinian life is exactly equal in value to a Jewish life. The tears of Palestinians and Israelis carry the exact same measures of grief. Their mothers love their children as much. Their fathers want only what other fathers want. Their children are just as frightened.

Constellations reveal the fundamental unspoken, un-thought, and un-felt structures that lie beneath the surface of our conscious awareness. On this dimension, we see that love both heals and harms, innocence is often a force of destruction and acknowledged guilt can be a source of healing and benevolent strength.

For five millennia, humans have survived by protecting their own and fighting their enemies. However, as Einstein said, "The release of atomic power has changed everything except our way of thinking" (1945). Whether by Messianic redemption, apocalyptic destruction, nuclear Holocaust, or through a fragile co-existence based on mutual tolerance and respect, wherever humanity is going, Jerusalem will get there first.

In the silent stillness of a constellation circle, we tune in to the resonance of our ancestors. They received animating existence, carried it along for some time, and passed it to us. If we attend to them, perhaps they will teach us something new about how to live in peace with our parents, lovers, children, and neighbors.

References

Anti-Defamation League (2001). *Advocating for Israel: An activist's guide.* Washington, DC: Anti-Defamation League.

Bennis, P. (2002). *Understanding the Palestinian-Israeli Conflict.* Orlando, FL: Trans-Arab Research Institute.

Boszormenyi-Nagy, I. and Spark, G.M. (1973). *Invisible loyalties: Reciprocity in Intergenerational Family Therapy.* Hagerstown, MD: Harper & Row.

Einstein, A. (1945). Retrieved March 30, 2005 from http://en.wikiquote.org/wiki/ =Albert_Einstein.

Hazzard, S. (1980). *The transit of Venus.* New York: Viking.

Hellinger, B. (2001). *Alpha and Omega.* Retrieved March 13, 2005 from http://www.hellinger.com/international/english/hellinger_lectures_articles/2001_new_york_alpha_omega.shtml.

Hellinger, B., Weber, G., & Beaumont, H. (1998). *Love's Hidden Symmetry: What Makes Love Work In Relationships.* Phoenix, AZ: Zeig, Tucker & Theisen.

Lawson, E.T. (1985). *Religions of Africa.* New York: Harper & Row.

Madelung, E. (2001). *The Dignity of the Perpetrators.* (M. Abernathy, trans.). Portland, OR: Human Systems Institute. Retrieved March 13, 2005 from http://www.human-systems-institute.com/ELSCIE/article8.html.

Rank, O. (1998). *Psychology and the Soul: A Study of the Origin, Conceptual Evolution, and Nature of the Soul.* (G.C. Richter and E.J. Lieberman, Trans.). Baltimore, MD: The Johns Hopkins University Press.

Roy, S. (2002). Living with the Holocaust: The journey of a child of Holocaust survivors. *Journal of Palestine Studies,* (32)1.

Schützenberger, A.A. (1998). *Theancestor Syndrome: Transgenerational Psychotherapy and the Hidden Links in the Family Tree.* (A. Trager, trans.). New York: Routledge.

Vegh, C. (1979). *I Didn't Say Goodbye: Interviews with Children of the Holocaust.* New York: Dutton.

7

Some Heretical Thoughts On Organizational Constellations

by Jane Peterson

*We sit around in a ring and suppose
But the Secret sits in the middle and knows.*
—Robert Frost

I was the first woman engineer to be hired in my department in a high-tech company. Perhaps because I was somewhat of an outsider initially, I quickly became aware that there was a difference between the written rules of the organization and "how things really worked." Even though Harry's name was on the official organization chart as the person in charge of the department, everyone I asked would say, "Go see Sally, she'll get it done for you." Many of you who have worked in organizations can relate to this story. While employed at this company, I eventually managed both projects and people, and understanding the *un*official organization chart became very important to my success. Since then, I've run two small businesses of my own, first a ceramic artist's studio, and over the past seven years, my own small consulting, training, and seminar/workshop business, The Human Systems Institute. The visceral lessons I gained during my employment in a large, complex, fast-changing company have served me better than any textbook or training in understanding organizational constellations.

"The Rules"

I will not attempt to describe the *procedures* used in setting and facilitating organizational constellations; instead, the reader is referred to an excellent and thorough article by Gunthard Weber, M.D. (2000). Additional excellent articles in English are available in the *Systemic Solutions Bulletin* published by Barbara Stones, which is listed in the References and on Bert Hellinger's Web site, www.hellinger.com. What we will explore here are some of the typical heuristics that tend to be repeated among organizational constellation facilitators, an unofficial "gospel" of constellation protocol.

Among the perceived "rules" are: Thou shalt not do constellations *within* teams or organizations because people will be constrained by internal politics and so cannot speak freely. The constellations will be "nice," but not truthful. The corollary is: Thou shalt set up constellations in workshops or outside of organizations whenever possible, as this gets around the problem described in the first rule. And, finally, if one must work inside an organization, one should bring in one's own representatives, who are untainted by the politics of the organization.

Breaking the Rules

These are very sensible rules. You, as a department head setting up a constellation among your peers, would certainly feel constrained by the potential backlash of other department heads if you did not portray them in a good light. You would have more freedom to set up the picture as you actually feel it should be in a workshop setting, where your peers would not be present, and the details of the situation would not be known. Team members watching representatives who are not aware of the internal politics will, of course, be more persuaded by the representatives' reports than by the possibly biased reports of their colleagues. So why would we break the "rules"?

First and foremost, the use of constellations is relatively unknown here, especially in business and organizational communities. We do not have the luxury of hosting workshops to which managers, executives, and board members will come to participate in the work. Most of our potential clients have no clue as to what an organizational constellation is, or even that such things exist. In addition, many of us don't have a handy possé of representatives who will travel to various companies to play stand in-roles. Further, most of those interested in doing this work with organizations are consultants, not therapists. Constellation work has come into the United States, at least, embedded in the language of therapy, and this is confusing, if not potentially off-putting, to many consultants who might find the work useful. Even though in our translations of the German articles on the subject we have changed the word "therapist" to "facilitator," many of the descriptions retain a therapeutic flavor. Finally, those consultants with therapeutic backgrounds know only too well that most managers will quickly show you to the door if anything you say sounds too therapeutic or "new age-ish." Human emotions, and for that matter, bodies, are relatively taboo topics in American business. Problems should be solvable through rational means, not emotions and, certainly not by having people stand around saying what they feel! But in spite of these restrictions, some consultants are successfully using constellations within organizations, and a number of us have been working with smaller teams and parts of organizations.

Approaches to Organizational Constellations

Executive Coaching Versus Organizational Consulting

As consultants, our clients often present us with two very different questions, depending on the situation in which we find ourselves. When we work with an individual client in a workshop setting or in a one-to-one session, the question tends to be something along the lines of: "What shall I do regarding situation W to get result X?" When we are brought in to consult for a management team, organizational board, or chief executive or department head, however, the question tends to be: "How do I get my organization to do Y with regard to issue Z?" In the one case, we are acting as a coach to the manager or executive; in the other, we are assisting in the management of the organization. In the former, one looks at the role and needs of an individual. The latter may include this tactic, but ultimately is concerned with how the consultant's intervention will benefit the organization *as a whole* versus what benefits the *client*. To put it another way, in coaching, the psychoanalytic view of internal individual psyches is a useful perceptual lens, whereas the consultant's field of perception is the organization, the perspective is systemic, and the measure of success is the effect of the consultant's input on the organization's performance relative to its goals.

To quote a colleague, Kent Layden (Layden & Peterson, 2001), who has had 35-plus years of consulting experience, primarily with nonprofit and government organizations: "My job is to guide management to better understand the working relationship of the organization to its external and internal environments. Constellations allow me to make those dynamics clear to the board, chief executive, or management team very quickly."

Three Useful Heuristics

I learned three key lessons during my time in management that continue to help me to be effective in facilitating organizational constellations. First, as a middle manager in a rapidly changing organization, I developed an instinctive understanding of who had the power in the organization to make things happen. This wasn't necessarily the person with "position" power, but the person whose integrity or connections translated into "influence" power. Second, a lived experience of interdepartmental relationships has proved very

valuable in understanding human behavior in organizations. I have a visceral understanding of "turf" and "territory" and the relationships they engender inside an organization. Finally, since I worked in manufacturing for part of my tenure, the relationship with the final goal of the company was clear. We either made our "widgets" on time, at a profitable margin and sold them, or we were out of business. Organizations, unlike families, exist to serve an external purpose. This purpose may be complex and multilayered — meeting shareholders' financial obligations (true for most U.S. corporations), producing and selling a product, serving the needs of a city, supporting an environmental/political agenda (the Sierra Club, for example), maintaining a functioning workforce, outranking other search engines (Google, for example) and garnering the highest price for ads on your Web site, and so on. A study of individual psyches will not prepare you to understand these organizational dynamics. To work with an *organization,* rather than with an individual client, takes a sociologist's grasp of systems to master the complexities that companies and organizations face today. Experience in working in companies is one way to gain a deep understanding of organizational dynamics, although certainly not the only one. This chapter is focused primarily on work with organizations and less on coaching situations. For information on working with individual clients who have organizational issues, in addition to Weber's article, also see the articles by Heidi Baitinger (2000) and by Gert Metz and Werner Messerig (2000), as well as those articles in the *Systemic Solutions Bulletin.*

Working with Organizations

Understanding family dynamics is helpful in this context since these can be a motivating force in the behavior of individuals in the work system. However, knowledge of family dynamics is not sufficient to understand organizations as self-organizing organisms with their own goals, interactions with their environment, and needs, including the needs of the individuals who comprise the systems. The key is that the organizational constellation facilitator needs to understand that the behavior of the *system* is not an arithmetic or mechanical sum of its parts. Even in a machine such as an automobile, one cannot really understand the function of a carburetor without the car. As an organizational consultant, you need a sense of the system as a whole since you will be asked to make changes in that living organism.

Students of organizational constellations who do not have this kind of life experience or a grounding in sociological or systemic thought tend to overlook obvious questions in their initial interviews of potential constellation clients: Can the person presenting the issue actually *do* anything about it, or is that person just complaining about upper management (a favorite pastime among middle managers and employees)? Is the work team so absorbed in its own internal politics that the *goal* of the organization is no longer in view? Is the leader *able* to lead given the structure of the system in which he or she is embedded? An eye to practical consequences is important in setting up organizational constellations, and the facilitator has to be willing to challenge the client, for example, with the fact that the desire to change the way in which the department head manages may be beyond the client's sphere of influence.

Working Within Organizations

Since we are breaking the rules, here are some strategies for using constellations with clients without ever mentioning that that is what we are doing.

The Spontaneous Tabletop Constellation

This is one of the simplest ways of using constellations in a coaching, or small group, consulting context. As an example, during lunch with a colleague, she mentioned a complex decision that she needed to make concerning a business partner and various projects the two were pursuing. We did a simple tabletop constellation using an "as if" frame. I asked her, "If you were the pepper shaker [handing her the pepper shaker, which she took without hesitation], and your partner was the salt shaker [handing her the salt shaker], where do you stand with each other right now? Show me your relationship to each other." My colleague immediately placed these two items on the table. Then I asked, "And where does project X stand relative to you and your partner [handing my colleague a spoon]?" I continued to do this until we had the whole constellation (and at least one place setting of silverware) "set" on the table. Once my colleague could see that her partner was only looking at one project, not the one in which she herself was most interested, the source of their miscommunication and conflict became clear. We did this without once using the word "constellation."

A variation on this method can also be used with a small number of team members or department heads (the most we've done this with was about eight people). Just as in a couple's constellation where one person sets up the constellation of the family and the other modifies it, everyone sees the different views of the organization. If you have a deck of cards or a number of small sheets of paper, you can have each member create his or her own tabletop constellation, and then let the team members compare their views. This allows the members to see where their perspectives on the organization may be out of synch. This very simple form of constellation shows the power of assuming that your client will know what to do when you act "as if" his or her business partner can be represented by the salt shaker and project X by the spoon, or the team by a pack of playing cards. The "game" context of playing cards can also help to suspend the normal working rules of an organization and permit team members to enter into an exploratory learning space together. Kent Layden and I used this method (with small laminated "people" cards) with a local Fire Department to uncover the differing "unofficial" organizational maps held by key members of the management team. People have successfully used a variety of objects to solicit these maps, and to do small, in-the-moment constellations.

Standing in the Other Person's Shoes

This is a way of inviting members of a team to learn more about their fellow members' experiences. Because people generally want to be understood, it is relatively easy to get them to cooperate. There are several ways to go about doing this. The tabletop constellations can be done first, and then the team members can take turns standing in the various constellations. We have also done constellations in which the manager set up the constellation, and then the team members rotated through the various positions. In one, the members said that it gave them a greater appreciation of the challenges that the other members' faced. Using simple language to invite team members to wonder what things might look like from the other person's perspective or telling a story about how taking the other person's perspective helped to resolve a conflict can introduce this idea to a small group. Here is a place where the "set up no more than five to eight members" rule is a useful guideline — to preserve the sanity of the facilitator.

Show Me What's Happening Here

Layden tells the story of being invited to a board retreat for an organization that was having a difficult time firing a high-performing manager for political reasons. Layden used his position as a "newcomer" to have the group do a constellation using members of the team. He asked the group, "I'm new here, and I know you are having difficulties, so why don't you show me how things stand between you?" He invited the group members to position themselves in the room according to how they thought things stood between them. The manager placed himself away from the main group, even though he had not been told of the board's decision. Although this was a tense moment for the group, once the facts of the situation became clear, the group could begin to move through the difficult situation together and take appropriate actions that honored the manager's contribution.

As a consultant and facilitator, if you are comfortable with tension, have rapport with and permission from the main power brokers and stakeholders in a group, and have good facilitative skills, you can work directly with a team that is in trouble. The team members already sense something is going on, as in the foregoing example, however they usually lack the courage to name the problem, and so get stuck. Such situations can be tense, and yet the experienced facilitator is not bringing in any new information, just providing a container for the team to use to work through what is already happening, with greater awareness and responsibility.

Blind Constellations

If you have permission from a work team, it is possible to set up a "blind" constellation in which only the person setting up the constellation actually knows who is representing whom. One easy way to do this is to utilize the ubiquitous adhesive-backed name tags that most organizations have available for meetings (or bring your own; they fit easily in a briefcase and can double as "people cards" for tabletop constellations). In assisting the client to choose representatives, we have the client select team members to represent someone other than themselves. The person setting up the constellation then uses a code — it could be a number or a letter of the alphabet — for each member of the team. In this way, the constellation can be arranged, the responses from the representatives are less likely to be biased, and information for the various team members can be brought to the surface in a confidential manner. This is also a helpful technique to employ in small towns or communities where confidentiality is important.

These are just a few samples of the creative ways consultants have found to work around the limitations of not having organizational constellation workshops available or groups of representatives at hand. Although we have not done formal research, those of us who have used these methods seem to be getting results similar to those of constellations done in workshop groups.

Working Covertly with Family Issues

As described in Weber's (2000) article, there are many ways to address the family issues that might surface in organizational constellations. Our estimate is that, in a coaching or workshop setting, family issues will show up between 30% and 50% of the time. The percentage is slightly lower when the focus is on the functional dynamics of the organization. We have evolved a fairly neutral language to address family issues indirectly, such as describing what is clearly a need for support from a father, "Imagine you have a resource behind you that will give you some backing to do what you need to do."

Why Organizational Constellations Are So Powerful

Managers can *feel,* but not *see,* many of the issues with which they grapple on a regular basis because they are too close to the issue or are part of the problem themselves. Organizational constellations allow the manager to get a different perspective on issues and to observe the structure of the organization or the effects of the behaviors of team members on the whole. Constellations also put this "felt sense" information into the preferred format for manipulating data in organizations (flip charts, PowerPoint presentations, graphic handouts — all visual aids for understanding). Now the manager can finally *see* what has been eluding his or her attempts at solution.

Finally the constellation process itself promotes "buy-in" from managers. It's *their* picture of their situation, not the consultant's interpretation. Because of their participatory nature, organizational constellations promote ownership on the part of the client. Assuming that the consultant maintains sufficient rapport with the client or work team, even difficult issues can be addressed via variations of the constellation format. Often a constellation allows the information that everyone knows but no one can name to surface and confirms the sanity of the manager and/or group. ("We're not crazy, there really is something going on here.")

In his recent book, *Blink* (2005), Malcolm Gladwell makes the case that we use our momentary initial impressions of available perceptual information to make what are often good decisions. On the other hand, as Tversky, Kahneman, and Slovic (1982) and other researchers meticulously show, many of our snap decisions and favorite heuristics are based in erroneous thinking. Constellations provide a system of checks and balances for the manager's hunches and hypotheses about what is going on in his or her department by connecting the manager to a larger field of information. For example, in a constellation that I did for the head of a services department, the former head of the department had been asked by senior management to step aside because her approach was dividing the staff and causing acrimony among the members of a previously well-functioning group. The former department head was, however, still part of the group. The current chair had several theories about why the group continued to be split along the lines that the former head had created, and it was clear that the previous department head still had considerable influence in the organization. Even though the new head had seniority and now held a higher position than the former head, he hesitated to use his standing and, instead attempted to "be friends" and to gain the former department head's support. When the staff members, including this former chair, were lined up beside the current department head, in the order of their seniority, this former head no longer felt so powerful, and the current chair felt the strength of his position. I could then suggest that he assert his "position" more, as the current chair, with the former chair, and keep the "person" (or friend) part of their relationship separate from the "work" part. Clarifying this distinction between the "positional" and "personal" roles visibly strengthened the current department chair.

Two other enticing possibilities speak to the potential effectiveness of using constellations in organizations. As many managers and consultants know, leadership training programs often fail to produce changes in participants. To quote an article in the *Academy of Management Executive Journal* (2004): "This very condition was acknowledged by Steve Kerr when he was asked about the basis for changing GE's Leadership Development program. 'It's Organization Development 101,' he quipped. 'You should never send a changed person back to an unchanged environment.'" In contrast to many leadership trainings, constellations uniquely facilitate collective learning in work groups, an approach that reaches them on multiple levels of experience, not just intellectual. Constellations quickly reveal the weakness or structural issues that underlie many common leadership problems.

In an article that recently appeared in the *Academy of Management Review* (2004), authors von Glinow, Shapiro, and Brett challenge the merits of the popular strategy of "talking things out" for conflicts that arise in multicultural work teams. In our global marketplace, these multicultural work teams are becoming increasingly common. The authors point out that not only do team members often lack exactly equivalent words for some of their experiences, but that in some cultures, the very act of talking about a problem might be considered aggressive. In Asian cultures, for example, saving face often necessitates the use of a third-party "go-between" to resolve issues fraught with emotional content. The authors suggest that nonverbal means of exploring conflicts within these teams might be more successful than attempting to bridge the gaps presented by language. Thomas Crum (1981), a black-belt Aikido master and organizational consultant, demonstrates the effectiveness of a nonverbal approach in his story of meeting a group of Soviet educators to explore the issue of U.S.— U.S.S.R. relations during the Cold War period. Crum describes the following scene, in which he nonverbally models the relationship between the Soviets and the United States at the time.

> "I asked for a Soviet to assist me in my explanation. I put my fist out to meet his fist. As our fists touched, I started to push. He immediately pushed back. Naturally. He didn't have to think about it. Instead of letting himself be pushed over, he started to push back...Humans tend to meet force with force. I then asked the Soviet to put his face within inches of his fist, and I put my face within inches of my fist and pushed even harder. I said, 'Now, how does that feel?' He looked at me and with his Russian accent said, 'Not good! *Nyet!*' Everyone laughed."

Constellations also offer a direct route into shared, nonverbal conflict resolution in work teams and organizations. Further investigation into ways of using constellations directly in organizational settings could yield rich dividends, both for developing systemic awareness among managers and employees, and, subversively, for undermining the lopsided dependence of current management on narrow, rational solutions to complex systemic problems.

How to Speak About Constellations So that Organizations Listen

Since organizational constellations are a recent branch of the family constellation work developed by Bert Hellinger and others, the language of constellations tends to be therapeutic in nature. One of the challenges facing consultants and managers who wish to introduce constellations into their organizations is to talk about constellations so that organizational leaders will listen. Feelings, bodies, emotions, and the irrational are all unwelcome guests in most organizations. This doesn't mean that people don't have these experiences; it simply means that these feelings and sensations operate underground. If you want to introduce constellation work to an organization, don't talk about "constellations." The word itself triggers images of astrologers and Tarot card readers. As illustrated in the above examples, sometimes it is better to do the constellation and then explain afterward what happened. Avoid feeling and emotion-based language. Instead of asking a representative, "How do you feel?" use such phrases as, "What's your sense of what it's like to stand there?" Talk about learning or change instead of process or transformation. Read the *Harvard Business Review*, the Academy of Management journals, or *Forbes*, or visit www.fastcompany.com to get a sense of the language of business and organizations. Almost all constellation jargon can be translated into acceptable "management speak." Metaphor is another way to discuss the undiscussable. The fire chief in the article Kent Layden and I wrote could not talk easily about his own feelings of stress, but he could use sports team metaphors to describe the behavior of his team and his own responses.

Science is still the reigning paradigm for understanding human behavior in a management setting. A quick check of the research articles in any of the mainstream management journals will show that *positivism* lives and quantitative research studies are still the norm. Science does provide some interesting examples that can be used for analogies to constellation work. Complex adaptive systems, autopoiesis, and the "strange attractors" that organize apparently chaotic systems are all examples of scientific metaphors that can be used to explain constellations to those who wouldn't be caught anywhere near a therapist's office (at least not if their boss or co-workers might know).

With a well-tuned ear for common expressions, we find that many of the situations demonstrated in a constellation are represented in our everyday speech. We speak of "not seeing eye to eye," or someone "breathing down our neck," or we ask a colleague to "watch my back." These phrases can be used to show managers that constellations are part of ordinary human experiences and help to make what they already know with their "gut sense" of a situation visible so that they can work with it directly.

Finally, be sure that a constellation is truly the best method for resolving the issue at hand. The consultant's downfall lies in his or her becoming excited about a new learning and wanting to use it when it might not be appropriate for the client, the situation, or the issue. To paraphrase Abraham Maslow's famous remark: "If the only tool you have is a hammer, you treat everything as if it were a nail." I remember one constellation I did in which the consultant was trying to persuade a client to allow the consultant to introduce constellations in a very staid and proper business environment. The manager clearly had little need for the new tool and was just humoring the consultant until he could move onto the issues that really concerned him. Coaching the manager on how to better implement the changes he had already begun to make might have been a better fit for the client's immediate needs.

Some Final Thoughts On Learning:

Chris Argyris, Peter Senge, Otto Scharmer, and Organizational Constellations

The constellation process provides for double-loop, or even triple-loop, learning. If we have the option of doing a constellation with team members, a full body experience of the team's situation is created. This encourages learning on a behavioral level; the movements and phrases of constellations allow participants to experience directly a new behavior (single-loop learning). Constellations also encourage participants to experiment with the process of change, and to provide opportunities for self-reflection, as participants have the opportunity to view themselves from a different perspective: the double- and triple-loops described by many writers, especially Chris Argyris (1974). This is transformational learning, and it often occurs at a deep level beyond the reach of the mind and words. This embodied learning can then surface at the appropriate time and in the appropriate situation. Constellations also provide a tool for implementing Peter Senge's (1990) learning pyramid, although in a top-down fashion. Constellations start with a holistic experience that demonstrates the interconnectedness of team members and the possible shifts in relationships. A constellation often exposes the structural influences that constrain the behavior of the members of the organization for good or ill. This allows the management an opportunity to build new cognitive structures and to establish new policies in response to the stimulus of the issue facing the organization.

Finally, constellations provide the method for implementing Otto Scharmer's (2004) "Theory U." Clues to future directions and "truths" emerge naturally from the constellation process. Proper action follows from a spontaneous reorganizing of perceptions and experiencing "what is" directly. Participating in a constellation offers team members an opportunity to, in Scharmer's words, "…learn from the future as it emerges…" and gives participants the chance to "…shift the inner place from which they operate." Constellations bring participants directly into contact with Martin Buber's "Grand Will" or Hellinger's "Mystery." Constellations are a way to implement Scharmer's ideas of presencing by combining "…into a single movement of seeing, sensing, presencing, and bringing-into-being" what is happening in an organization and allow what wants to emerge to be discovered.

I like to think that organizational constellations are a positive, subversive influence in shifting organizations from a rational, mind-dominated, and often inhumane environment for feeling human beings to one that is connected, relational, and embodied. I invite you, the reader, to explore new methods for introducing this systemic way of experiencing organizations into your workplace, and to share what you learn so that you can help this field grow.

References

Argyris, C. & Schön, D. (1974). *Theory in Practice: Increasing Professional Effectiveness.* San Francisco: Jossey-Bass.

Baitinger, H. (2000). Organizational Constellations in Individual Consulting Sessions — Emergency Solutions or a Good Solution in an Emergency?" *Praxis der Organisationsaufstellungen.* Carl-Auer-Systeme Verlag. English version trans. by J. Peterson & U. Luppertz.

Crum, T. F. (1981). *The Magic of Conflict.* New York: Simon & Schuster.

Gladwell, M. (2005). *Blink.* New York: Little, Brown.

Green, C. & S. (2003). Constellations: A Hellinger lens for viewing organisational relationships and change." *Systemic Solutions Bulletin, 4,* 10–20.

Hellinger, B. (1999). *Constellation Work in Organisations* (Chile, vol. 1 - 3). Videotape series. *Movements of the Soul.*

Kahneman, D., Slovic, P., & Tversky, A. (1982). *Judgment Under Uncertainty: Heuristics and Biases.* Cambridge, England: Cambridge University Press.

Layden, K. & Peterson, J. (2001). Organisational Case Study. *Systemic Solutions Bulletin, 2,* 45–47.

Metz, G. & Messerig, W. (2000). Setting of the inner team: a procedure for personal development, group coaching and organizational consulting. *Praxis der Organisationsaufstellungen.* Heidelberg: Carl-Auer. English version trans. by J. Peterson, & U. Luppertz.

Raelin, J. A. (2004). "Don't bother putting leadership into people. Academy of Management *Executive, 18, (3), 131.*

Scharmer, C. O. (2004). *Theory U: Leading from the Emerging Future: Presencing as Social Technology of Freedom. Draft version.*

Senge, P. (1990). *The Fifth Discipline.* New York: Doubleday.

Stones, B., & ten Herkel, J. (2000). Systemic solutions in organization. *Systemic Solutions Bulletin, 1,* 16–18.

von Glinow, M. A., Shapiro, D. L., & Brett, J. M. (2004). Can we *talk*, and should we? Managing emotional conflict in multicultural teams." Academy of Management *Review, 29* (4), 578–592.

Weber, G. (2000). Organizational constellations: basics and special situations." *Praxis der Organisationsaufstellungen.* Heidelberg: Carl-Auer. English version trans. by J. Peterson & U. Luppertz.

8

A Couple Is More Than Just Two: The Dynamics of Relationships

by J. Edward Lynch and Barbara Lynch

Introduction

Working with couples is considered to be the most complex and difficult area in psychotherapy. At the same time, a recent survey in *Family Therapy Magazine* reported that while first among those seeking psychotherapy were people with a diagnosis of mood disorders (23% of the total), that number was closely followed by couples' relationship problems at 21%. The remaining 55% of cases were seen under 12 diagnostic categories ranging from family relationship problems (12%), to personality disorders (3%). In general, relationship therapy is the second most commonly sought after form of psychotherapy. However, there are serious questions in the profession concerning the success rate of couple's therapy. In part this is due to the elusive definition of success in this form of therapy. In addition, it is well recognized that many couples enter psychotherapy at a stage when there is little left to salvage in the relationship; that is, they have waited too long to begin the healing process.

This chapter brings to the facilitator a body of information that forms the backdrop for working with family constellations. This knowledge makes up the informed field from which the therapist constructs and facilitates constellations. The chapter broadens the picture of the couple system to include all the pertinent factors that come together to make up what is actually a very complex system. In addition, the connections to family constellations and the works of Bert Hellinger and others will locate this information within the Family Constellation field. Finally, guidelines for working with couple systems in the Family Constellation frame will be presented along with case studies illustrating the process.

Systemic Foundations

The difficulty and complexity of couple's therapy has roots in the belief system of the therapist, the unique dynamics of the intimate couple system, and the process of psychotherapy. Couple's therapy is especially prone to projections of the therapist. Without being aware of it, the therapist may have a tendency to attempt to replicate personal, intimate relationships in an attempt to bring about repair. This replication-repair pattern may take several forms. The relationship of the therapist's parents is the one that is most likely to be the subconscious guiding force when working with couples. The therapist's personal intimate relationship is the next in importance along with the therapist's relationship with each parent. The acceptance of the potential for this type of unawareness to contaminate the working with couples is a strong motivation to uncover relationship patterns through Family Constellation work.

In addition to past generational relationship patterns, the therapist/facilitator has a belief system about relationships constructed from extraneous and often unacknowledged sources. These beliefs enter into all aspects of the therapist's work with couples and have the capability of structuring the process of therapy without regard for the *couple's* beliefs. The therapist's understanding of the definition of marriage, the acceptance of separation or divorce, and the hierarchical place of children in the couple system, are all influenced by his or her own experiences, beliefs, and exposure to various media. Family, friends, and personal relationships help structure what is "right," "wrong," appropriate, or unacceptable. Individuals often believe themselves to be open and accepting, when, in fact, the limits to this position are often unconsciously rigid and intolerant. This unaware position infects both the therapy and the couple system.

The therapist's definition of intimacy, along with a preconceived idea of the "amount" of intimacy that is required for relationship health, is another factor that directs the course of therapy. In addition, the faulty idea that relationship distance is a negative force governs the therapeutic process. Intimacy is learned in the family, and is the result of generational processes that are formed through the interaction of two similar and disparate families coming together. Couples choose partners who have a similar intimacy capacity and tolerance. The difficulty arises in the negotiation of acceptable and non-hostile emotional distance that is a requisite for intimacy. Distance has a natural affinity with abandonment. Therefore, primal abandonment anxieties become activated when an intimate partner makes moves toward (necessary) emotional distance. Respecting the need for distance as a vital process in the establishment of a functional and rewarding relationship may be a foreign concept for a therapist. The resulting position in therapy is replete with therapist entanglements. The therapist's tolerance for emotional distance has an impact on his or her ability to enter into the couple system and the amount and "kind" of distance he or she will allow the couple to manifest. Imagine, for example, the differences possible in the couple system if the therapist understands that emotional distance is a precursor for increased intimacy and that difficulty is inherent in the *means* of attaining distance rather than in the *act* of attaining distance. An understanding of the fear that comes with distancing, and being distanced from, and accepting both positions from a neutral stance gives the therapist a clean field from which to work. Family constellations can greatly assist a couple in confronting their abandonment fears, recognizing the "inherited" distance tolerance, and the individual differences between them, and respecting each other's tolerance levels.

Therapists often impose their belief systems onto the couple system, with or without intention. Unexamined beliefs are likely to interfere with the effectiveness of resolutions in therapy regardless of the modality employed. Family constellations are one of the most effective means to illuminate the foundations of the therapist's unaware personal ideology. The "clean" therapist will be open to the couple's movements of the soul and will be able to respond in a way that is healing.

The Components of the Couple System

Attraction is the driving force that initiates the energy toward forming an intimate system. This drive toward another person begins initially with the physical presence. Without realizing it, each individual usually has a composite picture of an ideal mate. Automatically eliminated are all the individuals who do not match this internal image. There are those who believe that each person looks for some aspects of the self in the countenance of the other, and that, like Narcissus, it is with ourselves that we fall in love. Whatever the root motivation for determining physical attractiveness, it is a powerful and extremely individualized force in partner selection. In addition, Hellinger and other theorists present the idea that individuals attempt to recreate their first introduction to love, the relationship with the mother, in their romantic interactions. Further, there is much speculation that the partner of each of the individuals is representative of an "ideal mother."

Beyond the physical, there are abstract attraction forces working in a powerful manner to bring individuals together. In *Supporting Love, How Love Works in Couple Relationships*, Bert Hellinger states: "That which is fully complete and perfect has no attraction for us" (p.1). In part, this explains the force that drives individuals to search out partners who seem to have valued traits that are unacknowledged in the self. The partners initiate their relationship with a sense that they "complete each other." Eventually, both people will need to reclaim the disowned aspects of self. This occurs when the couple has negotiated the relationship commitment and there is faith in the relationship's capacity to endure over time. Relationship faith and trust develop in a context of meeting challenges and struggling through difficult situations. Similar to building muscles, the couple exercises often enough to build up strength. One partner's unique skills complement the other. For example, a young couple faced a financial crisis; investments that were earmarked for buying a home were almost completely wiped out. Both the partners were devastated. The man approached the situation with negativity and despair. The woman was *respectfully and realistically* optimistic, taking into consideration her partner's natural tendency to see things at their worst. However, her skills did not include being able to build a realistic plan for the future, she operated strictly on faith. But she avoided minimizing the problem and he latched onto her faith and together they worked with their bank to devise a plan that would enable them to purchase a house, more modest than the original one, in a realistic amount of time. Throughout the process, each realized that the other had skills and abilities that enhanced the relationship. They began the progression toward building mutual respect for each other and their combined ability to resolve difficulties. The strength of the resolution was in their differences.

Commitment is the adhesive force in the intimate relationship. It is the contract under which all the parameters of the relationship operate. The terms of the contract between the couple are usually both overt and covert. The standard agreements or rules such as fidelity are the ones that are usually spoken aloud. Other rules commonly remain in the realm of "vaguely known but not spoken" until broken. Promises frequently include elusive conditions such as honor, love, happiness, and satisfaction. Although each of these concepts is valuable, difficulty arises when it is assumed that each individual in the couple system has the same definition of these qualities. Individuals build their internal knowledge of love, honor, happiness and the like based on their families of origin and their, often unacknowledged, ancestral learning. In the throes of passion, there is little time reserved for uncovering the core factors that have the ability to strengthen or destroy a relationship.

An erroneous assumption would be that the couple intends to remain in their intimate relationship for life. The reality is that most commitments are conditional, whether it is spoken or even known. Couples always have an escape clause in their commitment contract, and most often do not know or acknowledge it. There are two primary categories of relationship exit-conditions: one closely connected to an unrealistic expectation of continual satisfaction, and the other tied into family-of-origin history and the family scripts that are in place but often outside of awareness.

Expectations of the partner and the relationship are fashioned from several sources. The most common basis for relationship presumptions is the composite picture compiled from media and literature. Fairy tales are a flimsy foundation for long-lasting love. However, individuals frequently have an unspoken notion that the relationship will survive *as long as the individual is happy.* The problems inherent in this condition are obvious. The definition of happiness is elusive and subject to an unrealistic set of conditions. Further, happiness as a given is completely unattainable. Another underlying presumption among couples is that love is a "product" rather than a process, and that once love is attained, it remains forever, *without ongoing effort.* Under this condition, there would be no need to attend to factors that create and maintain a loving relationship. The notion that love is earned, nurtured, and supported does not seem to be one that is compatible with romance. However, working under the supposition that love is and should be earned, ensures a relationship that can and will sustain the couple and family in a rich nurturing environment.

Hellinger (2001 presents the underlying theory that forms the parameters of the connection between the commitment contract and family scripts. He states, "There is a deep need for justice and retribution within family systems" (p. 2). Hellinger makes the statement that couples marry each other's families. When considered with the fact that within systems there is a continuous exchange of giving and taking across generations to maintain balance, we begin to understand that commitment has an underlying purpose. The need to balance ancestors who remained in destructive relationships with current conditionally committed marriages is a factor that can be overlooked by therapists unfamiliar with the orders of love. Hellinger suggests, "In order for a relationship to succeed, each of the partners has to leave the original family, not only in the physical sense but also in terms of leaving behind some of the principles of the family" (p. 5). Much of what must be left behind is connected to the legacies left by previous generations pertaining to relationships. Family constellation work is a rich venue in which to explore and develop genuine parameters for *mutual* happiness uncontaminated by historical family legacies. A reduction of the number of conditions under which the commitment is formed greatly increases the couple's ability to trust the relationship, and within this context, all difficulties will become challenges to be met rather than causes for divorce. Ultimately, the couple will intentionally co-construct unconditional commitment wherein the orders of love flow freely.

Intimacy and distance are two sides of the same coin. Couples frequently come into therapy with a complaint about the amount of intimacy in their relationship. The novice therapist often believes that this statement is absolutely true, gives ideas and assignments about increasing intimacy, and is disturbed when these reasonable suggestions fail. But this presenting problem statement is full of misunderstandings. The therapist and the couple have been shaped by ancestral learning and experiences as observers of and participants in intimacy. Therefore, exactly what has to be increased is unclear. Further, in many cases with this presenting problem, the therapist is being led down an incorrect path, where the difficulty is not intimacy, but rather how to negotiate the withdrawal to self that precedes *and* follows intimate relating.

There are three main components to this aspect of couple systems: the capacity for intimacy, engulfment and abandonment anxiety manifested in the intimacy withdrawal cycle, and the reaction and response to each individual's need for distance. Individuals enter a relationship with capacity for intimacy "inherited" from the family of origin. Each finds another individual with a similar capacity perhaps slightly greater, or minimally less but overall, surprisingly similar. However, each may manifest this capacity in very different ways and together they construct a relationship with as much intimacy as they can manage. However, since their capacity is not exactly the same, one will strive for more intimacy, whereas the other, made anxious because the impossible is being asked for, or demanded, is led by the need to create distance. This "Dance of Intimacy," described succinctly by Eileen McCann in *The Two Step: The Dance Toward Intimacy* is played out in a pursuer–distancer interaction that has the outcome of maintaining exactly the same amount of intimacy despite which role which individual plays. The steps of this dance, and the accompanying words, have all been learned in the bosom of the families of origin. In the current relationship, they are so well learned that they appear natural.

In making the assumption that couples inherently know their capacity for intimacy and cannot and will not go beyond it, the task of the therapist becomes unclear. The overall goal, however, is to minimize the destructive ways the couple use to attain distance. In the normal course of couples' lives, there is a natural cycle of intimacy and withdrawal, usually governed by the axiom stating that the degree to which a couple is intimate is the degree to which they must distance. It is virtually impossible to constantly maintain a high degree of intimacy. Doing this would result in complete burn out on an emotional level. Every act of intimacy must be followed by an act of withdrawal. This withdrawal is into self. It is not a running away from the other. The purpose of withdrawal is to recharge, to integrate the fruits of intimacy to be able to return to the partner for more intimacy. The misunderstanding of withdrawal or distance comes from generations of witnessing unproductive ways of attaining this necessary distance and from internalizing the anxieties associated with distance.

When the need for distance remains out of awareness, the behaviors that speak for this need are usually negative. Expressions of frustration, disapproval, criticism, insults, and anger, have the effect of pushing away the partner. In general, this has the desired impact. The partner withdraws, hurt, and distance is achieved. However, the hurt experienced by the partner can have destructive aftershocks. A natural response might be to strike back, to seek revenge, to respond in kind. This could easily begin a spiral of negativity with significant harm to the relationship unless the retaliation is just a little less than what was given so love can continue to flow. Usually, the original partner who has initiated the withdrawal will apologize and the relationship might be temporarily repaired. However, when too many of these negative interactions occur, there is a risk of permanent damage. A further consequence could be that the partner, who is the designated initiator of distance, experiences shame and guilt about the need for distance and, in an attempt to understand or rationalize, finds self or partner at fault. The process of self or other condemnation negates the ability to build a sustaining, nurturing relationship and the ultimate outcome will be dissolution of the marriage.

There are predictable phases in a committed relationship where withdrawal is necessary in order to proceed to a stage that permits a greater level of intimacy and supports the personal awareness and growth of both partners. The initial stage of a committed relationship tends to be devoted to the establishment of the partnership. This task involves negotiating the parameters of the commitment, including the limits of the relationship, and discovering the fit of the partnership into all aspects of the couple's system. This stage, lasting anywhere from two to six years, is also one where competing roles, such as those of son or daughter, clash with the present roles of husband and wife. Hellinger describes the difficulty associated with this stage:

> When two people enter a relationship, they often have difficulties at the beginning because they come

from different families, each with a different family conscience.

The primary function of conscience is to bind a child to his or her family. This conscience is very sensitive to what the child is allowed to do or what the child must tolerate in order to belong to this family.... A particular condition for belonging to one family may endanger the right to belong to another group.

In order for a couple relationship to succeed, each of the partners has to leave his or her original family, not only in the physical sense, but also in terms of leaving behind some of the principles of the family. The new couple needs to work out new principles that will be fair to both families. On this new level, the couple can forge an intimate relationship (p. 5).

When these tasks have been completed, the couple is ready to move onto the next stage in the cycle; one that is marked by transitions, dispelling of illusions, and managing withdrawal. The relationship conflicts are about distance versus closeness, although this underlying conflict is masked by more mundane complaints. This stage generally occurs at a point when the couple has been together for about seven years and thus giving credence to the popular phrase, "the seven-year itch." This sometimes tumultuous period in the relationship actually marks the fact that the couple has established the foundation of the relationship and is ready to move on, but not without conflict. Withdrawal that is not accomplished *within the confines of the boundaries of the couple system* will be worked through by means of relationships, activities, or interests that break the boundaries of the system. The ultimate withdrawal is, of course, the ending of the relationship.

Equality is a vital component that enters into all aspects of the couple's relationship. The notion of a partnership has an built-in expectation of a nonhierarchical union. Some of the actualization of this nonhierarchical structure is a basic attempt to avoid recreation of the parent/child relationship in any form. The noted family theorist, Carl Whitaker, claimed that a 15-year age difference between the partners was the maximum that could be maintained without constructing a parent-child system. This idea was predicated on the fact that more than 15 years between partners could technically be the parent of the other. However, beyond that physical fact is the understanding that adults must negotiate stages of adult development and that they will be negotiating vastly divergent developmental tasks if they are more than 15 years apart. For example, a 25 year-old is in the process of differentiating from the family of origin and has begun to explore achievement systems. The primary struggle at this stage of individual development is between intimacy and independence. If the partner happens to be in a middle-age stage of development, the tasks are those of someone who must begin to accept the status of aging parents. It is a time of beginning introspection, questioning long-held convictions, and recognizing the relativity of belief systems. These natural and normal concerns are outside the realm of understanding of the younger partner. The couple will have difficulty with the compassion and respect that are hallmarks of a successful relationship. They will have great difficulty understanding each other's basis for decision-making and are likely to become impatient, frustrated, and annoyed with each other. These qualities are the antithesis of what is needed to promote the formation of a system of intimacy.

Equality is more than age dependent. There is no notion of superiority or inferiority in an equal partnership. Hellinger states, "The consummation of love expresses a full equality that must be carried over into the other areas of a relationship" (p. 4). Partners recognize each other's and their own strengths, appreciate the strengths manifest in the other, and recognize the complementarity of the differences. This is much easier said than done! Individuals have grown up in a society that seems to believe in and may actually encourage the superiority of one gender over the other while pretending that it does not. Each gender has inherent strengths and weaknesses and they need not become battlegrounds for status or hierarchy. Historically within Western cultures, women have been keepers, or rulers of the hearth, whereas men were rulers of the hunt. This has been transmuted into the modern idea that women rule affiliation systems and men are the rulers of achievement systems and women control relationships and men control commerce.

This is contrary to the idea that couples live in a patriarchic society. The notion is valid when viewing most systems that involve making money or policy decisions that remain the primary area of male dominance. However, in day-to-day functioning, meals, children, nesting, and the like, women control, either actively or passively. There is no problem with this *natural* condition as long as it emerges from a context of balance and equity. When a couple delegates aspects of decision-making (with consultation) to the person who is better in the position, it is operating from a foundation of equality. There is a realistic balance of give and take in all areas of their functioning. In these relationships there is an absence of overt or covert battles for power and control.

The facilitator may work with a couple where it is clear that there has been a pattern of transferring onto the partner to get childhood needs met, and the failure of this endeavor has created a chasm in the relationship. Usually, this is a result of traumatic pain in childhood. This pain fosters an intense sense of longing and as a result there is blindness to reality. An appropriate sentence, one that could lead to a resolution picture, could be "I am only your wife/husband, nothing more." The implication in this sentence is that the partner is *not* the other's mother/father/daughter/son. It is an attempt to clarify the structure of the relationship and to foster equality between the partners.

Relationship purpose is an often-overlooked factor in intimate relationships not only by therapists but also by the partners themselves. The question, "Why are you together?" usually elicits the answer, "Because we love each other." However, love is not enough to sustain a relationship through uncharted and often perilous territory. Without getting into a discussion about love, but at the same time acknowledging that it is a basic force that binds the individuals, purpose becomes a second but not lesser factor to be considered. If commitment is the foundation of the intimate relationship, purpose becomes the supporting beam. Purpose provides a direction for the relationship and structures decision-making to a large extent.

As an example, if the purpose of an intimate relationship is to have unlimited safe sex, and that is the only purpose, the relationship will flounder if and when one of the partners is temporarily uninterested in sex. If the purpose of the relationship is to raise children *only*, then children will not be allowed to differentiate and leave. The purpose of a relationship must be flexible, subject to change as the couple develops both on the continuum of adult development and consistent with the developmental cycle of relationships.

Purpose is unique to each couple system. In the development of a relationship purpose has antecedents in the intergenerational families of origin. It is a worthwhile exercise for partners to explore and expand their understanding of the purposes of their ancestors' relationships. In many ways, their own purposes will be garnered from these past relationships, and knowing them will assist in accepting those that are functional and discarding those that persist *only* out of loyalty.

The purpose of a relationship must be able to change throughout the couple's life together. It also must be based in reality with consideration of the age and the general conditions that are a part of the relationship. Couples who together devise relationship purpose with intentionality are doing so in a climate of respect. This kind of purposefulness becomes an act of love that fuels the relationship and ensures its endurance with joy and tenderness. Purpose can be the life force of a relationship even when confronting the death of a partner. There is honor in living in a relationship with purpose and of having it be a function of the love and respect a couple has for each other and their relationship.

Decision-making is another factor that is usually given little consideration by partners or by therapists working with couples. Many professionals seem to take for granted the decision-making process employed by a couple. An assumption is that the couple makes decisions from the same knowledge base that is used by the professional. The reality is that most couples, and individuals, do not consider what goes into their decision-making. They give little or no thought to what forms the basis for the decision, and sometimes not even to the impact of the decision on the significant other. Those who have been studying the family constellations method of working understand that decision-making can be profoundly affected by factors from the past, and the locus of the decision may not even reside in the individual or in the present. Attempts to balance or rectify past events and the need to create balance in the system through loyalties are just two of the covert forces behind many decisions that are made in the couple system. Such forces tend to remain out of awareness until the couple engages in the constellation process.

Individuals in intimate relationships should have only one basis for all decisions — what is in the best interest of the *relationship*. When this is a primary and agreed-upon condition of the relationship, trust is established. Under this condition, one partner can view the actions of the other with benevolence, and with the understanding that whatever has been done was undertaken with the intent of enhancing, strengthening, or supporting the relationship. When it appears to be difficult or impossible to do this, partners ask for explanations. They challenge each other, lovingly, and learn more about each other's process and about how the given decision was expected to serve the relationship. When both partners operate from this frame, the relationship has no questions about trust. However, this level of security is not accomplished easily. It takes work and concerted attention. How long it takes is unique to each couple system. Once established, this binding force will keep the relationship in safe waters throughout the course of life.

Couples' Constellations

Identifying problems that fall within the realm of appropriate work for couple's constellations is the first task of the facilitator. There are two primary avenues to traverse on the path of change in the system using constellations: working directly with the couple and facilitating one of the individual's constellations. The purpose of working with one individual while the partner witnesses is to remove a block to intimate relating. Such blocks include abortions or miscarriages that remain un-integrated into the current relationship. Other incidents that may have a negative impact on the current relationship may include murders, suicides, or abuse within the family of origin. In *The Art and Practice of Family Constellations*, Bertold Ulsamer refers to Hellinger's statement that the facilitator must be "Concerned with the naked, unadorned truth, no matter how horrible it seems at first" (p. 128). The facilitator must overcome any unaware tendencies to protect a partner from harsh truths, when undertaking a constellation with the other partner. Hesitancy on the part of the facilitator may also be a factor when considering Hellinger's statement that "Everything concerning previous intimate relationships should be kept secret from later partners and shouldn't be talked about" (p. 192). Therefore, the facilitator may be confronted with contradictions, but if the facilitator is guided by respect and an assessment of the system as strong, the constellation will be beneficial to the individual and the couple.

When the determination is made that the situation contains the set of conditions that comprise "daddy's girls and boys or mommy's boys and girls," it is appropriate to facilitate an individual constellation as a means to reorder the couple's relationship. The clues that this set of circumstances is operational are discovered in both a verbalization of the presenting problem, as well as nonverbal behaviors. Some version of the statement, "She (or he) is a flirt," is an indication of this pattern. Another hint may be found in the way the participant approaches the facilitator. The following are typical characteristics and the accompanying behavioral signs of this pattern:

Mommy's Boy Characteristics
Outstanding mother complex
Remains too long in adolescence
Savior and messiah complex
Secretly threatened by other men
Refuses responsibility for anything
Charming
Possible homosexual
Don Juanism

Behaviors
Impatient
Arrogant
Unstable job history
Engages in dangerous sports
Unstable relationship history
Rejects authority and rules
Sexual acting-out

Daddy's Boy Characteristics
Aggressive
Monogamous, stable, solid
Good soldiers
Concrete thinker
Has inner strength
Not charismatic
Conservative
Security oriented

Behaviors
Plays safe sports
Denigrates environmental causes
Relishes war
Not creative

Mommy's Girl Characteristics
Reality oriented
Stable, reliable
Internally fulfilled
Maternal
Grounded

Behaviors
Good workers
Solid performers
Loyal followers
Assertive
Strong leaders

Daddy's Girl Characteristics
Creative
Manipulative
Idealistic
Entitled
Threatened by other women
"Hysterical"
Coy

Behaviors
Seductive
Adventurous
Unpredictable
Energetic
Dramatic
Unreliable

Case Study — *An Individual Constellation with a Couple*

A couple came to sit beside the facilitator. The woman assumed the seat next to the facilitator without hesitation. The husband responded to the facilitator's question, "What is the issue?" with the clear statement, "She flirts with all men and doesn't seem to realize that it bothers me." With a few more questions, the facilitator ascertained that the wife was a "daddy's girl." With this in mind, the facilitator asked the woman to set up her mother, father, and herself. (She had no siblings.) The representative for the mother was placed with her back to the representative for the father, about eight feet away from him. He was in the center of the room. She placed her own representative in front of the father in what, to the facilitator, appeared to be a wife's position. There was almost a minute of quiet before the therapist asked all three representatives what they were feeling. The representative for the mother said that she was distant and uninvolved and more interested in looking at the wall, unaware of what was behind her. The father reported feeling warmth toward his daughter and as if he were invisible to his wife. The facilitator was moved to turn the mother's representative toward the center of the circle. She then reported feeling angry with her daughter. "She's taking my place," the representative said.

The facilitator allowed the emotions of the situation to be integrated into his being and then turned to move the father to the side of the mother. Now there was a triangle in the center of the room. The facilitator asked the mother to say to the daughter, "I am the big one and you are the small one." The daughter indicated that she did not like this statement, and she appeared to become larger as she let it be known. The facilitator, being cued by the daughter "puffing herself up," thought that his intervention might be futile. Nonetheless, because he was feeling internally led, he asked the girl to say to the mother, "I am the small one. You are the big one." The girl merely parroted the words. The facilitator decided to perform a ritual. He had the girl sit in a chair in front of her father who was also sitting in a chair, with the mother standing behind the father. Immediately, the girl's eyes went to her father and the facilitator suggested she look at her mother while the mother said, "I am older and more mature than you, and I can take care of your father in every way. Thanks for your help. I no longer need it from you." The representative for the daughter looked surprised and unconsciously looked to the father, most likely for the actions or signs from him that had led her to be a "daddy's girl" in the past. After several more phrases and sentences relating to the mother's caring for the father, the girl began to feel small, and she then was able to join the feminine ancestral lineage of her mother. This work for the wife set in motion a movement to reclaim some of her disowned "mommy's girl" characteristics; those that she had given up in service of the system's call to her to be a daddy's girl. As the daddy's girl loses both her mother and her father, it was a difficult constellation. A daddy's girl becomes a rival to her mother and a pseudo-wife to her father, a very dangerous place to be.

As the change was integrated into her functioning, and was supported by her husband, the couple system became balanced and the partners related to each other as equals. The charming aspects of the "daddy's girl" characteristics remained an integral part of the couple's relationship. These were some of the traits that initially attracted the man to this woman. However, as she accepted her place as a woman, the need to get validation from other men by flirting diminished.

In a discussion with the couple six weeks later, they reported rediscovering each other with the newfound dimensions uncovered by the constellation. The movements of the soul had opened aspects of their relationship that had previously seemed impossible to change. This was not a magic cure-all, rather it opened the door to more possibilities for change.

A Constellation with Both Partners — The Death of a Child

At a recent couples constellation workshop, a couple came up to take their turn. The facilitator observed something that seemed to suggest that they were carrying the weight of the world on their shoulders. They both were slightly hunched over and looked excessively sad. As they sat down by the facilitator, the woman began to weep, and the husband made no supportive gesture. "We should not have come up or even be here," she lamented. This couple system was engulfed in self-pity. An effective constellation would not be possible unless the self-pity was dispelled. The facilitator decided to approach the husband as he seemed to be more rational and, although still despairing, less mired in self-degradation.

"What's the issue?"

The husband replied, "We are getting a divorce."

"Why?"

"We are no longer intimate in any way, and getting along is becoming more difficult."

"What happened?"

"What do you mean what happened?" The man queried with some surprise.

The facilitator now thought that the husband was "playing dumb," since the man was attending the workshop and he should know what the question meant. This "playing dumb," more formally referred to as "neurotic stupidity," would block anything coming from and to be learned from the constellation. The facilitator thought about dismissing the couple because it seemed they weren't ready for a constellation. Just as he was about to say it, the man began to speak.

"Well, we lost a child eight years ago, but I think that has been resolved."

The facilitator was thinking that this was clearly something that hurt the soul of the child and the family. To be excluded goes against the natural orders of love. Everyone who belongs to the family has a place in the family and must be honored.

"Any other events?" asked the facilitator.

"No, but we used to have a good relationship with each other."

The facilitator took his time and then said to the wife, "With your husband assisting you, set up three people: you, your husband, and the dead child. You must be in agreement about who will serve as representatives."

The woman began to cry and the facilitator addressed her directly, firmly and with caring. "You are going to have to look at it. Any other children?"

"No," she said in a quiet and weak voice although she seemed to be collecting herself and getting centered.

The facilitator thought about getting them into an agreement and believed that they probably would have difficulty arriving at a decision that represented a collaborative effort. But after some quiet talking, and deciding, the couple agreed on the three people, and then selected them to represent.

The facilitator asked the wife to put them in place. She arranged them in the "field," with the husband facing the dead child and the mother behind and to the left of the dead child.

The wife was beckoned to sit, and the facilitator let a deep and long silence develop. Then he turned to the husband and said, "How would you change it?"

The husband got to his feet and went into the constellation and moved the mother onto the same side as the father, as if one side were death and the other life. Now, they both faced the dead son. The husband came back to his seat. The couple began to cry although they both had enough control to look deeply at the picture and to benefit from the constellation. They wept equally.

It was clear to the facilitator that the couple had not thoroughly grieved this important, deep, and painful loss. He went to the husband's representative and made some statements of empowerment. The most useful one was included in his instruction to the husband and the wife to say to the dead child "You will always have a place in my heart."

The husband's representative repeated the statement and he cried also. The facilitator did a similar piece of work with the wife's representative. Next, he had the couple themselves take their places in front of the representative of the dead child and they moved to a healing embrace. This lasted quite long.

Healing is generally a slow process and there are intrinsic factors that must be at the foundation of the relationship for this process to occur. This couple was supportive, present to each other and full of love and forgiveness. Their vibrancy following the constellation was palpable in the room. It was later learned that the couple had reconciled in a deep way and they had also became volunteers at the hospice children's division in their town.

Commentary

The untimely death of a child is an event that has devastating effects on the couple system. Couples, even those who love each other deeply, are profoundly affected by this event. The death of a child seems to go against the natural order of life and the rules that govern the parent–child relationship. Parents are supposed to keep their children safe from harm and die before their children. When this natural order is disrupted, it leads to deep wounds in the relationship. The resulting collateral damage is not receptive to healing through traditional talk therapies, even those that attempt to work with both members of the couple system. In general, there is an undercurrent of blame for this death that can either be directed at the self or the partner. A climate of covert blame results in less intimacy and more distance. A relationship cannot flourish in this environment. Eventually, the relationship languishes and quietly atrophies. The constellation frees the couple system from this fate and allows for the natural grieving and holding that must take place.

Also there is an unconscious need to balance the system with a compensatory death. There are examples on record that one of the parents of a dead child will develop a life-threatening illness that does result in another untimely death. Even when the compensation is not as direct, close inspection of the couple system can reveal some other "death" such as loss of sexual desire, the loss of a job, or the loss of a meaningful friendship. The untimely death of a child unbalances the system as well as goes against the natural order of life. There is a powerful drive to balance this loss with another loss. Often, the couple conspires, unconsciously, to kill their relationship in an attempt to create balance. The constellation remediates this compensatory loss and allows the couple to find an outlet of giving as a means of balancing the loss with giving of themselves (such as in the case where the couple volunteered at hospice.

General Considerations in Couples' Constellations

In the process of determining of the appropriateness of a constellation utilizing both partners there are general presenting problems that definitely point to working in this way. They include:

- ❖ The couple speaks of pervasive unhappiness in the relationship;
- ❖ One of the partners is excessively jealous;
- ❖ The role of parent has overtaken the function as intimate partner in one or both individuals;
- ❖ The partners have fallen out of love;
- ❖ They experience unproductive arguments about finances, living arrangements, work, or other issues;
- ❖ One treats the other as a child rather than an equal.

Each of these presenting problems must be seen as symptoms of deeper wounds in the soul. The facilitator needs to be sensitive to avoiding problem solving, and should have as a goal paving the way for insight and understanding as the initiator of lasting change. All of the knowledge of couple systems should be a part of the facilitator's foundational understanding of the problem as symptom.

In a 2004 seminar at ZIST, Penzberg, Germany, Jacob Schneider presented four typical couples constellation arrangements. These are manifest in the ways that representatives are set up. They are:

1. Man on left — often means weakness in the relationship
2. Face to face — frequently indicates confrontation, often unfriendly.
3. Man turned slightly away from spouse toward daughter or woman turned away from spouse toward son
4. Face to face but very close as if about to embrace

Conclusions

In *Insights: Lectures and Stories* Bert Hellinger presents an intensive understanding of the Orders of Love between men and women that is the core of working with couples systems and family constellations (pp. 92-105). The complexity of the couple system and the difficulties encountered in the development of functional intimacy is inherent in his discussion. The couple is presented as existing in a field that includes the past, the present, and a broad sphere of influence. He states, "The Orders of Love discussed so far can also be applied in our relationship to life in general, and to the world as a whole and the mystery we may glimpse behind it all" (p. 105). Therapists and facilitators who bring the richness of constellations and the concepts of systems together to free couples from the entanglements of the past, have a privilege and opportunity that is realized by very few in the field of psychological help. The influence of this type of work extends beyond the couple. A disentangled couple system allows for a greater degree of strength and freedom in the parental system, which then allows for children to develop more of their potential. This follows from the idea that, "Parents and children together form a unity of fate in which they are all dependent upon each other in a variety of ways" (p. 84).

Psychotherapists who have devoted their education to learning various models of individual, couple, and family therapy can deepen their work with the addition of training in family constellations. There is a high degree of compatibility among models that is readily evident upon an examination of the conceptual roots of Hellinger and the second generation of constellation facilitators. When facilitators are mostly free of their own entanglements and open to the impact of their spirituality, the movements of the soul flow freely. This deep soul work is the pinnacle of success when it is conducted with humility and centeredness. The couple system may indeed be the most complex and complicated of all human systems. Along with this, however, it must also be seen as the system most deserving of respectful and powerful healing. Through the rendering of family constellations with the goal of freeing the couple system so the orders of love can flow freely to children, kinship group, and beyond, this small system can have far-reaching and powerful effects.

References

Hellinger, B. (2002) *Insights Lectures and Stories*. Heidelberg: Carl-Auer.

Lynch, B. "Adult Development,"(2004). Southern Connecticut State University, New Haven, CT. (lecture)

Lynch, J. E., & Lynch, B. (2000). *Principles and Practices of Structural Family Therapy*. New York: The Gestalt Therapy Press.

McCann, E. (1985). *The Two Step: The Dance Towards Intimacy*. New York: Grove.

Neuhauser, J. (Ed). (2001). *Supporting Love, How Love Works in Couple Relationships*. Phoenix, AZ: Zeig, Tucker & Theisen.

Ulsamer, B. (2003). *The Art and Practice of Family Constellations*. Heidelberg: Carl-Auer.

9

When Professional Experience Gets Personal: Working One to One

by Daniel P. Gates and Mary M. Gates

Introduction

I (Dan) have been practicing family therapy for 18 years. I first experienced the family constellation work of Bert Hellinger in 2003. At that time, I was curious and searching for more effective ways to do my work. A mentor directed me to Dr. Edward Lynch of the Marriage and Family Therapy program at Southern Connecticut State University, who was offering monthly workshops in family constellations. I convinced my wife (Mary) and a friend to come with me and spend a Saturday at a workshop. Although I trusted the person who had made the recommendation, I confess that I did not expect much.

The workshop began with a brief explanation by the facilitator of the work of Bert Hellinger. I was intrigued by some of the concepts, especially the delineation of who belongs to a family's soul, including the parents, parents' siblings, and grandparents. In addition, he said that any miscarriages, stillbirths, or abortions also belong to the soul. I suddenly remembered that my wife had had a miscarriage approximately 20 years ago. I looked at her with tears in my eyes and said, "We had a miscarriage." She said, "I know." I felt something that I had not felt before. It was real and it touched me.

As the morning session passed, I witnessed the work of family constellations: what I now know are called "movements of the soul." I was deeply touched to witness love break through in what seemed to be the worst of situations.

After lunch, the facilitator asked if there were any questions or comments, and I raised my hand. I shared with him how moved I was by this work, and also how touched I was when I remembered my wife's miscarriage. The facilitator listened, and I will never forget what he said in response. "Would you like to see what your unborn child looked like?" I was speechless, and a bit anxious, as he asked Mary and me to sit beside him. He asked us a few questions, and then invited us to choose someone to represent our unborn child. We both agreed that the child was a boy, and in unison we pointed to the same young man. He agreed to represent our unborn child and the therapist directed him to sit in front of us. Immediately, my wife and I moved toward him. It felt both awkward and freeing. As tears flowed, I found myself telling "our child" about his two brothers and his sister and how much he would have loved them. I am not sure how long this conversation lasted. It felt as if time was suspended, and we were contained in a very safe and secure bubble. It appeared to be a state of trance where chronological time elapses and time in the moment is expanded.

As I looked back and forth between my wife and my unborn child, the quiet in the room deepened and we all waited. My wife said to our child, "I really never wanted you." I realized that I had felt the same. I also did not want another child at the time. More tears flowed as we made our confessions. Encouraged by the facilitator to stay with what was happening in silence, we were able to simply feel and allow the process to unfold. The group supported us by their quietness and willingness to offer compassion without judgment. The representative of our son, who was sitting, was asked to stand, turn around, and look at us. As we looked at each other with appreciation, the therapist said, "It was his fate, and he knew it." We knew it too. I felt the love and truth of the situation. It was okay. I felt the resolution of a situation that I did not even know needed to be resolved. There was a sense of understanding and peace.

The facilitator then directed our son's representative to move away from us as he selected two people to represent Mother Earth and Father Sky. Our son's representative stood between them as the facilitator said, "This is where he belongs now; this is where miscarried children go." There were no words to express how right it all felt. We were then encouraged to linger in this resolution picture, taking time to let it settle. As we returned to our seats, I experienced the support and care of many people in the room whom I had never met before. I also experienced a deeper bond with my wife, Mary. I claimed the truth that we had four children, not three, and that we all belonged in each other's soul.

Although Dan told the above story about our introduction to family constellation work, the story belongs to both of us. We were deeply moved by our first constellation experience, both through our individual work and as members of the group. In some way, both separately and together, we felt called to this work. We were already thinking about ways in which we could bring this work into our own practices.

This chapter is about how we brought our experience of family constellations in a group setting to our work with individuals, and how our work with individuals has, in turn, enhanced the group work. We will discuss what has worked and what has not, and what we have learned and are still learning.

Getting Started

Personal Experience

Before you can use family constellations with individuals, you have to experience the work for yourself. Even if you do not work on a personal issue, it is essential to go to a group constellation, and, at the very least, to have the experience of being a representative. Representing gives you a personal experience of family constellations that helps in understanding the underlying concepts. There is no way to bring the work back to your own practice if you have not experienced it firsthand.

Understanding Basic Concepts

Buddhists have a saying: "Buddhism isn't about beliefs, it's about firsthand knowledge." The same may be said for family constellations. Bert Hellinger's work is experiential. It is difficult to gain a full understanding simply by reading about it, however, it is helpful to read any of his books, especially *Love's Hidden Symmetry (1998),* in order to begin to comprehend the ideas. A brief discussion of some of these concepts follows but these definitions just hint at the essential meanings.

Family Soul: This is an intelligence that drives the evolution of the family over the generations.

Those who belong to the Family Soul: These include children, parents, and their siblings, grandparents, and anyone who has been excluded from the family system (i.e., miscarried, stillborn, or aborted children; perpetrators or victims; former lovers or partners of either parent; and any others who have significantly influenced a person's life for good or bad).

Order of Precedence: The family unconsciously shows preference for those who came first over those who came later (i.e., parents come before children; a firstborn comes before a second, etc.). When this order is honored, love can flow more freely, and everyone in the system feels better and more in balance.

Balancing Gains and Losses: The family soul seeks justice and balance, so where there has been gain at another's expense, payment of that debt will be required in a future generation.

Exclusions: Children are recruited by the family system over generations to bring the family back into balance. Unconsciously, they can be elected by the family soul to reclaim excluded members (i.e., alcoholics, perpetrators, or any alienated ones).

Primary, Secondary, and Meta-Feelings: Primary feelings empower us. They lead to action and come and go rather quickly. Secondary feelings weaken us. They never strengthen, but rather keep us going around and around, like a gerbil on the wheel. Meta-feelings are feelings associated with God. We cannot make them happen, but when we do experience them, they can bring us a sense of reconciliation and peace beyond understanding.

Systemic Entanglements: Sometimes one person in the family takes on the fate of another family member (i.e., a wife cannot have a fully functioning relationship with her husband because she is still bonded to her brother, who committed suicide, a child carries the fate of the deceased father, who spent time in prison for criminal activities, by following him into a life of crime). These systemic entanglements can be seen when one family member unconsciously takes on the feelings or role of an earlier excluded member, or when one member follows another into misfortune, or even death. In other words, "I'll go instead of you." Out of love, a child will take on a parent's fate. This is done unconsciously to keep the system in balance.

Movements of the Soul: For Hellinger, the soul, or "knowing field," extends beyond the individual and guides the individual, as well as actively seeking and finding resolutions in the family soul (Hellinger, 2001). The work of family constellations is to find harmony in the soul. We cannot control the movements of the soul, but we can take the time to be with the soul.

Phenomenological Approach: In *Love's Own Truths*, Hellinger writes: "There are two inner movements that lead to insight. One reaches out wanting to understand and control the unknown. This is scientific inquiry... The second movement happens when we pause in our efforts to grasp the unknown, allowing our attention to rest, not on the particulars, which we can define, but on the greater whole." This second movement, which orients itself to restraint and inwardness rather than reaching out, is the phenomenological approach. Hellinger believes that the two approaches complement each other.

Orders of Love: There are hidden natural laws that exist in all families. They are invisible laws that guide the behavior of human relationship systems. It is in the orders of love that resolutions can be discovered and movements of the family soul can occur. Hellinger contends that love can only succeed when we align ourselves with these natural laws. For example, everyone has the right to belong, even those who are often excluded (i.e., alcoholics, the insane, those who commit suicide, perpetrators, victims, etc.). These orders of love hold that everyone in the family system has his or her own fate. Meddling in the fate of another imbalances the system. Fate includes illness, life and death issues, so called good and bad luck, and debts and compensations.

Understanding Trauma

Trauma is a significant life event involving actual or threatened serious injury or death, to which the individual responds with feelings of intense helplessness, fear, or horror. This experience can be triggered or reexperienced in numerous ways (*DSM-IV*). This trauma causes a disruption in the person's reaching-out movement toward love (i.e., a child's reaching out toward the parents is interrupted when abuse occurs). Understanding how to work with trauma is important. The therapist needs a variety of tools in order to support and help the client reprocess these past events. We believe that there are varying degrees of trauma, we call them small t's and large T's. Although it is not the goal of this writing to educate the reader about trauma, we know that many clients present with trauma issues, and so it can be very helpful to know how to deal with them. We also believe that family constellations are effective in helping clients to process past traumas.

When Is Using Family Constellations the Appropriate Intervention?

We use family constellations with most of our clients to some degree. They can produce beneficial results by opening insights into the family system. At the very least, they provide pictures that can further the understanding of presenting problems and what lies behind them; at best, they can point the way to resolution. We use them whenever we perceive entanglements, exclusions, or a family system that is out of order (i.e., parentified children, a younger child who has taken on the role of the firstborn). We also use constellations when there are family secrets or the client presents with past traumas. We have used them with clients who find it difficult to make decisions or to move on from a problematic situation. Through the use of family constellations we are able to give clients a visual sense of the problem, which sometimes will allow them to resolve the issue. In determining whether or not using family constellations is an appropriate intervention in a given situation, we find it helpful to ask: "What is the soul trying to manifest, resolve, or balance through these symptoms?"

Targeting An Issue

Effective therapy starts with listening to the client and targeting an issue. Family constellation work has a unique orientation in this regard. It is phenomenological, so we need to ask the right questions if we are looking for family secrets or the invisible systemic conscience of the family. We often start by simply asking, "What would you like to look at today?" It is important to meet the client in the present moment and determine whether the presenting issue has enough energy to be explored or it is merely curiosity that the client brings. We look for whether the issue has primary feelings attached to it, and if the client is experiencing it powerfully in the body. If the answer to these questions is Yes, the issue is probably worth looking at. Hellinger has stated that the client will often give you the issue in the first sentence or two.

Sometimes the issue we target does not have enough energy for us to work with it, or the client is unsure and wants us to select an issue. We use such situations as opportunities to educate clients about family systems and intergenerational patterns: the larger picture. If we choose an issue for the client, we find that we usually lose our perspective and get in the way of the work. We have never yet seen a resolution picture emerge out of this kind of situation.

Becoming Centered

Orienting yourself to this work requires that you center yourself in such a way that you are open to the field in the present moment. What does this mean? When you are at your best, you are relaxed, grounded, and tuned into your body. You are attentive and willing to be open to any information from the field. It is helpful if you are able to put away any preconceived ideas about what the problem is and what the resolution should be. Unlike psychodynamic work that requires you to analyze, this work requires you to tune into what you are feeling and experiencing in your own body, and as you tune in, to try to distinguish between your own feelings and what you are experiencing that is related to the constellation. You begin to test what you are experiencing, by asking questions, or by moving small figures, if that is what you are using. And you listen deeply to your client's feedback.

It is easy to impede the work if you try too hard to find a resolution. The ego gets in the way when we try to be too helpful or try to prove how insightful we are. Staying in tune with your body, however, can help you to check your own needs and to step back from them, thus allowing the constellation to unfold. If you have your own agenda, you will obstruct the field.

In *Love's Own Truths* (2001), Hellinger writes that this work requires us to "let go of all our intentions, conceptions, preferences, influences or needs to convince others." He challenges us to go into this phenomenological work fearlessly. I like to think of this as the Zen way of letting everything go where it naturally wants to go: being in the moment and trusting the force, the intelligence of the system, love's hidden truths.

In his training, Ed Lynch teaches four essential principles as guidelines for the therapist: No intention, no judgment, no fear, and no memory, an emptying of oneself in order to be in the moment. That is essentially what becoming centered in this work requires.

Working With Figures, Feelings and Virtues

Educate and Explain the Process

We usually start by asking if the client is willing to try something, never forcing, simply offering. We talk with clients about the process into which they are entering, explaining that the client will be attempting to create a picture of the family as he or she experienced it. This is the client's reality, how it feels. This is not a re-creation, it is a present centered therapy that brings the client into the field in the moment, it is phenomenological. We explain that there is no right or wrong way to do this. We tell them that they should tune into their bodies and observe any sensations or feelings that they are experiencing as they view the constellation. We keep our explanations simple.

How We Proceed

We have a table in our office that is 18 inches high, 24 inches wide, and 48 inches long. This table is easy to move and works well as a conventional piece of furniture. The table can hold many family pieces, feelings, and virtues. We place it in front of our clients as we sit across from them. If the client has agreed to do a family constellation, we bring out our bag of figures, feelings, and virtues and place it near or on the table. It is sometimes necessary to answer questions or to calm the anxiety aroused by this new situation. We try not to talk too much, as the work tends to explain itself better than we ever could.

Choice of Figures

We provide a variety of figures. Our standard kit has four grandparents, four adults, four children, and one baby. It also includes nine wooden rounds that we use to represent feelings and virtues. The essential figures are dressed differently and are of different sizes in order to distinguish them from one another. Our figures were selected to represent, as closely as possible, real people.

We begin by asking the client to choose a figure to represent himself or herself. The client will then choose figures for each of the family members needed for the particular issue at hand. (For instance, a client may only need herself and her mother, or perhaps both parents but not the siblings. In other cases, all the family members may have to be represented.) The client selects the figures and then places them in relationship to each other. We emphasize that this placement should be done from a feeling place, in the present moment, with the presenting problem. (This is similar to family constellations in a group setting where the individual is asked to place representatives in relation to one another according to his or her inner movement.)

We encourage the client to choose figures one at a time, building the system step by step. This helps both the client and the therapist to avoid becoming overwhelmed by the system, which is particularly important for the therapist who is new to this work.

The Problem Picture

After the client has set up the problem picture a period of silence follows, in which both the client and the therapist may observe the picture and tune in to what they are experiencing. The therapist also tunes into the client's reaction to the picture, and then both look at the picture together and talk about what they see and experience. The therapist may share observations of how the client reacted to the pictures. (For example, the therapist might observe that the client smiled or became teary as the picture took shape.) This sharing of observations will likely lead to deeper exploration.

Stem Sentences

The therapist can also suggest the use of stem sentences for individuals represented in the constellation, observing the effect these have on the client (i.e., a father who died when the client was young may be asked to say to the son, "I will always be your father, you will always be my son.") Stem sentences, also called statements of empowerment, are statements that strengthen the client, and help to move the problem picture toward the resolution picture. Not realizing that others who do individual work use stem sentences, we were not sure they would work in this context. When working with individuals, the representatives are figures, and we wondered if having the therapist say the stem sentence would be as effective as having the human representative speak it. Through experimentation, we have discovered a number of our own ways to use stem sentences with individuals. Sometimes we speak a sentence as a representative without checking with the client first. Sometimes we ask, "Can you imagine your mother saying ...?" Sometimes we have the client speak the sentences of one representative to another. In doing this, we are continually observing the reactions of the client to determine where the field wants us to move next, always looking for movement toward a resolution picture.

Adding Feelings and Virtues with Figures

We discovered the use of feelings and virtues in the work during a group workshop on family constellations when the facilitator suggested that a client imagine strength standing behind her. We were intrigued by the change that this created in the client and the picture, and began to think about how adding other qualities to the work might help the movement toward resolution and strengthen the outcome. Through experimentation, we narrowed the number of feelings and virtues to nine. We use double-sided wooden rounds that have the feeling or virtue on one side and its opposite on the other side. For example, love/hate, hope/despair, courage/fear. However, we are not tied to these qualities, we often use other feelings and virtues if they meet the needs of the client.

Feelings or virtues may be added to the picture at any time to help move the constellation toward a resolution or to strengthen a resolution picture (i.e., a client who feels hopeless may be aided by adding hope or courage, or perhaps both, to the picture). As with stem sentences, the therapist is always observing how any change in the picture affects the client.

Case Study

Anna is a 55-year-old woman who came to treatment with mild depression and a variety of complex life choices that made her confused and anxious. Having recently returned to work after raising two children, she was about to embark on a new career. She had been married for more than 20 years and her husband was not happy about her return to work. He was an active alcoholic, who liked having his wife at home. She had participated in one family constellation in a group setting, where she worked on family-of-origin issues. In treatment, however, it became increasingly clear that her relationship with her husband, his drinking, and her guilt about going back to work were the major causes of her anxiety and depression.

Anna agreed to do a constellation. She was given the bag of figures and she chose an adult female figure to represent herself. She then chose figures to represent her husband and three children. Interestingly, she chose adult figures for her grown children, but for her husband, she chose a young male figure, much smaller than any of the others. She then placed herself and her husband face to face, so close that their noses were almost touching. She placed the children behind the parents in a semicircle, lining them up by descending ages.

As we looked at the picture, the size discrepancy between the husband's figure and all of the others was hard not to overlook. I asked her about this. "Oh yes, it was deliberate," she said. "I think of him as smaller. He really can't take care of himself. He's kind of like one of the boys, but they are more grown up." I also noted that the husband and wife figures were very close together. I said, "It's almost like they are breathing the same air." I noticed an "aha" on her face as I said this. "It's funny you should say that," she said. "Sometimes, when we lie in bed at night, I feel a though I can't breathe because his face is too close to mine. He's taking up all the oxygen. I make him turn over. 'I can't breathe,' I say, 'I can't breathe.'"

As I looked at the problem picture, I wondered what would happen if I replaced the "small" husband with one of normal size. Without asking Anna I chose an adult male figure and put it in place of the smaller husband figure, maintaining the same distance, nose to nose. I asked Anna how this felt. She pondered for a moment, and then said, "That feels better, but I think it would be even better if we had some space." She took the husband and wife figures and placed them shoulder to shoulder. Again, I asked how this felt. There was a noticeable change in her demeanor, her shoulders dropped, there was a hint of a smile on her face. "What a relief," she said. "This is what I hope for." She then said, "The figure you chose looks like a professor. My husband is such a good teacher. If he could only make some changes, I know he could be a great professor."

Anna made it clear that as much as she liked looking at this picture, she did not believe it could ever happen. I picked up the disc with the word HOPE printed on it and showed it to her. "What would it be like," I asked, "if I placed this here?" I laid it in front of the husband and wife figures. "That feels so good," she said with a big smile. I suggested to Anna that she hold this picture in her mind and heart, and that she revisit it every day.

When Anna returned a few weeks later, she told me that although she had not noticed any significant changes at home, she was feeling better about her work. She did not feel so guilty about enjoying what she did away from home. She also said that she did notice that she was trying to allow her husband to take more responsibility. If there were tasks to be done around the house that were his chores, she no longer felt that she had to do them when he did not. She was seeing him as less helpless.

Using Figures as a Diagnostic Tool

Using the figures diagnostically follows the same process just described. The process is explained to the client, keeping in mind that the therapist's belief in it allows the client to feel safe. One of the things a client should know is that you will be seeking to identify the problem from a systemic viewpoint.

Again, the client will choose figures and place them in relationship to each other so that it feels right in the present moment. We explain that there is no right or wrong way to do this, and that

When Professional Experience Gets Personal: Working One to One

the client is creating a picture of what is, as opposed to what he or she wishes it could be. The therapist and client look at the constellation together, until they get a feel for the system. The therapist submits to the problem picture and notices the energy of the system and where it is moving. To what is one's attention drawn? On what do one's eyes immediately focus? There is a felt sense of the direction in which the movement is going: is it toward life, or toward death? The therapist also checks his or her own feelings and intentions. (For example, is his or her own anxiety getting in the way of the system by trying to force a resolution?)

The therapist can further assess how the problem picture affects the client by asking, "When you see this picture, what feelings do you have?" And, "What emotions/feelings can you imagine it would bring up for others in the family system?" We are looking for entanglements, exclusions, family members out of order, secrets, past traumas, guilt, innocence, and blind love.

Another period of silence follows as the therapist allows the client to sit with these questions and any emotions that have been activated by this process.

Often this is enough work for a client to do in one session. We do not move toward a resolution picture at this time, but use the picture to help guide our future work. The therapist "parks" any issues that have emerged for the client so that the client feels safe, and the issue feels contained, but can be revisited at another time.

Case Study

Chris was brought to therapy by his parents because he was experiencing anxiety and sleeplessness. The anxiety arose most often on Sunday afternoons, and again on Monday mornings, when he had to go to school. Chris was also sad because his older brother, who was an eighth grader and had been his best friend, was no longer interested in spending any time with Chris, who was in the fourth grade. With the parents and older brother in the room, I asked Chris to choose figures for himself, his parents, and his brother. I then asked him to place the figures so that they made a picture of his family. Chris created a picture with family members extremely close to each other in a circle. What was most noticeable was that the father figure was half of the size of the brother figure. This was a revealing insight for me, and also for the parents, especially the mother, who had been carrying most of the stress for Chris. (After asking each family member how he or she was affected by the constellation, I replaced the father's figure with one that was taller than both boys' figures and moved the mother and father across from their boys. The child's mother expressed a sigh of relief, and the father stated, "I never realized that I was needed more.")

Using the figures to help diagnose the problem gave me, as well as the parents, a clear picture of the work that was needed to strengthen their relationships and put the family back in order.

Using Figures to Revisit and Strengthen the Resolution Picture

We often invite clients to participate in a group family constellation. Most of them have described it as a profound experience, and it becomes a very meaningful aspect of the therapeutic process. We have found that is it helpful with many clients to revisit any resolution picture that emerged during the group experience in our individual work. We begin by listening to the client's experience of the group and answering any questions. We then invite the client to choose figures and recreate the resolution picture. A quiet period follows as the client is allowed to revisit the resolution. More often than not, clients will smile or look pleased. For the client, this process provides an opportunity to strengthen the new picture; for the therapist, it is an opportunity to receive feedback, and to continue to assess for issues for which further movement might be needed.

We find that, for some clients, the problem picture is so familiar and the resolution so foreign, it is all too easy to return to the old picture. When we feel that the client is having a difficult time with integrating the new picture, we often use Eye Movement Desensitization Reprocessing (EMDR) to help with that integration process.

Most of our clients do not have any trouble entering into this work, in fact, they find it interesting and helpful. At times, if this is their first experience of family constellations, some people dub it a little "kooky." It is not unusual to hear something like, "We're not really going to play with dolls, are we?" For clients who do have trouble, we help them to become centered by using breathing techniques, integrated meridian therapy, EMDR, or other body-energy therapies.

Using Paper As Representatives

Our first experience in using family constellations with individuals was in a training group where the leader instructed us to use pieces of paper as representatives of family members. We typically use white paper, but the use of colors to represent individuals is also acceptable. We were taught to draw an open-sided triangle for men, and an up-ended one for women.

We have since found that it is easier to keep family members straight in our minds by writing their names on the pieces of paper.

We proceed as with figures, inviting the client to select the people who need to be in the constellation. After putting these names on the papers, we ask the client to arrange them in relationship to each other, on a small area rug that we use to contain the field. Some time is allowed for the client and the therapist to observe the picture and, to note any reactions they are having. We then ask the client to stand on each of the pieces of paper and to tune in to what they feel in their bodies. We hope to discover where the energy is in the system and if there is a movement that needs to be made. Awareness and compassion toward the other members of the system may be accomplished by standing with them, literally "stepping into another's shoes." For example:

> A woman who came to therapy because she learned that her husband was having an affair was asked to place papers representing herself and her husband on the floor. She placed herself next to him, but a little behind.

> She said that she felt he was moving away from her and was leaving her behind. When she stood on the paper representing her, she said that she felt sad and afraid, "kind of like a little girl." When she stood on the paper representing her husband, however, what she felt was tremendous grief. Her reaction was strong and spontaneous, "Oh my God, I didn't realize how sad and overwhelmed he feels. I think he might be more scared than I am." Following this experience, the client was willing to take the therapist's suggestion to bring the husband to the next session, something that she had previously been unwilling to do.

We also use papers in situations where a client is having difficulty making a decision. We ask the client to use papers to create the problem picture by placing them on the floor in relation to each other. As with figures, we then move the papers while watching for the client's reactions. We are looking for movement toward a resolution picture. Often, it is not even necessary to move the papers; simply seeing the picture and standing on the papers within the field brings movement for the client. For example:

> A second-year college student came to us. She was very unhappy at school and felt that she was a failure, but would miss out on something if she came home and attended a local college. We used papers on the floor to represent herself, her current college, and the local college. As she stood on each of these representations, she realized that the local college eased her anxieties and made her feel more centered in herself. She was able to get out of her head and begin to recognize what she really wanted, as opposed to what others had been telling her to do.
>
> This young woman knew what the resolution was within herself without any movement of the papers.

> She had been torn between growing up and doing what she knew was best for her and loyalty to the family, which wanted her to finish at the school that several other family members had attended.

When Clients Need Help Tuning Into Their Bodies

We live in a culture that is dominated by the head. We have found that it is often necessary to help clients tune in to their bodies in order for them to be open to the deep work of family constellations. We have learned several effective methodologies to help clients: Integrated Meridian Therapy, Eye Movement Desensitization Reprocessing, and breath awareness.

Integrated Meridian Therapy

Integrated Meridian Therapy (IMT), a component of the larger field of energy psychology, is based on the concepts of traditional Chinese medicine. It uses specific tapping sequences to balance the body-energy system. In a high percentage of our client population, it restores a sense of harmony, fosters calm and reduces stress so that we can continue with the work. It interfaces with family constellations as a way to center the work or reinforce the resolution picture. It has also been proved to assist clients in gaining insight and moving forward from a given problem. IMT can be used at the beginning, in the middle, or at the end of a session. It also can be used as a resource between sessions. Because it is active and body-centered, IMT does not interfere with the movements of family constellations. We know this work through acupuncture, acupressure, and applied kinesiology. We are grateful to our friend and colleague Arnold Morgan for developing and teaching it. For example:

> Mark was so enraged at his biological father for abandoning him that he could not place any of the figures on the table in order to work with them. I invited Mark to start with a clearing statement, a sentence that helps restore balance and harmony.

He was directed to say, "Even though I'm enraged, I'm okay." It was to be repeated several times until he could accept the truth of it. As Mark started to nod that saying the sentence was okay for him, I began a series of tapping sequences to center and calm him. During the sequence, the clearing statement was repeated gently again and again. Although it took several sequences, Mark eventually began to relax so that he could begin to place the figures and move into the family constellation work.

Eye Movement Desensitization Reprocessing

Eye Movement Desensitization Reprocessing (EMDR) is a trauma-based psychotherapy developed by Francine Shapiro. It is an integrative model that incorporates many aspects of other models, and can be both an accelerated and an adaptive information-processing system in the hands of a skilled therapist. One of its central components is activating the neurological systems of the brain by asking specific questions pertaining to an image or picture. Processing to an adaptive resolution means that a new picture with positive beliefs and a different body sense is attained. Because an essential ingredient of family constellations is the resolution picture, EMDR and family constellations can be very complementary. One of the goals of this approach is rapidly to metabolize dysfunctional residue from the past and transform it into something useful in the present. Like family constellations, it works with problem pictures that involve negative beliefs and body sensations. It builds and strengthens resources and empowers the client to live fully in the present and to be able to move forward. It is a therapy of compassion and healing that encourages movements of the soul.

One of the most effective ways in which we have utilized EMDR in conjunction with family constellations has been in reinforcing the resolution picture. For example:

Kevin came in for an appointment a week after experiencing his first family constellation in a group setting. After some discussion, I invited Kevin to recreate his resolution picture, and he set it up using figures. As Kevin viewed the picture, he sat quietly, nodding his head and smiling. After several moments of silence, I began to move my hand slowly back and forth in front of him, inviting him to follow the movement with his eyes while continuing to hold the resolution picture in his mind. (A note about the procedure: The therapist, sitting across from the client, raises his or her hand and moves it back and forth across the midline of the client as the client moves his or her eyes right to left, causing a bilateral stimulation of the brain. This movement processes information.) Some researchers believe that it may engage REM sleep in a waking state (Shapiro, 2001). After 12 to 15 back-and-forth sets, I stopped and waited while looking for any reaction from Kevin, and then I asked, "What's happening now?" Kevin answered, "I feel stronger and the picture is clearer." I repeated the process, and then asked, "What's happening now, Kevin?" Kevin responded, "I am stronger and clearer about my past, and I can move forward knowing that I am loved and supported from the past. Even though I was adopted, I'm okay."

Breath Awareness

Breath awareness is as simple as it sounds, being aware of one's breathing in the moment. Breathing in and breathing out. Helping clients to become aware of their breathing grounds them in the present. The simple exercise of putting their feet on the floor, feeling the ground beneath them and their bottoms sitting on a chair while breathing in and out, can help them to settle into their bodies and to be more open to the deep movements that are produced by family constellation work. There are a number of health professionals who discuss breathing work, such as Andrew Weil, and Ursula Franke (2003).

Conclusion

The work of family constellations has proved to be so powerful in its ability to lead us to healing, and ultimately to freedom, that we want to share it with everyone. We continue to believe strongly in the group experience; however, there are times when a group either is not available or is not the right choice. In the part of the world in which we live, the opportunities to participate in group experiences are infrequent, with time and distance obstacles to the work. Safety is also an issue. For many of our clients, their anxiety is too great to allow them to participate in a group constellation with an open heart and mind. For them, the familiarity of doing the work in our office provides a sense of safety. In writing to Ursula Franke (2003) to congratulate her on her book on using family constellations in individual therapy, Hellinger commended her for furnishing a protected setting for individuals, while still offering them new possibilities and insights. We have found the sense of safety inherent in the protected environment of individual work to be invaluable, as well.

Education is another benefit of using family constellations with individuals. It affords us an opportunity to answer questions that a client might be shy about asking in the group, and to prepare clients for participation in a group constellation.

As we have described, family constellations can be a very effective means to diagnose problems. What better way to observe a person's reaction to a situation than to see it in front of you? One of the most beneficial things about the use of figures is the fact that they provide a way to visualize relational dynamics within an individual setting. Our clients receive an image that effectively engages the neurological system in a different way than in talk therapy. What appears to be a trance state, an altered state of consciousness, occurs for many of our clients as they fixate on the figures that represent various members of their family. This state of consciousness sets up the framework for the movements of the family soul.

Working with individuals also gives therapists the opportunity to practice constellations in a simpler setting, without having to contend with the dynamics of group interactions. Although such dynamics can be invaluable to the work, they also can complicate it for the novice constellation facilitator. We even suggest that therapists in training produce an audio or videotape (with permission of the client), to be used in supervision.

We thought of entitling this chapter, "Seeing is Believing," because to us that is the essence of family constellations work with individuals. So often in our work there are roadblocks to healing, and although it may be the resistance of the client that is an obstacle, many times it is something unseen that keeps the work from moving towards resolution. These obstacles are the hidden entanglements of the family system that we are simply unable, or unwilling, to see. In many cases, family constellations have allowed us to uncover these entanglements by showing us a picture of *what is*, as opposed to what we would like to see, or what we are told to see. The Indian philosopher, J. Krishnamurti (1969) once said, "The primary cause of disorder in ourselves is the seeking of reality promised by another" (p.11). Hellinger, like sages from many spiritual traditions, understands the truth of that statement. He is insistent that only when we see *what is* for ourselves, our own reality, will we begin to trust our own soul and allow it to lead us to freedom (1998, p.330). We have found in our work that this willingness to see what is, and to trust our own souls and those of our clients, has led to healing and resolution in wounded lives. We are privileged to share family constellations with our clients. And we feel blessed to be working and studying with our friend and colleague, Ed Lynch, as we continue to deepen our understanding of this work.

References

Franke, U. (2003). *In My Mind's Eye: Family Constellations In Individual Therapy*. Heidelberg: Carl-Auer.

Gallo, F. P. (1999). *Energy Psychology: Explorations at the Interface of Energy, Cognition, Behavior, and Health*. New York: CRC Press.

Hellinger, B. (1998). *Love's Hidden Symmetry: What Makes Love Work in Relationships*. Phoenix, AZ: Zeig, Tucker, & Theisen.

Hellinger, B. (1999). *Acknowledging What Is: Conversations with Bert Hellinger*. Phoenix, AZ: Zeig, Tucker, & Theisen.

Hellinger, B. (2001). *Love's Own Truths: Bonding and Balancing in Close Relationships*. Phoenix, AZ: Zeig, Tucker, & Theisen.

Hellinger, B. (2003). *To the Heart of the Matter: Brief Therapies*. Heidelberg: Carl-Auer.

Krishnamuri, J. (1969). *Freedom From the Known*. San Francisco: Harper.

Morgan, A. (2000). *Integrated Meridian Therapy* (workshop materials). Lincolndale, NY: CIFT.

Shapiro, F. (2001). *Eye Movement Desensitization and Reprocessing* (2nd ed.). New York: Guilford.

10

Listening to the Wisdom of the Body

by Dale Schusterman

The emergence of complementary medicine has brought to the fore the concepts of the mind-body connection. The relationships among the body, mind, and emotions are now well documented. Much research exists that demonstrates the mind's healing and destructive effects on our health. When we include the soul, especially the family soul, new tools for healing and well-being emerge. In this chapter, we will look at physical health conditions through the lens of the unique systemic approach of Bert Hellinger. These new insights add great depth to the concepts of the mind-body interaction.

Observations made while leading family constellation groups, and from my chiropractic practice, have led me to conclude that all chronic physical problems have systemic roots. Even old injuries from "accidents" are locked into place by systemic forces. When these energetic patterns are rerouted, an amazing healing force becomes available, which may even alter longstanding health issues. This chapter will explore the systemic principles, taught by Bert Hellinger, that are the key to resolving chronic health conditions. It is possible to demonstrate the effect of these systemic issues on the body by using kinesiology, or muscle testing. Moreover, one can start with a physical problem and often trace it to its systemic roots with muscle testing and proper declarative statements, as we shall see.

As a chiropractic physician, my view of healing is structurally based. However, early in my practice, I found that the greatest leverage for stabilizing the body's structure — spine, skull, and extremities — lay in addressing the multiple aspects of a person, including nutrition, lifestyle choices, and his or her emotional and spiritual needs. Over the years, I learned how to incorporate treatment modalities to meet these different needs, or at least to recognize which area(s) were necessary to address in order to regain health. If a patient didn't respond quickly to mechanical treatments, then I immediately shifted to nutrition or emotional work. My success rate improved dramatically with this approach.

Since 1983, I have been researching the Kabbalah, or Jewish mysticism, as a way to understand how consciousness works through the body. I have been developing hand signs, or mudras, that act as energetic keys that open the body to the various healing dimensions of the Kabbalistic Tree of Life. In other words, when I met Bert Hellinger in 2000, I already had many healing tools at my disposal. There were many wonderful ways to diagnose and treat structural, biochemical, and psychological imbalances. My "comprehensive" approach to treating people was in place, but I was in for an awakening. I met Bert Hellinger. I had never seen myself or my patients as other than individuals. I knew how complex and multilayered we were, but I had never considered the family fields in which we are all embedded. However, since that first encounter, exploring the family field in healing the body has become my passion and focus.

Family constellations provide unique insights useful to both clients and facilitators. Constellations are intriguing and they are high art. Everyone loves a great story, especially stories about themselves. Unfortunately, most people carry around personal stories that are inaccurate, limited in scope, and designed to prevent inner movement, or growth. The stories that unfold within family constellations tend to be highly accurate, broad in scope, and definitely designed to stimulate inner movement toward healing and resolution. They often reveal something surprising, which is another aspect of a good story — that we learn something new about ourselves.

I have used family constellations in several ways in my practice. People who have chronic health issues may be referred to group constellation work. A constellation usually offers great insight into the hidden forces behind their problem. Often, it is enough to begin the healing process and nothing else needs to be done. However, sometimes I find that several months, or longer, after a constellation has taken place, the information obtained still needs processing by the patient. Occasionally, several years later, the revealed patterns remain in place and need a "push" to get them to move. This is where new healing modalities can help unlock the patterns. This will be described in more detail later.

I have also found the constellation work to be extremely useful in treating patients in one-to-one work in my office. They may not have experienced a constellation, but it is possible to question them and their bodies to create a window into the hidden forces behind their illness. This is an illuminating process for both the doctor and the patient. An understanding of the systemic forces and how they affect the body and mind is one of the greatest weapons a physician or therapist can have in his or her therapeutic arsenal. The rest of this chapter will discuss this process.

Applied Kinesiology[1]

Applied kinesiology (AK) is a system used to assess function in the body. By testing the strength of muscles before and after a stimulus, it is possible to observe the body's response. A stimulus can include anything that causes a nerve to fire. In other words, it can be a touch, a mechanical thrust, a biochemical substance placed upon the tongue, a visual or auditory input, or even a thought. When a stimulus causes a strong muscle to weaken, or vice versa, then it is considered a positive test — a change in the state of the muscle as a result of the stimulus. The doctor can then use this information, in conjunction with other data, to determine how to strengthen the body so that the stimulus no longer causes a muscle to inhibit.

Applied kinesiology was developed in the chiropractic profession, although it is now practiced worldwide by healers of all persuasions. Although the procedure as described here is meant only for physicians and others with licenses to diagnose illness, there are many kinesiology systems available to the layperson. Hundreds of techniques have been developed based on this unique ability to interact with the intelligence of the body. Many of these approaches deal with the diagnosis and treatment of the body's alignment. It is possible to test the muscles, the soft tissues, the extremities, the spine, and the cranial bones. Such testing has improved the accuracy and effectiveness of many medical treatments. There is also a wealth of information on how to deal with nutrition and toxicity in the body. For instance, sometimes a chronically weak muscle will only strengthen when a specific nutrient is placed on the tongue. In this case, it becomes apparent that the muscle problem was secondary to the nutritional deficiency. Finally, research on how to treat psychological issues is now in full bloom, and this will be discussed further.

Psychological Reversals

A psychological reversal (PR) is a positive statement that causes the inhibition, or weakness, of a previously strong, or facilitated, muscle. For instance, challenge a muscle to ascertain that it is strong and then make a positive statement, such as, "I feel centered in my heart when I am at work." If the body/mind is in agreement with this statement, the muscle will still test strong. If, however, there is some inner discordance with that statement, the muscle will test weak. (The muscle doesn't actually lose strength, but it changes momentarily to a state of weakness termed inhibition. Likewise, a strong muscle is considered to be facilitated. Because the terms strong and weak may imply a judgment, the neurological terms are preferable, as well as more accurate.) For example, if there has been some stress at work, or if it is not the type of environment that encourages the heart to remain open, or there is some negative association with someone in the office, muscle testing will reveal that the emotional flow (at the very least) is not healthy there. If we make this statement — "I feel centered in my heart when I am at work" — and the muscle inhibits, it indicates that there is some imbalance in the system that we can address with our healing methods. The inhibition from this psychological reversal will last only a few seconds before the system recovers and readapts to a positive, strong veneer.

Dr. George Goodheart, the founder of applied kinesiology, first observed in the late 1960s that thoughts and emotions can affect a muscle test. When a person thought of a problem, it would cause a previously facilitated muscle to test inhibited. Later, Dr. John Diamond, an Australian psychiatrist practicing in New York who had studied with Goodheart, expanded on these concepts. He noticed that by using muscle testing, it was possible to observe the body's response to a spoken word or phrase. He also correlated different emotions to the various acupuncture meridians. In addition, he found that sometimes positive statements would cause inhibition in muscles. It would seem to make sense that making a positive statement, such as "I choose to be happy in my relationship with my wife/husband," or "I choose to be healthy," would cause a strong muscle to remain strong. However, Dr. Diamond also observed that sometimes these statements would cause people to weaken or demonstrate inhibition in a muscle test.

In the early 1980s, Roger Callahan, Ph.D., a student of applied kinesiology, further developed the use of muscle testing for treating psychological problems. He also worked with these positive statements that caused paradoxical responses in people. When a person demonstrated muscle inhibition in response to a statement, such as, "I expect good things to happen to me," he called it a "psychological reversal." In other words, it is a reversal of the normal psychological status. Callahan wrote several books on this subject, including *The Five Minute Phobia Cure* (1985)[2], and *How Executives Overcome Their Fear of Public Speaking and Other Phobias* (1986).[3] In these books, he provides a highly effective treatment protocol, using the acupuncture meridians to eliminate the psychological reversal. This procedure would often produce dramatic results in complex psychological and physical conditions. Dr. Jim Durlacher wrote an excellent book on Callahan's techniques called *Freedom From Fear Forever*.[4]

I first heard Callahan speak at an applied kinesiology conference in the early 1980s where he presented papers on the concepts of psychological reversals.[5] His observations made a big impact upon me and I have used this simple concept ever since — that the body will tell you (via muscle testing) when it is not congruent with Truth.

Others have been similarly stimulated by these ideas, as there are now numerous systems of healing based on Goodheart/Diamond/Callahan's discoveries linking psychology and muscle testing: Neuro Emotional Technique (NET),[6] Thought Field Therapy (TFT),[7] Evolving Thought Field Therapy (EvTFT),[8] Emotional Freedom Techniques (EFT),[9] and so on. Common to most of these procedures is their reliance on the acupuncture meridian system for treatment and/or diagnosis. Different algorithms of tapping acupuncture points are used to reset the body so that the psychological reversal is corrected — in other words, the statement no longer inhibits a strong muscle. Based in chiropractic, NET uses a spinal tapping procedure to make the corrections. The Association for Comprehensive Energy Psychology (ACEP)[10] is an organization of therapists who teach and use many of the above methods to link body and mind in energy healing.

My preferred method of balancing the body is with the Kabbalistic hand signs as detailed in my book *Sign Language of the Soul*.[11] This energetic balancing treatment brings the body/mind into alignment with the Tree of Life, which is a map of the soul — a map of consciousness. I find that this works especially well when dealing with the family soul.

The Body Doesn't Lie

It is often said that the body does not lie. With muscle testing, it is possible to unlock the truth of the flesh. A person may think that he or she is not experiencing any repercussions from his diet or lifestyle, but a few simple muscle tests might confirm the opposite. The same is true of the psychological reversal. When a person says that he or she is "not afraid of spiders," an inhibition may result in the muscle test's showing that the person is in fact fearful, and that the phobia is active.

Hellinger has said that the "flesh is wise."[12] And experience has shown me the truth of this statement, as the body will always see what we are unable to see in our awareness. Illness always represents something that we are unable, or unwilling, to see. Therefore, the body sees it for us, but in a way that is painful.

Imagine that a woman is unconsciously connected to the trauma of the death of her great grandmother's, which happened as she was giving birth to the child who would become the woman's grandmother. She might have severe menstrual pain, ovarian cysts, or a host of so-called female problems. The repercussions of this kind of trauma in the family field can be dramatic. The family of the great grandmother, who died in childbirth, is often unable to deal with the pain surrounding this event. The surviving child never knows his or her mother. The great grandfather might even be seen as responsible for what happened, as a murderer, since he got his wife pregnant. This woman, the great granddaughter, might unconsciously feel the need to connect with her great grandmother. However, her loyalty to her own mother, or possibly to other family members, might require that she not "see" what happened. She may not even be aware of the great grandmother's fate. One way that she might stay connected to everyone involved would be to quietly develop female problems. In her mind, she can remain "blind" to the fate of her great grandmother, but in her body, she can show the close bond between them. The body truly sees what happened.

This woman would need help from allopathic medicine, as well as from complementary medicine (herbs, vitamins, acupuncture, etc.). She might even seek counseling for pain management or for issues surrounding her relationships with men, or with her mother. All of these things might be appropriate and useful courses of action for her to take. The hidden cause is generally not dealt with, as there are plenty of symptoms to keep both patient and physician fully engaged. However, when she finally does meet someone who can facilitate her family constellation, all these hidden patterns are revealed. Now, her symptoms begin to abate, and the physical treatments, which are still necessary, have a more lasting effect. Without the systemic insights, her case could be managed, but with the newfound realizations, she has a chance to get well.

Diagnosing Psychological Reversals

When a potter makes a group of pots, he or she will often test them after the firing process by tapping them to see if they are strong and intact. If there is a flaw in the wall of one of the pots, the pot will shatter, or make a sound that indicates an inconsistency in the material. Similarly, we can tap the body to see if it responds in a way that indicates strength and consistency, or the opposite. Unlike pottery, however, the body is highly sensitive and will respond to a broad range of stimuli.

The tool we will use to test the body is the human voice. Voice is very powerful in its effect. It creates a resonant field in the body with which all organs vibrate. This can be both a positive and a negative experience, depending on the words chosen and the emotional energy behind them.

The different Energy Psychology protocols (TFT, EFT, NET, etc.) incorporate their own set of questions that they pose to the body/mind and evaluate with the muscle test. There are specific sequences of the statements that they use in order to unravel the psychological defense mechanisms that develop as a result of trauma and injury. It would be useful for anyone who wishes to do individual therapy to study some of these methods in order to understand the idea behind testing for psychological reversals. However, once you have identified the issue, it is important to begin to think of it from a systemic perspective. Who in the family system really has this issue? Who is really saying this sentence? To whom does the client feel closer when making this statement? The family constellation facilitator has an edge here, because he or she already knows how to listen inside the system for the sentences that heal.

Systemic Psychological Reversals

Standard statements that are used for psychological reversals are ones that say something about the person. "I choose to be healthy." "I acknowledge why my lower back hurts." "I enjoy being free of pain." — These statements concern only the individual. When they cause muscle inhibition, the various therapeutic protocols can be applied, often with outstanding results.

Systemic statements have a broader scope and include previous generations. The individual is linked to something greater than himself or herself: "Dear Mom, I honor you when I am healthy." "Dad, when I acknowledge why my lower back hurts, I am closer to you." "Grandfather, I leave your pain with you, and maintain a loving connection to you when I am pain-free." "Mother, I am too small to carry your pain, as I am just your child." Implicit in these statements is that one's current situation is related in some way to what happened before. Here the individual still receives attention, but he or she is connected to something else at the same time. The muscle inhibition that occurs with these statements can be cleared, thus restoring balance to a person and helping him or her connect to a deeper place within. One of the fundamental principles of systemic work is that everyone has a right and need to belong. When someone is excluded for any reason, stress develops in the group that excluded him or her. Therefore, systemic statements are always designed to create connection and inclusion.

When a client presents a problem, it is important to listen to him or her with systemic ears. As the client talks about his or her family, we listen for who is excluded, or in some way, diminished in stature. The illness usually represents someone or some event that is denied acknowledgment. Not only does the illness keep us connected to what happened in the past, but it also gives us an unconscious feeling of being important, because we think we are helping to remedy the past through this connection.

Muscle testing is an effective tool for performing an interactive investigation with a client of his or her illness. Of course, one needs to keep in mind that muscle testing is not infallible, and so one should not make major assumptions based on muscle testing data alone. Nevertheless, there are certain protocols or statements that can direct us toward understanding some of the systemic factors behind a physical problem.

The Basic Statements

The place to begin is with the mother and father. Following are the basic statements for investigating whether or not a problem has roots in the family field — in the experiences of previous generations.

> "Dear Mom, when I am free of (illness/problem), I am connected to you and your ancestors with great love."

> "Dear Dad, when I am free of (illness/problem), I am connected to you and your ancestors with great love."

The client is tested to find a facilitated muscle. The client makes these statements, and after each one, the muscle is retested. If one of them inhibits the test muscle, we can identify a connection between the illness and the past. Although only one side of the family usually tests positive, it is conceivable that both sides might be involved. Now we can question the client about what happened on that side of the family, and even craft new statements to see if the specific issue the client has voiced is related to the problem at hand.

Sometimes the standard set of questions that are asked by those testing for psychological reversals cannot reveal the deeper issues, because they are hidden to the client, and, as a result, to the therapist. There is no permission in the client's system to expose the issues. The conspiracy of silence is a subconscious loyalty often found in family systems that makes it hard to expose certain patterns. This is where the understanding of systemic dynamics and the dynamics of the soul becomes invaluable. Sometimes, a family constellation in a group setting is required to bring up the hidden issue. But there is also a way to phrase a psychological reversal to help deal with the problem in an individual setting.

If neither of the previous basic statements causes a strong muscle to inhibit, the client may not have permission to acknowledge the issue. The following statements will help the client to alter his or her unconscious need not to see the issue.

> "Dear Mom, when I see why I have (illness/problem), I am connected to you and your ancestors with great love."

> "Dear Dad, when I see why I have (illness/problem), I am connected to you and your ancestors with great love."

These statements, when positive, indicate that the client is loyal to his or her ancestors by remaining ignorant of the pain or trauma that occurred in the past. There is an unspoken agreement within the group to keep the issue hidden. In these cases, the body readily shows what the person cannot show. We are often surprised when misfortune befalls us. However, if we were aware of the deep inner forces operating in silent agreement to events of the past and the present would become clear. But if we were aware of these things, we would not have problems! In this way, illness and misfortune, when understood, are really gifts, which can help us return to wholeness.

The psychological reversals of "not seeing" the issue must be cleared before further healing can occur. The clearing comes from using one of the techniques mentioned earlier, such as acupressure, or spinal tapping (TFT, EFT, NET), or Sign Language of the Soul. Once the body/mind has been balanced, the sentence will no longer act as a psychological reversal. Now, however, if we go back to the basic statement, on the same side of the family, we find that it is positive, whereas it was negative before the blinders were removed.

> "Dear Mom/Dad, when I am free of (illness/problem), I am connected to you and your ancestors with great love."

This statement is now the focus for a treatment. Once this statement has been treated, the client usually feels better. Now we can use systemic statements to investigate the specific dynamic being uncovered, such as, "Mom, you are the right one for me," "Dad, you are big and I am small," "Dear Uncle, I give you a place in my heart," and so on. If these statements inhibit a muscle, we apply the appropriate balancing. In this way, we can do a full one-to-one session with a client by testing and balancing his or her body in the process.

The statements just given are useful as a beginning conversation with the body/mind. It is a way to establish to which side of the family the illness relates. There are thousands of possible statements one can test after the direction that needs to be taken becomes clear. Choosing these statements requires an understanding of systemic dynamics and the ability to feel one's way into the client's family soul. Since we are working one-to-one, it is necessary to question the client concerning the family history. A formulaic approach may suffice to begin, but it is important to continue on a phenomenological basis, if possible, and to react to what comes up in the client. We can validate suppositions by muscle testing the healing sentences and looking for psychological reversals.

Example

Let us illustrate this by looking at the woman with chronic lower back pain. I test a strong muscle and have her say, "Dad, when I don't have low back pain, I am connected to you and your ancestors with love." Then I retest the muscle. If there is no change in the state of the muscle and it remains facilitated, I have her say the same thing to her mother, "Mom, when I don't have lower back pain, I am connected to you and your ancestors with love." If the muscle becomes weak, then there is probably a connection between the back pain and something that happened on her mother's side of the family. Now, I ask her about the history on her mother's side of the family and question her about traumatic events that happened, especially those relating to life or death situations. There may be multiple clues, but I listen for the one that has the most energy behind it. This should all correlate with muscle testing.

Let us suppose that the woman's mother was schizophrenic. A traditional therapist might stop here and develop a complete therapeutic approach based only on this information. A standard psychological reversal might deal only with the back, "On all levels of my being, I choose to have a healthy, pain-free back."

However, we understand systemically that schizophrenia often has deep roots in violence in previous generations. Using this knowledge, we can question the client to see if she has any knowledge about what happened. We can craft statements with which to test the body, such as, "Mom, when I see the violence that occurred and give it a place in my heart, I am connected to you with love." Or, "Dear Mom, I am too small to carry the burden that you are carrying. I am just your little girl." Or, "Dear Mom, I honor your burden and leave it with you, with love." Each of these statements is tested to ascertain which, if any, cause muscle inhibition. If the back pain is related to the previous familial experience, these statements will probably cause inhibition in the muscle. If she touches her lower back when she says these statements, the muscle will not inhibit, showing the connection between the lower back condition and what happened in the past. Using the statement, "On all levels of my being, I choose to have a healthy, pain-free back," does not address the intergenerational aspect of this problem and does not connect the woman to problem's root. The client needs to see her mother as part of a bigger picture, and to remain small to her mother so that she does not assume the same pattern. Any of the statements that you have learned or heard in the various family constellations can be used in this manner.

Case History 1: Aaron

Here is an example of how systemic issues might be involved with a physical problem. Aaron came to me for treatment of chronic pain in his right shoulder blade area. Sometimes, he could barely lift his right arm. There was no history of injury to the area, but his is an intense "type A" personality who has suffered much stress and aggravation in his life. He has a very high cholesterol level of 300 for which he is taking a statin drug. He also has tried many diets, none of which has made a dent in his cholesterol level.

As a chiropractor, I evaluated his spine, tested muscles, and gave him some treatments. He said he felt much better after each one, but that his pain would return within a few days. I have learned that if a problem returns despite good manipulation therapy, then other issues need to be examined.

Knowing that Aaron has high cholesterol and that the muscles around his right shoulder correlate with liver function, it was not difficult to figure out that he needed some specific nutrients to support his liver. The liver manufactures most of the cholesterol in the body, so that link is fairly clear. Once Aaron began the nutritional supplementation, his back pain started to ease. Although it has not completely disappeared, there is a definite improvement.

On a subsequent visit, I asked him about the histories of his ancestors on his father's side. Psychological reversal testing showed that his liver imbalance pointed to his father's side of the family. He tested strong on the statement, "Mom, when my cholesterol is normal, I feel connected to you and your ancestors with love." But he tested quite weak when the same statement was directed to his father. This told me that something had happened in the past on his father's side of the family to which he was unconsciously drawn. He explained that his father was never there for him, and it was obvious that he felt contempt for his father. Upon further investigation, I learned that both of his father's parents had died in an automobile accident when his father was five years old, and that his father had been raised by an aunt.

It is not difficult to see why his father had been emotionally unavailable as a parent. His father had experienced a great trauma as a child, and an experience such as this often makes it difficult for a child to move on. As this man's son, Aaron is also caught in an emotional trap — the loss of his grandparents. Even though he never met them, he unconsciously feels his father's feelings. As a way to be closer to his father, he takes on his father's hurt and anger and internalizes them. This manifests in his life as impatience, and a driving, obsessive type A personality.

The effect of these intense internal emotions on his liver was to block certain detoxification enzymes. When I had Aaron visualize his father and his grandparents behind him, he becomes emotional and uncomfortable. The liver reflexes, which I had just strengthened, suddenly became active again. While he held this inner image, I applied my balancing methods to correct this stress on his liver. By having Aaron focus on the trauma of his father and grandparents, I was able to access a very deep, and until now generally ignored, aspect of his internal experience; a major factor in his liver dysfunction. It became necessary to craft very specific statements for Aaron to say, in conjunction with his visualizing of his father and grandparents. One of the more important statements centered on acknowledging the drunken driver who was responsible for the accident: This brought about the most important release of tension in his body.

Aaron's Statements

A facilitated muscle inhibited to each of the following statements, after which I performed an energy-balancing treatment. Some of the statements required multiple treatments for resolution. It might have been better in the long run to do a family constellation on his issue, but as a one-on-one therapy in a 20-minute office visit, this was all that could be accomplished. And much progress was made with this method.

> "Grandfather (father's side), I give you a place in my heart."
>
> "Grandmother, I give you a place in my heart."
>
> "Grandfather/grandmother, I honor your fate."
>
> "Dad, if you won't see the drunken driver, then I will."
>
> "Dad, I now see your love for your parents."

To the drunken driver:

> "I see you and give you a place in my heart."
>
> "I honor your fate."
>
> "I leave the consequences of your actions with you."

Each statement inhibited a strong muscle, so I made an energy correction following the statement. Occasionally, three or four repetitions were required to balance one of the statements. Some of them brought up deep emotions. In the end, Aaron was very peaceful, relaxed, and able to see his childhood and relationship with his father in a different light. Also, his liver reflexes were much stronger. In subsequent visits, other parts of this pattern emerged. I had him visualize his father behind him with his grandparents behind his father. I then told him to say to his wife, his son, his mother, and his boss, "I feel the strength of my father and his parents" and "I honor the fate of the drunken driver."

The important aspect of this case was that, over several sessions, Aaron made significant changes in his world view. He changed his work ethic and began spending more time with his family. His need for the nutrients diminished, and gradually his cholesterol began to improve. The shoulder problem was gone, except when he became riled up over something at work. Aaron's case shows how the structural problem (shoulder) was a subset of the biochemical problem (liver/cholesterol), which was a subset of an ancestral pattern (untimely death of grandparents). Aaron could have spent endless money on chiropractic adjustments, massage, statin drugs, psychotherapy, anger management, and so on. However, an integrative approach that supports the body structurally (one or two chiropractic manipulations), biochemically (nutritional supplements), and psychologically (systemic therapy) has been shown to provide a solution that empowers him and balances him. In six months and five treatments, he had vastly improved.

Constellation Versus Individual Treatment

We make the same statements in family constellations that we use in psychological reversal testing. In the constellation the statements themselves have the healing power, as they are in contact with the experience of the client, who is in contact with the other person. Nothing more is needed. This is not true, however, when the same statements create inhibition in a muscle test, indicating incongruence. In this case, they act diagnostically, rather than as a therapy, unless a manual or energetic treatment to correct the imbalance is applied. The best way to help the client is to facilitate contact with the person to whom he or she is unconsciously connected. Here, the statements have great significance. But even in a constellation, there is often deep internal resistance to the statements, and to the full feeling of the words. Often the representative is able to say the statement, whereas the client has difficulty doing so. This is the reason why it can take months, or even several years, for some issues to be resolved following a constellation. In these cases, the use of psychological reversals can be of tremendous value as follow-up care.

Systemic psychological reversals can be used in conjunction with a balancing method as a one-to-one therapeutic approach when the issue is straightforward, or if a group is not available to do the constellation work. Many smaller issues do not require a full constellation, but are quite amenable to individual work. However, a greater benefit of this approach may be that the systemic psychological reversals can be used as follow-up therapy to help a client process some of the deeper blocks. My observation is that most people really have no concept of the depth of these systemic patterns, or of what is required to fully resolve them. Many people make a slight inner movement, and then stop. In these instances, some focused one-to-one work using specific statements can be quite helpful. In one individual session, I had the client say the same statement 21 times, each one followed by a treatment. It required more than an hour to clear this deep pattern, but the time was well spent, as it brought him to a never-before experienced sense of inner peace.

There are times when both approaches (individual and group work) are potentially appropriate, and it is up to the therapist to be flexible in deciding which one to use. Correcting a few systemic reversals can make a client more amenable to the constellation work, as it can ease some of the resistance inherent in his or her system.

Sometimes, in a constellation, the healing statements are enough to move the client toward resolution, and sometimes they are not. When they are not, it can be quite helpful to use the statements as psychological reversals to expose the pattern so that appropriate energetic or physical balancing techniques can be applied. This integrative approach enhances the potential for the new positive pattern to be folded into the body/mind of the client.

Case History 2: Larry

Larry came in to be treated for narcolepsy — a condition that causes a person to fall asleep at inappropriate times during the day, such as while eating or in the middle of a conversation, or even while driving a car. One can see that this can be a debilitating, or even dangerous, ailment. Common medical treatments include stimulants such as Ritalin to keep the patient alert. Unfortunately, like all drugs, these medications have side effects and other consequences.

I examined Larry and gave him a treatment that included structural and energy-balancing approaches. I also gave him a nutritional supplement to take at about the time he would normally start to have narcoleptic symptoms. The nutrient had a very positive effect on him.

On a subsequent visit, I could not find any structural or energetic imbalances in Larry's system, so I began to evaluate systemic effects to ascertain what was behind the narcolepsy. I asked Larry to say the basic sentences, and I tested a strong muscle after each one.

> "Dear Dad, when I don't have narcolepsy, I am connected to you with love."

> "Dear Mom, when I don't have narcolepsy, I am connected to you with love."

His arm remained facilitated to the father, but dramatically inhibited with the statement to his mother. This showed that the narcolepsy was connected in some way to the mother's side of the family.

I asked Larry what had happened in his mother's family. I wondered who was excluded, and whether he knew the reason. After a few minutes, he said that his mother's sister had died as the result of a botched abortion. She bled to death. But he didn't know much about her, as she was seldom discussed. I immediately asked him to imagine his aunt and to say to her, "Dear Aunt, when I stay awake, you have a place in my heart." This made a strong muscle inhibit upon testing. Then I had him say, "Dear Aunt, when I fall asleep, you are remembered." This statement caused his test muscles to remain very strong.

In addition to his aunt, there were three other excluded persons in this particular scenario. The aborted child and the father of that child both need to be honored and remembered by the family.

The person who performed the abortion was certainly excluded from the hearts of the aunt's family. I had him say the two statements to each of these other three persons, with the same muscle-testing results. When these people are not remembered, or perhaps even shunned by the family, it causes an energetic reaction that can have terrible consequences for the following generations.

Larry developed narcolepsy in an unconscious, although not very successful, attempt to remember the excluded persons. In a way, the illness caused him to seek treatment and he was able to find his way to reconciling these hidden patterns, but for most people, the hidden dynamics behind illness remain elusive. Most illnesses are treated on the level of the body, which is where the effect of the dynamic plays itself out for the individual.

This client's treatment consisted of having him look at the four persons in his mind and make the statements that caused the inhibition to occur in a strong muscle. When I heard from him two days later, he said that he was feeling much better. There were also a number of other issues in his life that were related to his aunt's fate.

As an interesting aside, Larry came to the office about a month later for further work on this issue. His son was with him. From a kinesiology standpoint, narcolepsy often shows up in the reflexes of the small intestine. When I had him make some more statements about the fate of his aunt, it not only inhibited his small intestine reflexes, but it also showed up in his son's. The son's small intestine muscles also inhibited as well. As soon as I balanced the father, the son's muscles became strong. This shows how connected children are to their parents and the currents that flow in the family system.

Eventually, Larry had a constellation focusing on the narcolepsy and the fate of his aunt. There was not a lot of energy in the constellation, because much of it had already been worked out. But the chance to see his aunt, her child, the father of the child, and the abortionist brought him to a new level of completion on the issue. Even with the constellation and the one-to-one work, Larry might still require nutritional and other physical therapies to support the deep inner changes that are taking place. Healing is a process, not an event.

Summary and Conclusion

Family constellations are a wonderful tool for understanding and healing physical ailments. The observations of Bert Hellinger are invaluable in getting to the root of physical problems, and in my experience, they provide the most essential part of the healing process. The body, mind, and soul are one integrated system. When something is not allowed to live on all levels, one part of the system takes on more than its share in the expression of that which is excluded. Invariably, the emotional or physical system is jeopardized. The body sees what we denied, and in that truth, we can honor illness as a gift that is designed to bring us into wholeness.

There is danger in making systemic work into a formula, as that is against its phenomenological nature. The work should unfold in a natural way, revealing truths as they are, without the censorship or manipulation of the conscious mind. Nevertheless, with this in mind, we can use certain basic statements to point us in the right direction to begin a systemic investigation with a client. We must allow our inner pictures to guide us as we unravel the patterns in which the client is caught. Muscle testing can be a tool, in the right hands, to help facilitate this clearing process. By balancing the statements that show incongruence in the body/mind, it is possible to break down internal resistance and to heal the blocks that prevent health and happiness. This can be done in individual therapy, as a way to help prepare someone for constellation work, or as follow-up care after a constellation. In all cases, it is up to the client to allow the movements of his or her soul to take place. All we can do as facilitators of constellations, or practitioners, who correct systemic psychological reversals, is to help bring clients to a point where they can fly on their own.

References

1. International College of Applied Kinesiology. Retrieved from www.icakusa.com.

2. Callahan, R. (1985). *Five Minute Phobia Cure.* Wilmington, DE: Enterprise Publishing.

3. Callahan, R. (1986). *How Executives Overcome Their Fear of Public Speaking and Other Phobias.* Chicago: Dearborn Financial Publishing.

4. Durlacher, J. (1995). *Freedom From Fear Forever.* Tempe, AZ: Van Ness.

5. Callahan, R. (1981). *A rapid treatment for phobias and psychological reversal.* Lawrence, KS: Collected Papers of the International College of Applied Kinesiology.

6. Neuro Emotional Technique. Retrieved from www.netmindbody.com.

7. Thought Field Therapy. Retrieved from www.tftrx.com.

8. Evolving Thought Field Therapy. Retrieved from www.tftworldwide.com.

9. Emotional Freedom Techniques. Retrieved from www.emofree.com.

10. Association for Comprehensive Energy Psychology. Retrieved from www.energypsych.org.

11. Schusterman, D. (2003). *Sign Language of the Soul: A Handbook for Healing,* Cranston, RI: The Writers' Collective.

12. Hellinger, B., Weber, G., & Beaumont, H. (1998). *Love's Hidden Symmetry.* Phoenix, AZ: Zieg, Tucker & Theisen.

11

Hellinger Meets Shapiro: Constellations and EMDR

by Andrea Stuck

These are exciting times in the world of therapy and family systems' work. Many therapies are being combined in a nexus of treatments inducing rapid changes in people's lives.

Constellation works has been shown to be a viable one-on-one process in addition to its better-known use in group settings. Many writers have offered ways in which individual constellations may be done (Franke, Madelung, and J. Hemming). This chapter talks specifically about how to utilize Eye Movement Desensitization and Reprocessing (EMDR) therapy with Orders of Love as an individual constellation practice. The utilization of EMDR and the "releasing statements" of constellation work afford remarkable relief for clients.

Constellations: What Are They and What Is Their Purpose?

A constellation is a multi-pronged process that names a problem that inhibits a longing from emerging; positions that problem in facts rather than emotional judgment of those facts; provides a spatial picture of the problem, as it is carried by the client; allows for actual tangible data to emerge from the representatives of the family members or business; allows for the release of the problem; offers plausible paradigm shifts by "acknowledging what is"; and opens a path for relief or change.

Perhaps the most striking phase of a constellation is the actual physical, spatial representation of a person's "fixed gestalt" or dilemma. A constellation is a picture of how a person carries his or her espoused dilemma in their daily life. Through spatial representation of his or her family or organizational system, a constellation shows us how this person's way of being is encumbered. A constellation taps the energy of the "knowing field," or a collective soul, and allows this energy to inform. It makes tangible that which we have been unable to see and allows for realignments, releases, and fluidity within the system.

What is the purpose of a family constellation? For a family system, it seems that the sole (and soul) purpose of the constellation is to let life flow from generation to generation, and within the generation at hand. A family constellation has at its core right place, inclusion, humility, respect, love, and LIFE.

What is the purpose of a business or organizational constellation? For an organizational system, it seems that its purpose is alignment. At the core of an organizational constellation rests right place, right people, right give and take, and right norms for continuance of the organization with respect, humility, and caring. Why? The answer: to support the organization so the organization may last.

The process of doing a constellation includes

1. The presentation of the dilemma or longing by the client to the facilitator. This is often referred to as the interview in which the facilitator is collecting factual data that may account for what is happening to the person seeking the constellation.

2. The spatial arrangement of the pertinent persons to the constellation as determined by the facilitator from the data presented.

3. The collection of the phenomenological data from the representatives by the facilitator.

4. The beginning of realignment via position and through releasing statements, given to the representatives by the facilitator.

5. The placing of the person with the original issue in the "right place" in the family system, to allow him or her to feel relief originally sought.

The entire constellation process relies on factual data from the client, phenomenological data collected from the representatives, and the realignment of the system on the basis of the "orders: time, space, belonging, give and take, and family conscience." The facilitator keeps in mind what the client longs for, the phenomenological data from the representatives, and the alignment of the orders to release the system.

What Is EMDR and What Is Its Purpose?

Eye Movement Desensitization Reprocessing (EMDR) is a therapeutic technique originally utilized in the relief of post-traumatic stress disorder (PTSD) Francine Shapiro (2001) notes that the technique does not merely provide relief or "desensitization" but also anxiety, she states that it is used in:

1. Helping the client learn from the negative experiences of the past.

2. Desensitizing present triggers that are inappropriate or distressing.

3. Incorporating templates for appropriate future action(s) that allow the client to excel individually within his or her interpersonal world.

EMDR is a comprehensive approach that includes careful attention to images, beliefs, emotions, physical responses, increased awareness, and interpersonal systems.

EMDR is a structured-treatment approach guided by an information-processing model. Although eye movements are often referred to as the definitive feature of the approach, it includes alternating sounds, touches or combinations of eye movements, sounds and touches. EMDR, as a trauma therapy, utilizes many other psychotherapies, such as psychodynamic, cognitive-behavioral, person-centered, body-based, and interactional therapies (Shapiro, 2002). Shapiro's (2001) adaptive information-processing model hypothesizes that when the information related to a distressing or traumatic experience is not fully processed, the initial perceptions, emotions, and distorted thoughts are stored in the brain fundamentally as they were experienced at the time of the trauma. These unprocessed experiences are understood to become the basis of current dysfunctional reactions and symptoms and can contribute to the onset and maintenance of many forms of mental disorders. EMDR therapy works directly with the cognitive, affective, and somatic components of the stored memories. It reprocesses the old stored experiences and helps to facilitate the forging of new associative experiences and more adaptive information. The simplest way of stating the goal of EMDR is that it allows the client to live well and fluidly in the present.

EMDR relies on the following process/protocol:

1. Delineating the presenting target or triggering event.

2. Naming the negative cognition (NC) that accompanies this target or triggering event. (NC's are statements such as "I am bad"; "I am worthless"; "I am weak.")

3. Assessing the strength of the negative cognition and the SUDS level (subjective units of distress). This level ranges from 0-10, with zero being no distress and 10 being high distress.

4. Eliciting the positive cognition (PC), or what the client would like to think and feel about him or herself. (A PC may be something like, "I am strong"; I am worthy"; "I am worthwhile.")

5. Assessing the strength of the PC known as the validity of cognition (VoC), which ranges from 1-7 with 1 being a completely false statement and 7 being a completely true statement.

6. Accessing the feelings of the client.

7. Using eye movement sets, where the client focuses on the named triggering event, NC and the bodily sensations/feelings, and follows the therapist's fingers of light bar back and forth for a set number of times.

8. Using cognitive interweaving, which is a reframing technique that posits alternative views of what the client thinks or feels or could think or feel. Cognitive interweaving is, in essence, a way to help present an alternative paradigm for the client to think about or feel around the triggering event.

9. Testing the SUDS level once the EMDR is completed for that session.

10. Installing the PC with short sets of eye movements (one to seven trips).

11. Testing the VoC for the strength of the PC.

Once again, EMDR is a process utilized to relieve present-moment negative cognitions and emotional distress. It presents possible alternative ways of feeling and thinking about one's self once a trauma has obliterated, prevented, or distorted positive beliefs and feelings.

Both, family constellations and EMDR provide effective relief. They work independently and, when combined swiftly produce remarkable results.

A Comparison of Family Constellations and EMDR

Family Constellations	EMDR
1. Interview: determine the dilemma and what the future would look like if the longing were achieved	1. Interview: determine the dilemma and what the future would look like if the dilemma were gone
2. Select representatives	2. Name the triggering event, the NC, and the SUDS level
3. Set up the constellation	3. Begin the eye movements
4. Have the facilitator collect phenomenological data from the representatives	4. Have the client report to the therapist current thoughts, visions, feelings, body sensations, smells upon ending the set of eye movements — the phenomenological data
5. Begin releasing statements and realignments	5. Reframe and begin next set of eye movements
6. Continue until the family system has been released and there is relief for all members	6. Continue eye-movement sets until relief is achieved; check SUDS level
7. Place the person with the issue, the client, in the constellations to feel the longing met	7. Reprocess by installing the PC
8. Thank everyone	8. Check VoC for the PC
	9. End the session

The real power of combining constellations and EMDR emanates from using "releasing statements" as formulated by Bert Hellinger as cognitive interweaves within EMDR. Reframing or cognitive interweaving depends on the data, the phenomenology of the client during EMDR, as realigning and releasing statements depend upon the phenomenology of the representatives in constellations. Releasing statements that "fit" the phenomenology of the client in EMDR represent, to me and to my clients, the most powerful and effective cognitive interweaves available.

What Are Releasing Statements?

According to Metzner (2002), Bert Hellinger is, in German, what is called a *Seelsorger*, a caretaker of the soul. A *Seelsorger* is one who "ministers to people's deepest spiritual questions and difficulties." Bert Hellinger and Judith Hemming (my teacher and mentor) are both *Seelsorgers*. Both have the unique capacity for daring to go where other therapists or clergy may not go. Both have the startling and amazing capacity for naming exactly what the soul of the system needs in order to be freed. Both go directly to the heart of the matter; both pierce the soul with clear reality and enduring love. Both change people swiftly and forever. Both utilize "releasing statements, or statements of power," with the precision of surgeons.

When using statements of power or releasing statements, Metzner (2002) suggests that Hellinger, Hemming and, indeed, every constellator, becomes a *Wahrsager*, a truth speaker or soothsayer. "These statements, when spoken, name what is with intense, soul-piercing precision, having the effect of soothing the anxious or tormented soul."

Statements of power seem to be statements of factual accuracy with family and business constellations. The following are examples of statements of power.

Partner to Partner

1. I take you as my wife/husband/partner and all that you come from.

2. In our children, I respect you and I love you.

3. I take you and all that life brings.

4. I love you and I want you.

5. We will bear this together.

Parents to Children

1. I am entrusting you to your mother/father.
2. In you, I also love your father/mother. She/he is still here for you through me.
3. I loved your father/mother very much, and if you become like him/her, I will agree to it.

Children to Parents

1. You are big and I am little.
2. You give and I take (receive).
3. From you, I accept everything, all of it.
4. From you, I take my life, at this price, with love.
5. I see the price you paid for your life.
6. I will make something of my life, for your pleasure and in your memory, so nothing has been in vain.
7. I take you as my mother (father) and you can have me as your child.
8. I will pass it all on as you did.
9. You are the right father (mother) for me and I am the right son (daughter) for you.
10. If it helps, I'll carry it too.

All of these statements are designed to allow the child to take the right place in the family system, as a child and not an equal of his or her parents. It is just a fact, children follow parents, they do not come before parents. Without parents, there are no children. Therefore, children are second forever and forever thankful for those who have gone before them, for without those who have gone before them they would have no life. I often say to my clients, "There are six billion people on earth and only those two, your mother and your father, could have created you. Without those two people, there is no you. So no matter how terrible it is or was, you always owe them respect and love for your life. It is your life; make something of it to honor them."

Siblings to Siblings

1. You are first, thank you for making my life easier.
2. I am second.
3. I am your sister/brother.

All of these statements of power come from *On Life and Other Paradoxes (Hellinger, 2002)*.

The purpose of statements of power is to name the truth in a very concise and clear form, piercing the soul of the client. How the client sees the dilemma and feels the fluidity and power of life are forever changed. This allows clients the new choice of living more fully and lovingly with the support of all who have gone before them. This is no small task and is a small, courageous truth that is named once and for all.

Case Studies Combining Family Constellations and EMDR

The Case of a Bulimic Woman

On her first visit to my office, this 50-year-old woman informs me that she also has another therapist, whom she sees twice weekly, a dietician, whom she sees once weekly, and a medical doctor with whom she has video conference sessions twice weekly. She finds all of them helpful and supportive, and she was "sent" to me for EMDR as all of her team of professionals felt she was stuck.

She tells me that her mother was an ineffective woman who could show no emotions and that her father was an eruptive, volatile man who scared her to death. She tells me she didn't like to even think about them ever. Rather, she prefers to concentrate on her successes as a bulimic. Once weighing 250 pounds, she is now anorexic and bulimic, staying "at the low end of her allowable weight range."

I ask he what troubles her the most. She tells me that food makes her incredibly scared. I suggest we start with food as her initial target. I ask her if she has a place she feels she could go to in her mind that would help her feel safe and stable if she were to become overwhelmed or frightened during the EMDR. She says she does and describes it to me. I install it with eye movements until it feels solidly in place.

The mere thought of food creates enormous anxiety in this woman. I ask her what negative thought (i.e., her negative cognition) she holds about herself when she becomes so frightened about food. She tells me that she is bad and weak. It is a very strong sense she has of her badness and her weakness, clearly a SUDS level of 10. I ask her what she would like to think and feel about herself in relation to food. She struggles telling me she has never been asked anything like this before and has never thought like that and isn't sure. I suggest that if she feels bad and weak might she like to feel good and strong around food. She clearly likes the idea but believes there is no way to think or feel that way because she has never done so before (VoC of 1).

We begin the EMDR session with the presenting target, "Food makes me bad and weak." She knew to allow anything and everything that enters her experience to come and go. All of these things appear for good reason. We do several sets of eye movements wherein she experiences within her body, considerable anxiety, rapid breathing, and sweaty palms, yet she says she is experiencing very little. We utilize her body sensations as the presenting phenomenology and do more eye movements. At one point, her mother appears and isn't helping my client in any way with her father's raging. My client is clearly frightened and fairly judgmental of her mother.

I suggested that we start the next set of eye movements with, "Dear Mom, you are big and I am little." She does so, and begins to see and report that it is clear that her mother had no real idea of what to do in this situation. She feels relief and sees that it is just a fact: her mother had no skill with which to help her.

We begin another set of eye movements with, "Whatever it was, it was terrible and I take my life from you and dad at this price." She sees and feels relief again. She says to me, "My mom would want me to live well, I know it."

This set of eye movements begins with, "I take my life from you with love and respect. And I will not waste another day of it consumed by food." She begins her set of eye movements. At the end of this set, she looks at me and says, "I think I can go get a chicken and eat normally today."

I ask her how she feels about food and buying a chicken. She tells me that she feels oddly strong. I ask her if her statement, her positive cognition, "I am strong and good," still fits. We install this "reprocessed" belief with two sets of short eye movements. One session is over. She feels lighter, stronger, and more able.

I realize, as a therapist, that EMDR, itself, will really help this client. I also know that because we utilized statements of power, releasing statements from family constellations work, this client is proceeding much more freely and quickly than she would have without them.

The second session begins with her telling me that she actually bought the chicken, prepared it, and ate well without so much fear. So I ask her what she would like to use as the target for this session. She chooses to begin with, "Weighing myself is an all-consuming daily event." Her NC is, "I am unlovable," with a SUDS level of 10. Her PC is, "I am lovable," with a VoC of 1, that is a statement that is totally inconceivable to her.

We begin the eye movements with "Constant weighing is consuming me and makes me feel unlovable." This first set of eye movements brings her father into her life when she is about four years old. She is in a closet, shivering with fear. I suggest we begin the next set of movements with, "Dear Dad, whatever it was, it was horrible for you. I see your fate, and it belongs to you not me." This brings her to a calmer place when she stops. She says to me, "I never ever think about him, he's so frightening, but I have done it, and I am calmer now."

We begin this set with, "Dear Dad, I am no better than you. You are the right dad for me and I am the right daughter for you. If being mean is how I have to behave to belong, I'll pay the price." Again we proceed with eye movements.

She stops me and says, "He doesn't want that does he?"

I ask her how she feels when she says that. She tells me, "Totally amazed. I never thought any of this before."

I ask her to begin the next set with, "I am just the daughter. I did it all out of love for you both and it didn't help." As we stop this set of eye movements, she tells me that she really loves her parents. I ask her to begin the next eye movements with, "Dear Dad, I am staying. Look kindly on me as I stay, please."

She isn't so sure, and yet she presses on, courageously. Ending this set, she asks me, "This was never about me, was it?"

We close this session with, "I am lovable." And she feels it for the first time.

This is a small representation of what is possible to accomplish in less than an hour utilizing EMDR and statements of power, acknowledging what is from family constellation work. The client isn't free and clear yet. She is very different than she was at her first presentation just three weeks earlier. Her own phenomenology is combined with acknowledgment of reality and releasing statements, and she is on her way.

A Case of a Biracial Woman with a Half Brother who Committed Suicide

This client is a 29-year-old biracial woman who appears to be Caucasian. She comes from a blended family, an African American father, a Caucasian mother, and an older half brother, who is also African American and has committed suicide. At this point, her father has died and her brother has been dead since she was 14 years old. She presents with overwhelming anxiety. This young woman has done two previous constellations and has experienced enormous change, and, yet, anxiety still surfaces. She is in graduate school and anxiety seems to have been worsening since she returned to graduate school in the fall of 2004.

Her presenting target is that she thinks and feels that it is not okay for her to succeed. She says that she thinks this continuously now. I ask her if there are any particular events that create this feeling of lack of worth. She tells me that she feels it chronically, and that she feels somehow out of place and that it is out of her control.

I ask her, "Who would smile on you knowing that you were and are suffering like this?"

She says, "My brother."

A great deal of history is known about her brother and her relationship with her brother. She adored him and he her. He also left her with a friend of his, who subsequently molested her. There is clearly much that one could talk about and process in regular talk therapy. Yet, to me, most likely most of it is not worth chasing.

We begin the set up of EMDR. She sees her brother's face and it is forlorn. I ask her, "What is the negative thing that you feel and think about yourself when you see his face?"

She tells me, "I am unworthy." It is a SUDS level of 10.

I ask her, "What would you like to feel and think about yourself?"

"I am worthy." She smiles, even though she doesn't believe it.

We begin the eye movements of EMDR with the face of her brother and her thinking and feeling that she is unworthy. As the first set ends, she tells me, "I am doing it for him."

I ask her what she feels when she hears herself say that she is doing it for him. She tells me, "Arrogant."

We begin the next set of eye movements with, "You were first and I am second. Thank you for being first, it made my life easier."

We begin the eye movements. The set ends and she says, "He feels relieved and so do I."

I suggest that we start with, "Dear brother, you are dead and I am alive. I'll come in time. Please look kindly on me as I stay."

The set ends as she says, "I am fine and so is he. I am done now."

This client is very sophisticated. She knows a great deal about energy work, constellations, and therapy. She is "easy," as it were. She grasps things quickly and wholly and moves through dilemmas with very little help.

Conclusions

I am thankful that Bert Hellinger sees things as they are and that he provides releasing statements that have so many valid applications that help so many people so quickly.

I am equally thankful that Francine Shapiro developed EMDR. EMDR can be creatively combined with many other forms of therapy and knowledge to help people more quickly and clearly.

Why combine family constellations work with EMDR? My answer is, quite simply, "Why not?"

All I am trying to do is provide the most direct path for my clients to reclaim their lives, take their right places, live well, and move forward in a more fluid manner, feeling and knowing that they are absolutely fine.

I do not use EMDR all of the time. I do not employ full-blown constellations all of the time. I combine these therapies because it "is" and it reaches, as Bert Hellinger would say, "the heart of the matter." I would be remiss, knowing what I know, being who I am, and not making this available to the lives of all I contact. The moment I saw both of these works, family constellations and EMDR, they changed me forever. The more I learned about family constellations work, whether from Judith Hemming, Bert Hellinger, himself, Hunter Beaumont, Fran Boring, Guni Maxa, Eva Madelung, Ursula Franke, and Jacob Schneider or from reading, or watching, and being a representative, the more I knew it had to be used and made available to everyone.

References

Franke, U. (2002). *The River Never Looks Back*. Heidelberg: Carl–Auer.

Greenwald, R. (1999). *Eye Movement Desensitization and Reprocessing (EMDR) in Child and Adolescent Psychotherapy*. Northvale, NJ: Jason Aronson.

Hellinger, B. (2002). *To the Heart of the Matter*. Heidelberg: Carl-Auer.

Hellinger, B. (2002). *On Life and Other Paradoxes: Aphorisms and Little Stories from Bert Hellinger*. Phoenix, AZ: Zeig, Tucker & Theisen.

Hellinger, B., Weber, G., Beaumont, H. (1998). *Love's Hidden Symmetry. What Makes Love Work in Relationships*. Phoenix, AZ: Zeig, Tucker & Theisen.

Hellinger, B., Weber, G., Beaumont, H. (1998). *Love's Own Truths. Bonding and Balancing in Close Relationships*. Phoenix, AZ: Zeig, Tucker & Theisen.

Hellinger, B. (1999). *Acknowledging What Is: Conversations with Bert Hellinger*. Phoenix, AZ: Zeig, Tucker & Theisen.

Parnell, L. (1997). *Transforming Trauma: EMDR*. New York: Norton.

Parnell, L. (1999). *EMDR in the Treatment of Adults Abused as Children*. New York: Norton.

Shapiro, F. (2001) *Eye Movement Desensitization and Reprocessing: Basic Principles, Protocols, and Procedures* (2nd ed.). New York: Guilford.

Shapiro, F. & Silk Forest, M. (1997). *EMDR: The Breakthrough Therapy for Overcoming Anxiety, Stress and Trauma*. New York: Basic Books.

12

Hurting for Love: Three Cases of Self-Abuse

by Mark Wolynn

The slashes on Sara's calves and ankles remind me of the Crayola sandwiched between red violet and plum — the one the color of a dark red grape. Without really counting, I estimate about 70 or so separate incisions.

"That's an interesting place to cut," I say, pointing to a barely-healed, seven-inch slash following the length of her shinbone.

"I wanted to see what the bone looked like."

"Were you successful?"

"Yeah."

Sara had come seeking hypnotherapy. At 24, she had already seen her share of psychiatrists, ingested enough drugs on a daily basis to sedate a rhino, been confined to institutions for more than a month on a few separate occasions, and had even been treated with electroconvulsive therapy. All to no avail. Nothing could reduce the pleasure she derived from the razor's weight.

Sara's not proud when she tells me about the cutting. She sinks down into herself, embarrassed, her voice small and flat. I'm much more interested in having her show me than she is in showing me. But we both look, and we talk, and make casual comments about the colors of the scars, the feeling when cutting, after cutting, the payoff of the pain. She appreciates that I'm not afraid to talk about this.

"What does your boyfriend say when he sees these?"
"He's never seen them."
I nod, although I find that hard to believe.
"Does he know you cut?"
"No, I don't think so."
"Would you be willing to show him, and tell him about the cutting?

She agrees to do this.

I like Sara. I work with many young people who cut themselves, or pull out their hair, or throw up their food, but Sara somehow seems different. She's a very gentle person, a serious person, who respects life, music, art, books, and the people in her world. What strikes me most is how deeply she loves and respects her parents, a quality uncommon in the other self-abusers with whom I work, who often blame their parents, in some way, for their pain. Her parents, she tells me, are best friends who truly love each other. "They love me deeply, and have given me everything," she told me. Sara volunteers at hospices, out of a desire, as she puts it, to give something back, because she feels she has received so much.

In our first session together, Sara talked about her past suicide attempts. Before I agreed to work with her again, I asked her to bring me a note from her psychiatrist supporting our work together. With so much respect for life and her parents, I had only one question. To whom was her love flowing? To which family member was she being loyal when she mutilated herself like this? In the family system, two generations back, we would find our answer.

Given her age, her medication regimen seemed excessive: Effexor, Wellbutrin, and Lithium for depression, as well as two antipsychotic drugs: Seroquel and Zyprexa. Whether it's the effect of the drugs or the consequence of her depression, Sara's vitality appeared to be muted, almost zombie-like, as though she were cloaked in a dull mist. But get her talking about Steely Dan, a band she loves, or about hospice work, and she becomes quite animated. I realized that later she could control her affect, regulating any joy she might feel, by not allowing herself to experience more than what she believed was her quota of happiness. She told me in a session once, "If I'm too happy, I'll lose my compassion, and someone else might suffer." Another time, she said about the cutting, "If I don't cut myself, I feel guilty." More about this later.

Commonly viewed as a diagnostic indicator for borderline personality disorder, self-mutilation has also been observed in individuals — the majority of whom are middle- to upper-class adolescent girls or young women — diagnosed with bipolar disorder, obsessive-compulsive disorder, eating disorders, multiple personality disorder, and schizophrenia. The increased observance of self-harming behaviors has many mental health professionals insisting that self-mutilation be given its own diagnosis in the *Diagnostic and Statistical Manual of Mental Disorders,* as the phenomenon is difficult to define and can be easily misunderstood (Zila & Kiselica, 2001).

Individuals who harm themselves have often suffered sexual, emotional, or physical abuse from someone with whom there had been significant connection, such as a parent or sibling. Such abuse often results in a perceived loss or disruption of that relationship. The behavior of self-mutilation is then experienced as an attempt to escape from intolerable or painful feelings (Levenkron, 1998).

Stanley, Gameroff, Michaelson, and Mann claim that those who self-mutilate often have difficulty experiencing feelings of anxiety, anger, or sadness, and thus use the cutting as a coping mechanism. The injury created by the cut is intended to assist the cutter in dissociating from immediate tension (2001).

Aside from her flat affect, which I observe mostly when she's lost in thought, and believing what her thoughts are telling her, I find Sara capable of experiencing and expressing a full range of feelings. When something touches her deeply, her eyes reveal it, although she says she doesn't cry much. Even so, she appears to move easily between emotions, feeling at once saddened and angered by what she envisions as inequities in the world: those with a lot who do nothing to help those with little, "the children who are starving, abused, or abandoned." We talk about how she might one day make a difference in the world through her writing, her drawings, through hospices, or by helping children.

As I listen to her talk, I envision someone helpless inside her who also knows what it's like to feel abused and abandoned.

At night, during the "cutting hours" between midnight and 2 a.m., she claims that she can feel the presence of spirits who want her to die. She feels that they call to her, pulling her, coaxing her not to stay with the living. She feels like she belongs with them, among the dead. "It's like I'm already dead," she told me. Several weeks later, she would bring in her sketches, underworld images of tortured faces and twisted bodies, drawings of people cutting or shooting themselves.

In the process of taking her family history, we found a devastating trauma in the system. When her father was eight years old, his 27-year-old father was hit by a car and died of multiple lacerations. The sudden and violent death of her grandfather left a wound in the family that rendered the grandfather "missing" from the system. Missing, as well, was the driver who caused the accident.

I thought back to a workshop I attended in Washington, D.C., on June 5 and 6, 2004. There, Jakob Schneider gave a lecture about traumas and their effects on a family. In such a trauma, a deep wound is created in the soul, as well as in the body, where the pain is so intense that it cannot be tolerated. The body responds, in what appears to be a good way, by going into shock, or numbing out, so that the pain is not felt so strongly. Thus, surviving family members, like Sara's father in this case, are able to function and continue with life. But generally, they don't function with a full set of emotions or a full awareness of their physical bodies.

As a therapist trained also to work with bodies, I remember the hundreds of bodies I've touched, where such a trauma had muted the vibrant quality of the muscles and flesh. In its place, a deadness or coldness or denseness was perceived in the tone of the soft tissue.

Bracing against pain — physical or emotional — is the body's instinctive reaction. At some level, something inside us believes that we can successfully shield against it. But we can no more subdue torrents of pain than we can prevent a dam from flooding by placing a finger in the dike. The pressure in the system, too powerful to be contained, will seek another outlet, perhaps through an illness or a physical problem, or through what many of us who work with Bert Hellinger's theories experience, a systemic identification. Someone who comes later in the system will attempt to carry or balance what is unhealed in the system from someone who came earlier.

In this case, Sara, the child, could "carry" for her father what he could not let himself feel. In another interpretation, Sara could attempt to replace her father's father by appearing "dead" herself, and by cutting herself in front of her father. Both of these behaviors could have the effect of forcing her father to come into contact with his dead father, who himself was cut to death in the accident. That was my theory as Sara and I began to move more deeply into the trauma.

As we experience emotions somatically as sensations felt in the body, numbing our bodies after a trauma has the effect of distancing us from our feelings. Victims of the Holocaust, for example, often reported going numb, not feeling anything, in order to survive their ordeal. Victims of an accident often describe something similar. They cut off from remembering the accident, blocking what they saw or felt in order to dissociate from the trauma.

To distance from the pain of a trauma, a family member may cut off his or her feelings, especially compassion and empathy. In this way, Sara's father may have shut himself off from his feelings of love for his father. If he allowed his love for his father to flow, then along with that love would come the feelings of pain, and perhaps even the violent images of his father's death in the auto accident. Instead, he shields himself, and in this way, leaves his father out of his heart. He knows in his mind that he loves his father, but it can't be felt, as the images of the grief and the death are too intolerable, and cannot be dealt with.

"A child who loses one of the parents isn't strong enough to bear the grief and sadness," Hellinger says. "Instead the child reacts with anger. Anger is a child's way of grieving. Later, when she wants to get into contact with her grief, she cannot find it, and she experiences anger instead" (Hellinger, 2001).

Then, later on, a child down the line — like Sara, in this case — may become angry with the parent who is not emotionally available. Perhaps Sara's father was not able to show his love for Sara, for in his love for her, is also his love for his father. And in loving Sara, the pain for his father could be felt. Sara assures me that this is not the case. Her father, she says, was very loving with her, and she feels only gratitude and deep love for him.

Schneider has observed that such a trauma may repeat itself later as an illness or symptom, whether physical or psychological, which forces the love for the missing father to emerge. Stephan Hausner, at a workshop in Washington, D.C., on September 11 and 12, 2004, elaborates: "If a father dies when a child is young, there is a great longing for the father and a fear that, 'if I love him, I will have to go the same way.'" This image stands in the way of the love. Hausner goes on to say that often it's easier for the child to have an illness. "With an illness, it's easier to look at the father without having to feel the grief." The solution, of course, is to be able to love the father without being sick. In constellation work, we bring the client into contact with the father, so that the client can see that the father wants his child to continue with life and to be healthy. The client then has a chance to move on in a different way, by honoring the fate of the father, and by taking life from him fully, exactly as it was given, with all of the consequences of that particular fate.

In our work, symptoms are always viewed positively, as arrows or signals that may be directing us toward a traumatic event in the family. We ask ourselves: "How does this symptom make sense? To what or to whom is it pointing? How might the cuts on Sara's body connect to the lacerations that killed her grandfather?"

In our second session together, we confronted the car accident. Behaving both like a perpetrator by cutting into her skin, and like a victim by suffering from the wounds, Sara was asked to look at both her grandfather and the driver of the other vehicle. With these two forces alive in Sara, victim and perpetrator, it felt right to have her search for her compassion for both men.

With her eyes closed, Sara saw the two men embracing each other. Both men were crying. A deep reconciliation appeared to be taking place in both men and inside Sara. In this same image, her father, who had been watching the whole thing — he, too, was crying — embraced both men. Sara then backed away.

"Dear Grandfather," I had Sara say out loud, "my father misses you so much, that I tried to appear dead like you. I cut and mangled myself, so my dad would see you and your death through me. But I'm so small, and it's not my place to act so big. And it certainly hasn't been helpful for anyone involved. I respect your fate and your tragic death. Please see me with love when I let myself feel alive and happy."

To the driver, I had her say, "Dear Driver, I have tried to hurt myself, making myself bleed, so you, too, could be seen by my dad. Now he sees you, and I can back away. You have a special place in my heart."

To her father, she said, "Dad, there's nothing I can do to help you. This is your fate to have lost your father. I'm too small to do anything here. I can just love you the way it is, and try to let myself be happy, even though at times I may feel a little guilty, being happy having you as my dad, when you grew up without your father."

I handed Sara two small wooden figures to take home and place on a bookshelf or some place where they could be seen. I suggested to her that they represented her grandfather and the driver of the other vehicle, and that they belonged together. I asked her to light a candle for each of them to show respect.

Sara came back for the next session reporting that the work had had a profound effect on her. "I think about my grandfather now. Before, he was just a picture. The whole thing made his existence more real." When I asked her about the driver, she told me that she felt some type of closure inside, and that when the two men had embraced in her inner image, each was at peace with what had happened. This put her into a deep peace she couldn't explain.

For the rest of that session, we worked with meditation techniques designed to shift her awareness away from her heavy ruminations. I taught her to give her body sensations more importance than her thoughts. First, she started with focusing on the sensations of energy currents in her hands. Then she gradually allowed other body sensations to arise into her conscious awareness. By the end of the session, she was able to hold in her awareness the energy sensations in her entire body, simultaneously, as a single sensory experience. She reported being able to attach less importance to her thoughts. She was learning for the first time that she was not her thoughts; she was part of something much greater. Practicing techniques like these, nightly, would play a significant part in her healing process.

In our first session together, I had asked Sara when things had begun to go awry. She said that everything had started for her at age 17. She recalled swimming for the high school swim team in a competition, and being suddenly struck midway in the water with the overwhelming feeling that she couldn't go any further. "I failed… I couldn't make it," she told me, "I had put in so much time and had let myself down."

After that, Sara talked about how she had struggled with anorexia, and occasionally had to be hospitalized to attain a proper weight. By age 21 or so, Sara's weight would remain steady. With an extra 5 or 10 pounds on her frame, Sara now says she doesn't care so much about her weight.

The cutting started soon after that. Cutting her ankles and wrists became a nightly ritual.

"Here's my pen," I told her. "Pretend it's your razor and show me how you cut yourself."

As Sara traced one of the scars with the pen, her aliveness appeared to dim.

"What are you telling yourself at this moment? What do you hear inside you?"

"I'm already dead."

"And who are you who's already dead," I asked, not having any idea where this question might lead.

"I'm dead. I shot myself."

Having no information about anyone in her family history who had committed suicide, we followed the energy that presented itself, without judging its content.

"I'm a girl," she said, "I'm 17 and they don't notice me." Sara began to tell a story about what appeared to be some other person, a young girl, who also felt isolated. "I sit in my room... I hate myself... I can't be happy." The girl then said that she found her father's gun, and shot a bullet through the roof of her mouth.

Without judgment, just seeing where the energy would lead, I asked the girl, who at this point called herself "Karen," what would happen if she saw her death again, and just "allowed" it. Karen reported that a light she hadn't seen before, "a window of light," was opening over her dead body.

"Who's there in the light?" I asked.

Karen reported she could see ancestors, uncles and aunts, other relatives, and even some she didn't know, reaching for her, coaxing her to go to them. Karen went with them.

"It's so calm... I feel big, expanded," Karen reported, as she appeared to leave Sara, who, at this point, was relishing the expanded, calm feeling.

If we take this story at face value, it might seem as if Karen, a discarnate spirit, had attached herself to Sara for a purpose that appeared unclear. However, concluding that Karen is an entity separate from Sara would limit other perceptions.

In the next few sessions, we worked with other voices inside Sara, other characters or spirits. None of them appeared to be connected, at least consciously, with anyone in her family. In my opinion, it's not important to speculate about the "who" or "what," whether we are working with discarnate energies, archetypal metaphors, or unintegrated personality fragments. All that felt important to me was one question: "Did it have a good effect for Sara?" After each session, Sara reported feeling lighter, less preoccupied, and, what's most important, she began to cut herself less often.

One can never say for certain that what happens in a session directly results in a client's improvement. Certainly, a myriad of other factors weigh in. However, it appeared that Sara seemed to gain inner strength and more freedom from her pattern of self-injury the more we proceeded.

Sara seemed to feel as though we were helping people who were lost, people who were like her, who were neither "here" on the earth nor "there" at home on the other side. This felt to me like the right direction to pursue. It was as though a door had opened inside Sara, and something could now be set free.

In one session, Sara reported feeling huge and obese. She closed her eyes and began to connect with the energy of an extremely overweight woman in her mid-40s who hated herself and the way she looked. The woman reported she had been alone her entire life without friends, and had died in a similar way, alone in her chair in her cluttered apartment. She didn't realize she had even died. When I asked her how she came to be this way, she said that she had taken on her mother's pain. I asked her to imagine seeing her mother coming for her to take her home. As her mother held her tightly in her arms, she cried away years of loneliness and pain. And then she, with her mother, left. I thought back to Sara's bout with anorexia. Could this "story" have been connected in some way?

In another session, Sara described a young woman "with" her who had died after slicing her wrists. "Overlooked and forgotten, like she wasn't important and didn't belong anywhere," the woman said she was connected to an earlier relative, a grandmother who had also committed suicide, and then beyond that, to a man in the family who had been a murderer. Ancestors began to surround them all, and a great healing had begun to take place in that family. Strange as it seemed, it appeared as though I were facilitating a family constellation through Sara, with a family that had passed on a long time ago.

Other characters told their stories through Sara. One was a scruffy man in ragged clothes who had died of an apparent heroin overdose. He did not know where he was. Once he saw his body lying in the alley, he realized he might be dead. He began to tell his story. As a 10-year-old boy, he had witnessed his parents being shot to death during a robbery. This event, he said, had ruined his life. "After that, I did anything to hurt myself," he said. It seemed that the drugs helped to put him into contact with his dead parents, as though to say, "If you suffered so much, my dear parents, so will I. I will shoot myself with heroin to be out of life like you." Apparently, the heroin had served its purpose. I asked him to envision himself resting in the arms of his parents who then escorted him home.

After each session, Sara would light a candle for the "spirits." As part of her homework, she was asked to light the candle at night, during cutting hours, for their safe journey home, and also for what was beginning to open up in her. "The first night that I lit the candles," she told me, "a strange thing happened. I started to cry. It was a relieving sort of cry, a feeling cry, an understanding type of cry." She said she had never before felt a crying like that.

"As I light a candle for the spirits, I take a moment and reflect. And then I feel relief that lighting the candle may change somebody's situation or ease somebody's pain." She was talking about what was happening inside her. "I feel lighter," she said, "I'm able to notice now when I drag myself down."

Instead of going into her ruminations, I asked her, as part of the nightly candle-lighting ritual, to use that time to focus on the energy sensations in her body. I also asked her to keep a journal of some of the messages and feelings that came to her during her meditations, and to write down some of the things for which she felt grateful. She was also required to have two days of "fun" during the next week. I held Sara responsible for her homework. She consistently kept her agreements.

"I'm almost afraid to get better. Then I could get hurt again," she said once.

We talked about how staying "dead" was akin to staying "safe." How there's no risk involved in staying safe, and that it's often easier to die than it is to live. Sara understood that, and agreed to try something new — to celebrate the gift of life she had been given. That week was also the week when she agreed to show her scars to her boyfriend.

"He didn't *say* anything," she was almost crying, "he just bowed down and kissed them. I'm so glad to be with him and thankful for the time we spend together."

Sara was no longer cutting every day. During that week, she was able to enjoy two full days of happiness.

Then, one of the "spirits" or characters who seemed to be most distressed showed up in the next session. That day, Sara came to the office saying that she didn't deserve to live. "I need to cut myself," she told me. "If I don't cut myself, I'll feel guilty." I had her say the sentence again, "I don't deserve to live."

"What did you do?" I asked. "What makes you so tortured that you don't deserve to live?" I thought about her father, and how he might feel guilty fully engaging in life when his own father had bled to death from his wounds. Then she said this:

"I killed people."

Sara told the story of a man, 30-something, who had murdered the woman he craved. She had stopped seeing him because she, as he put it, "found better people to hang around with." So he broke into her home and murdered her and her new boyfriend with a knife, and then cut his own throat.

"I'm evil," he went on. "Nobody could love me. I'm a disgrace. Now I'm alone in the house where I killed them. I sit and I think about what I've done."

Sara watched, in her mind's eye, as the man confronted his two victims. Emotions of remorse and reconciliation began to emerge. Then the man found a deep peace, as his own father, whom he had never met, came to escort him into the light. Sara imagined giving the razor she used to cut herself to the man's father, saying, "I thought I needed this, but I don't. It's not mine." Then Sara saw herself withdrawing and walking away.

At that moment, I imagined Sara handing over her pain to her own father. By recounting the killer's story, she was making peace with the perpetrator shadow inside herself, and, therefore, could more fully integrate the killing in her own family.

It feels important at this point to say something about these characters and their plights. I've found, after having facilitated numerous cases like Sara's, that from inside most of us, especially when we're in our pain, an image or a story can arise — often quite spontaneously. It feels as though we're dreaming, but we feel awake at the same time, like we're having a "waking dream." The Dutch Reincarnationists call this phenomenon "elliptical consciousness." In these images or stories, we seem to be living someone else's life. The surroundings are different. The characters are different. We may even look different, feeling male when we're female. These may be our memories from a previous life. These may be the memories of other people's lives that somehow we're able to tap into. Perhaps they may even be the memories of people who've died with whom we seem to resonate in some inexplicable way. Maybe they're metaphors or archetypal parables that seem to mirror our present-day conflicts. Maybe we're tapping into what Jung refers to as the Collective Unconscious, or simply remembering the events of our forgotten ancestors. All we really know is that many of us carry within us a story like Sara's that has the power to help us heal. When told, it contains a key that can unlock buried emotions and release entrenched physical patterns.

If we go further and venture to say that discarnate spirits are somehow able to affect the living, as might be the case with Sara, then these spirits must come to us because they need our help. And perhaps, too, we need theirs.

The Tibetan Buddhists, who have studied "bardos," the after-death realms, teach us that the mind is very much alive after death, reliving the experiences of the life just lived. Sogyal Rinpoche discusses this phenomenon in *The Tibetan Book of Living and Dying*:

"In this state, the mental activity is very rapid: thoughts come in quick succession, and we can do many things at once. The mind continues to perpetuate set patterns and habits, especially its clinging to experiences, and its beliefs that they are ultimately real" (p. 289). In this state, he says, "We believe we have a physical body and that we really exist" (p. 290). He goes on to say, "The mental body can linger near its possessions or body for weeks or even years. And still it may not dawn on us [that] we are dead" (p. 289).

I have often wondered whether, in this death state, one might have an effect on one who is alive. Psychiatrist George G. Ritche, in his book, *Return from Tomorrow* (1978), recounts a near-death experience he once had. He saw spirits of the dead trying to influence the living by entering their electromagnetic fields. These spirits were unaware that they were dead and could be neither heard nor felt.

Perhaps it follows that, if the dead can, in fact, influence the living, then one who dies — especially one who dies in an anxious or tormented state with strong emotions such as terror or vengeance, remorse or regret — might look for relief through a living person who has a similar wound. The living person, because he or she has a body with which to work the wound through, has the opportunity to heal in a way not available to the dead person. Clients such as Sara often report sharing a similar emotional resonance with the characters they describe.

It could go something like this: The spirit who is in distress joins with the client, drawn to him or her by a certain magnetic quality or similarity. This "joining" has the effect of augmenting or driving the client's neurosis up, just a notch or two, but enough to impel the client to seek professional help. If the therapy is successful, then both benefit by becoming freer to move on.

I find it hard to believe that there is such a thing as a spirit possession beyond our will. If something like this were actually going on, then it would have to be with the agreement of both parties, as both ultimately gain an advantage. The relationship then possesses a genuine reciprocity. At some level, we agree to help them, and in so doing, we are able to help ourselves.

With every story she told, every character she helped, Sara became lighter.

For the next week, Sara was given the task of having seven days of happiness, and if possible, and only if it felt right to her, seven days without cutting. The intensity behind the cutting, she said, was gone. We were now working with neuropathways generated by the act itself — memory imprints of an ingrained three-year habit. We talked about an image of a well-trodden path flattened in a meadow, and how we might take a different route.

We talked about continuing the nightly healing rituals, and how not to be so available for the pain and loneliness between the hours of midnight and 2 a.m. If the pain ever became too intense, she knew she could just leave her room, or sleep at her boyfriend's apartment.

Every time she lit a candle now, she felt as though she were opening a doorway into the higher realms. In that space, she felt she could offer up her sadness, or bring forward healing for herself, or send light for all those who might be lost in the dark.

Sara was now reading Eckhart Tolle's, *The Power of Now,* and putting it into practice by focusing on the energy, whether painful or pleasurable, inside her body. We talked about the idea of letting her body become a factory for thoughts and feelings that arise and pass away, not becoming too fascinated with them, but simply allowing them to be there or not to be there.

We also talked about movies. I suggested the Albert Brooks movie, *Defending Your Life*, and also *The English Patient*, neither of which she had seen. Listening to Steely Dan or watching a movie at night could be a good adjunct to her nightly ritual. She thought so, too.

When Sara returned the next week, she reported having cut herself only once. That would be the last time. Cutting, she said, felt empty to her. "I didn't get out of it what I used to. I asked myself, what am I doing?"

She shared some of her journal entries, and talked about her meditations, how they made her feel "peaceful and attuned." In one meditation, she reported being approached by an old Tibetan man with a worn face, who lovingly touched his forehead to hers. "I saw myself as a baby," she said, "and felt how much my parents love me. I know I'm never alone, and that just 'being' is worthy of being alive. It feels so comforting." The next night this same Tibetan man told her, "It's OK to laugh and enjoy life." He told her that she could go to him in her meditations, and that he would always be there to help her.

Several weeks later, she would say, "I feel different. My outlook is completely turned around. When something happens, I no longer go into a downward spiral, into past and future, worrying about what I should have done or what I should have said. Instead, I can let it go. I see that my thoughts are transient. I know now the thoughts or feelings won't last too long." She continued, "And because of that, I can connect to people better. I guess it's not about me so much anymore. I've been noticing other people and wanting to know more about them."

Sara was now going out more, doing more, visiting more often with friends and family, and even planning a vacation to Thailand with her boyfriend. She was eager to reduce her drug intake, and was discussing doing so with her psychiatrist.

At this writing, it has been more than five months without a slice.

I met with Sara yesterday. She was now lighting candles for her hospice patients. She talked about how people rarely take the time to listen to their stories, and what it's like to hold their hands as they die. Then she said this. "Death is only a transition, like birth, into something much greater. We fear it because we don't understand it."

For several minutes, I had nothing to say. An image of Sara returning home from the underworld to guide the dying was more than enough.

* * *

Just as Sara had scarred her legs to awaken her father's love for his father, Samantha had similarly marred her legs out of a special love for her mother.

At 18, Samantha was a beautiful and happy young woman, with many friends and loving parents. She had been with the same boyfriend, a college football player, for more than three years without having had sex with him. Referred to me by her psychiatrist for trichotillomania (obsessive hair-pulling) Samantha had been tearing the hairs from her thighs and calves for years. Her legs were raw, with ugly, raised, red patches, especially on her inner thighs where she did the most pulling.

Her psychiatrist was baffled. In all other ways, Samantha was doing well. She was popular. She was interested in school and life, and she adored her parents, who accompanied her to her sessions.

Again, I asked myself, as I had with Sara, to whom is she connected when she makes her legs so unattractive? An important fact soon became apparent. Her mother, Judith, who spoke first in the initial session, revealed that, as a girl, she had been sexually abused by her grandfather from the age of 8 through 15. From what I could tell, Judith appeared to be doing well. She was in a happy marriage, with four children who were also doing well. Samantha's hair-pulling seemed to be the family's main concern.

In all probability, Samantha identified with her mother, attempting to protect her mother who, as a child, couldn't protect herself. Hellinger refers to this phenomenon as a "double shift," where both the object and the subject are replaced. Samantha pulls the hair on her own legs to make them unappealing, when it is her mother's legs that are desired. That's the shift in object. And the fact that Samantha makes her own legs uninviting to her boyfriend, and refuses to have sex with him, when it is the grandfather she wants to push away from her mother, that's the shift in subject.

I asked Samantha, who had learned about the abuse two years earlier (that's when the hair-pulling began), if she felt that she needed to take care of her mother, and if she felt that her mother was able to take care of her own pain. Yes and No were the answers, in that order. Judith was stunned to learn that Samantha felt as though she were the stronger of the two of them. My decision was to work with Judith in front of her daughter, using wooden figurines and healing phrases. If Judith could maintain her strength and dignity in front of her daughter, and embrace the grandfather, Samantha could feel perhaps freer.

Samantha watched as her mother, with eyes closed, visualized her grandfather in front of her. I gave her healing words to speak out loud.

> "Dear Grandfather, what you did to me was wrong, and now I see that you have been left out of the family because of it. That's not right either. You belong. I see now that I did it for you as my way of being loyal in the family. I was too young to know how to say 'No.' I leave all the responsibility with you. You are the one who must carry the shame and guilt. (In her image, the grandfather appeared ashamed and remorseful.) I give you now a special place in my heart with love."

Then Judith addressed Samantha.

> "This is my grandfather," she said, pointing to one of the wooden figures. "He sexually abused me when I was small. For my part, I was trying to do what I thought was required in my family. Now I see I was not to blame. I don't regret what happened. You need to know this. Out of what happened, I developed my strength and my character. I became a good mother and a strong person. So, in retrospect, I wouldn't change a thing. It shaped me. From here on in, I'll take care of it. There's nothing you can do for me. In fact, you're

fired. I'll take care of everything. And I'll take care of you. You're not to take care of me anymore."

At this point, Samantha had tears streaming down her face. She appeared to be very touched and relieved by what was happening, even chuckling a little in the middle of crying when she was told she was fired.

"Dear Mom," now Samantha was crying very hard, barely able to get the words out. "I have always felt like I needed to take care of you, that you couldn't take care of yourself. I always told myself that what happened to you wasn't fair. And I told myself that I would be angry *for* you, and that I would never let what happened to you happen to me. I told myself that no one would enjoy my legs the way Great Grandfather enjoyed yours. That I would make my legs red and raw so no one could desire them the way Great Grandfather desired yours."

"That's not your job," Judith replied. "I am stronger than you, Samantha, and I'm bigger than you. It's not your place to take care of me. I will take care of you. That's the only way it's going to be from now on. You relax and feel small, and I'll take care of you."

At this point, I gave Judith instructions to rub Samantha's legs to heal the raw, red areas. Samantha, soft and crying, absorbed all her mother's love.

At the end of the session, I asked Samantha to light a candle, asking for God's help and protection to stop the pulling. Afterward, Samantha said that she felt she would be able to quit.

The psychiatrist who referred her reported that Samantha hasn't pulled her hair since the session—it's been four months—and when the impulse arises, instead of pulling, she lights a candle. A few days ago, Samantha sent this email: "It's been just like you said; the wind in the sails is gone. It's still hard to resist the habit, but it's different now. Lighting the candles has been very inspirational, and

I know God is helping me. Thank you so much for everything, my mom and I really appreciate it. We will keep in touch."

★ ★ ★

Not all self-abusers, like Sara and Samantha, harm themselves physically. Paula could do it with fear.

In the work I do, it feels important to expand the definition of self-abuse to include one's self-destructive thought patterns. While some people rely on physical behaviors to harm themselves, destructive thoughts are an equally effective means of self-abuse, especially when the thoughts are abusive and repetitive in nature. Once again, Eckhart Tolle in his book, *The Power of Now,* states: "This kind of compulsive thinking is actually an addiction.... You no longer feel you have the choice to stop. It seems stronger than you. It also gives you a false sense of pleasure, pleasure that invariably turns into pain" (p. 18).

Mentally, Paula was quite tortured. Believing that her neighbor had been breaking into her home and assaulting her while she slept, Paula woke up each morning with a dogged hypervigilance, a watchfulness that could detect the slightest change on her body or in her home. Once she awoke to find that her leg had been cut, "as though by a razor." Another time, she was certain that a portion of her eyebrows had been plucked out. In her home, she believed that her new leather jacket and purse had been scratched, and a charcoal drawing of her had been erased and redrawn to make her look "dead, with black circles under the eyes." Each time she noticed something new, her husband, a retired high-ranking officer in the Air Force, made improvements to the home's security system, adding a camera in the bedroom, or rechanging the locks. No intruder had ever been discovered. But still, Paula suspected the neighbor with whom she had been fighting for months. "She's terrorizing me," Paula told me. Her husband, seated next to her at our first appointment, squeezed her hand and looked downward. A couple in their early 50s, they had raised four grown sons who were all doing well in life.

When I first received Paula's phone call, I didn't take the case right away, preferring to wait a day or two to sit with whether or not I felt a session would be helpful. She was requesting a hypnotherapy session with me to determine if she had been waking up in the middle of the night, and, without conscious awareness, harming herself. When a cancellation opened a space in my schedule two days later, I followed my intuition to contact her, and found her eager to come in that same day. While constructing a genogram of her family, I had a suspicion that something violent might show up, similar to how Paula described her neighbor's attacks. A strange series of tragedies began to become evident.

After becoming widowed in Italy, her great grandmother, Maria, her mother's paternal grandmother, came to the United States, taking her son with her, and leaving a baby daughter whom she never saw again. When I asked Paula why she would leave her daughter in Italy, she responded: "Oh, that's the only way *her* mother would allow her to go, if she left the daughter with her mother."

Often, the stories that pass down through the generations live like myths or fairy tales in our families, where the actions of the hero or heroine, the protagonist and the antagonist, are rarely questioned or examined for accuracy or authenticity. Paula's mother had only recounted what had been reported to her. Suspicions about who may have been the father of the baby girl, and questions about what exactly had happened in Italy that made her want to leave her country, Paula could not address.

After moving to America, Maria married a widower who also had two children — two small boys. Within a year of their marriage, both toddlers died, one falling down the stairs and the other falling into a vat of boiling water. The circumstances surrounding their deaths were peculiar, as they died while Maria was watching them. The couple then had a child together, my client's grandfather, who all his life was terrified of hot water. Her grandfather told the family that he never felt safe with his mother, fearing she would one day kill him. As a joke in the family, the children would often tease the grandfather, chasing him with cups of hot tea and coffee. The grandfather's daughter, Paula's mother, had given birth to a stillborn baby girl, when Paula, the firstborn, was three years old. The sister was never named, and never spoken about. In fact, she had never even had a burial. Instead, the body was removed and disposed of. My attention went two places: to the girl left in Italy, and to the idea of a sacrificing or a balancing in the system for the deaths of the toddlers.

I facilitated two sessions with Paula. Her husband came to both. Holding hands, they appeared to be very much in love. He was supportive with her in a gentle and loving way. He knew the neighbor had not been breaking into their home, but he gave Paula all the space she needed to come to this fact on her own.

In our first session together, as in most first sessions with clients, I took a family history by constructing a genogram. Extending back three, or maybe four, generations, we note the traumatic events, the tragic or early deaths, the losses, the leavings — the painful experiences where the loving energy in the family may have become impeded. I ask many questions designed to create a new awareness or to allow blocked feelings of grief to resurface. My questions are intended to help the client chip into the unchallenged myths in the family. I might ask something like: "What do you think your grandmother might have been feeling when her mother left the family for another man?" Or, "How do you imagine your grandmother looked at your mother, when all the children before your mother died in infancy? How might your mother have wanted to take care of her mother in such a situation?"

When we encounter feelings in the system that are blocked, clients are often surprised to discover that love is the culprit. They're surprised to learn that numbness is a defensive response meant only to block the pain, yet it blocks the love as well. It's easy to blame or label members of our families who are shut down emotionally as, "cold or mean" when they simply hurt so much because they love so much.

I then ask many questions about the client's parents, siblings, and children, and how they're all doing in life. I explore the client's marital or relationship history, and discuss in depth his or her presenting issues or symptoms. I also ask that the client give me a list of adjectives and phrases describing each parent.

I find that one's attitude toward one's parents is a crucial determinant in one's healing process. The more one rejects the parents, the more ingrained are the symptoms. I almost always find this to be true. So I dig with more questions. I might ask, for example, "What's the worst thing you remember witnessing or experiencing with your mother, something she said to you, or said to someone else, or something that was said to her, or something you witnessed happening to her, or you heard had happened to her?" I ask the client to pick the earliest memory. I then ask the same questions about the father. By asking these types of questions, the real feelings toward the parents begin to surface.

Then we look back in the system for what I call, "turning points," times when the love energy couldn't move forward. When no relevant information is available, we go prospecting for gold nuggets in the family stream. I ask questions meant to pry open the back door, questions such as: "What is the secret that's not talked about in your family? What's the information that was talked about maybe only once when you were small?" By asking these, and the other types of questions, I begin to formulate my hypothesis, a direction in which we might proceed for healing.

After I formulate a hypothesis, I let it go. I forget about it, allowing myself to be surprised by whatever shows up. I become quiet and listen to words, hunches, and intuitions that seem to appear spontaneously inside me, without thinking, or without thinking too much. I've learned to trust the voice inside me that leads me to ask a question, or touch a shoulder, or say something that appears to be bizarre or absurd.

In general, during an individual session, I ask more questions than I might when doing constellation work in a group. With the use of representatives in the group, I apply more the principle of "show me, don't tell me," observing the placement of representatives, their expressions, their body language, their internal and external movements, as well as my perceptions in the field, before continuing with my questioning. I ask, at first, for only enough information to determine what or who is needed in the constellation. Then I sit back and trust the work as it unfolds.

For me, less is always more: the fewer people in a constellation, the more concentrated the energy, the greater potential for a healing movement.

In our second and final session together, Paula and I proceeded to set up a family constellation using the small wooden figurines and a tabletop. Even without the resource of live representatives, both the client and therapist have access to the morphogenetic field of the family system via the figurines. The figurines seem to have an entrancing effect as they are placed into relationships with one another. They appear animated and alive. They seem to take on the characteristics of the family members they represent. The field, as well, becomes alive. Holes, empty spaces in the system, heavy emotions, as well as hidden family loyalties, can all be perceived or discerned, as both the client and the facilitator enter a miniature doorway into the dynamics of the family system.

Often, at the beginning of an individual session, I might ask a client to choose figurines to represent the present family, or family of origin, and to create his or her internal image on the table, before I take any other information. In this way, I get a snapshot of the family dynamics, and how the client may be entangled.

Paula picked figurines from the box, and placed them on the table in a manner consistent with her internal image. After a series of movements, where she acknowledged the forgotten family members with healing phrases, and arranged the figurines in a positive way, Paula started to cry. All the missing children who had not been grieved for in this family were now lined up in their rightful places. She gave a special place in her heart to all of them: the girl left behind in Italy, the two toddlers, and the stillborn sister — all of whom had been forgotten.

To the toddlers, she said: "Dear Children, I have nothing to do with what happened to you. I am only the great granddaughter.

Please look kindly upon me when I'm not harmed or frightened like you."

To her great grandmother, she said: "My dear Great Grandmother, Maria, please give me your blessing as your great granddaughter. Please be kind to me when I don't torture myself the way you might have tortured yourself."

In the session, we concentrated on Paula's fear of being harmed, a fear that lived in this family for four generations, by honoring those who were most likely to feel great terror and pain. Paula connected these feelings with her great grandmother and the two dead stepchildren. She was able to look at her great grandmother with warm feelings, brought about by an image of Maria as a young girl playing outdoors. After acknowledging the guilt Maria must have felt, the burden Maria had to carry as part of her fate, Paula imagined that Maria could only be peaceful when her figurine was positioned among the dead children. In her inner process, Paula reported that Maria and the children were all together in heaven, and appeared to be at peace with each other. All four children, including the stillborn baby, were now with her. We then finished the session with a process in which Paula, with eyes closed, thanked her neighbor for leading her to find healing in her family, bowed to her, and ended their rivalry. Paula was finally at peace. Several weeks later, Paula called my office to report that she was doing really well, and that her fears of being assaulted had disappeared.

★ ★ ★

In all three cases discussed above, it was important in the healing process that the clients looked respectfully at both the perpetrators and the victims who were not acknowledged in their families. For Sara, the image of her grandfather and the driver who killed him embracing affected her in a profound way. Samantha was able to find peace when her mother held the grandfather who raped her in her heart with love. Imagining Great Grandmother Maria in heaven together with the two dead boys and the daughter she left behind created the energy needed for Paula's obsessive fantasies to quiet. With both energies operating in a self-injurer, perpetrator and victim, healing can occur when missing family members are honored and given a place in the system from which they've been excluded.

In the end, it seems that those who are most able to trust their inner images are those who are most capable of making profound healing movements. When we can respect our inner processes, our healing images, and envision them as part of something greater, perhaps even something divine, then our entrenched attitudes and perceptions have a chance to shift. Healing images come to us freely. We don't go to them. We don't create them or make them up. They seem to arise spontaneously, much like visitations or gifts from the higher realms that, when fully trusted, have the potential to bring us true peace.

References

Hellinger, B. (2001). *Love's Own Truths*. Phoenix, AZ: Zeig, Tucker & Theisen.

Levenkron, S. (1998). *Cutting*. New York: W. W. Norton.

Rinpoche, S. (1992). *The Tibetan Book of Living and Dying*. San Francisco: HarperCollins.

Ritche, G. (1978). *Return from Tomorrow*. Grand Rapids, MI: Zondervan.

Stanley, B., Gameroff, M. J., Michalsen, V., & Mann, J. J. (2001). Are suicide attempters who self-mutilate a unique population? *American Journal of Psychiatry, 158(3)*, 427-432.

Tolle, E. (1999) *The Power of Now*. Novato, CA: New World Library.

Zila, L. M. & Kiselica, M. S. (2001). Understanding and counseling self-mutilation in female adolescents and young adults. *Journal of Counseling & Development, 79*, 46-52.

13

Spiritual Dimensions of Illness and Health

by Bert Hellinger

If we stand in our places as members of a family, we feel immediately better when we look at certain other members with whom we feel in tune. By the same token, when we look at family members with whom we are not in agreement — or whom we reject rather than love —we feel uneasy or angry or sad. Both love and rejection are felt in the body, causing us to feel better or worse as they take hold.

The Family Field

However, it often is not a personal matter; that is, we are not, as individuals, in agreement or disagreement with others in the family. It is the family as a whole, comprising not only its living members but also those who have died, that has a particular dynamic stance. Because a family is part of a field that is made up of both the living and the dead, they are all in resonance with one another, for better or for worse. In this field, none of the family can be excluded or lost, and the field is in disorder if members are rejected or forgotten.

These individuals exercise a strong influence on the present family and on the health of its members. This influence often shows up in illness. What does this mean? It means that an illness often represents an excluded member of the family. Put another way, this illness or malady encompasses the excluded member, forcing us, through the pain that it causes, to look at the excluded and to acknowledge his or her right to belong and to take his or her place among all the other members of the family. Therefore, while we may feel that an illness is in dissonance with our body, we become aware that it is actually in resonance with another person.

Perhaps you'd like to check this now for yourselves. You may close your eyes if you wish and come in tune with your body. Then you go to the organ or muscle or bone that hurts. You connect with that organ, become one with it. You allow yourself to look in the direction it wants you to look. Perhaps the person with whom this organ is in resonance comes into view. You look at that person with love, open your heart, take the person into your soul, and give him or her a home in you. Then, after a little while, you allow yourself to feel whether there has been any change in the organ that hurt, and you thank that organ for directing your attention to the person who had been missing from your soul.

Illnesses very often are connected to the fate of another member of the family that has been excluded or forgotten. Health, on the other hand, is restored when this excluded person is welcomed back into the family. Illness results when one person becomes entangled with the fate of another family member, who may have died many generations before. Thus, health is made possible when the neglected family member is received back into the family with love and when reconciliation with that person has been achieved.

Essential Insights

On the surface, this seems to be a very practical approach. Does it also have a spiritual dimension? Yes. It presupposes that in our soul we acknowledge that all people, irrespective of any moral judgment, have the same right to belong. This runs contrary to many religious beliefs, for instance in Christianity, where the predominant idea is that some people are chosen by God to be close to him and blessed, and that others are rejected by him and condemned.

On the familial level, some members of a family are considered to have the right to belong, whereas others have forfeited this right and are excluded. But the earth that supports and nourishes us supports and nourishes all beings, whether we consider them good or bad. The sun shines upon the good and the bad equally, and rain falls upon the just and the unjust equally. Therefore, the creative movement that keeps everything going is kind to everything and supports everything. To tune into this movement in every phase of life is what I would call spiritual. To give everything and everybody a place in our souls and in our hearts tunes us into this fundamental movement. To be in tune with everything as it is — this is spiritual. From this spiritual attitude and stance, we gain essential insights with regard to illness and health. When we are in tune with these insights, we help people in a spiritual way.

Illness and Conscience

There are other aspects of spiritual healing that I want to discuss briefly.

In the work I do, it becomes apparent that many illnesses are connected to the idea that we can save somebody by taking upon ourselves the illness or the fate of that person. We observe this especially with children. Very often a child wants to take upon him- or herself the illness of the mother, for instance. Such children become sad like the mother, become ill like the mother, want to die like her or in place of her. If they wish or do this, they feel innocent and good. They feel in tune with their conscience, because they do this out of love. Therefore, they get ill with a good conscience. Their conscience supports their illness and their wish to die.

I offer an example. In a workshop for teachers and difficult students in Mexico, a teacher presented the case of a 12-year-old boy, who refused to learn any more. In a constellation, I placed the boy next to his teacher with his parents opposite. I looked at the boy and said to him, "You are sad." At once, he began to weep. I looked at the mother and saw that she too began to weep. From this, I concluded that the boy's sadness was connected with something that had happened in his mother's family. I asked her and she answered that she had a twin sister who died at birth.

I placed a representative for her twin sister at some distance looking away from the family, and then asked the mother to stand behind her. I asked her how she felt in this place. She said, "Here, I feel better."

What does this show? In her heart, she wanted to follow her twin sister into death. This is a very common dynamic, which comes to light through family constellations. It is a dynamic that leads to illness and death. A person says in her heart: "I follow you into death."

Then, in this constellation, I asked the boy to take the place of his mother behind her twin sister and asked him how he felt there. He, too, answered, "Here, I feel better."

What does this mean? He said in his heart to his mother, "I die in your place." This, too, is a common dynamic that leads to illness and death. The movement revealed why the boy no longer wanted to learn.

Healing Movements

The question now is, "How can this dynamic that leads to illness and death be stopped or reversed?" Obviously, the twin sister of the mother was in a certain way excluded from the family. Perhaps the pain of her loss was so great that they did not grieve for her in an appropriate way. The solution would be that she is received back into the family.

The movement that will achieve this is very simple. In this constellation, I placed the representative of the twin sister next to the mother. They looked into each other's eyes and embraced with deep love. Then the mother turned to her husband and said, "Now I will stay." Then she looked at her son and said, "Now I will stay." The boy's face lit up with joy. He was no longer sad. Once the twin sister was received back into the family, neither mother nor son was compelled to follow her into death any longer. And, of course, the father also was happy, because he too had felt that his wife wanted to leave the family.

Uniting with the Divine

So, now the question becomes, "What about this might be considered spiritual?" My initial response is that it is the idea that nobody is excluded or forgotten, that everybody who belongs to the family is given his or her rightful place in the family. In the second place, it is that everybody is left to his or her own fate and destiny, and that nobody attempts to get in the way of life and death. Finally, it means that nobody assumes that he or she has the right to take upon themselves a responsibility that must be left to God; however we may define that word. This conviction is the result of an insight — of a spiritual insight — that our destiny and our illness and health are in the hands of forces that are beyond our understanding and beyond our hopes and our fears.

How can we then help those who are ill? We can only help when we remain in tune with these forces, when we do only that which they permit us to do — and if we allow them to work through us. Such helping and healing is humble. And yet, it can heal not only individuals, it also can heal a family, a clan, and even a whole nation. All the great spiritual men and women were also healers in this wider sense. At the same time, healing in the deepest sense is uniting with the divine. It brings peace to the body, to the soul, to the family, and even further. Therefore, spiritual healing is going with a movement of love that is beyond merely personal love and personal concern. It is doing and non-doing at the same time, allowing something greater to take over. It is common and rare, humble and vast. What does one call this way of helping and healing? I call it spiritual.

About the Contributors

J. Edward Lynch, Ph.D., is Chair of the Marriage and Family Therapy Program at Southern Conn. State University in New Haven, CT. He is coauthor, with his wife, of *Principles and Practices of Structural Family Therapy* and has been a contributor of chapters to several other books. He also has had many articles published in the United States and France. He has been leading family therapy and gestalt therapy workshops since 1979 in France, Spain, Belgium, Germany, Italy and Moscow. He currently is training therapists in family constellations in Connecticut. (www.hellingerct.com)

Suzi Tucker is Editor-in-Chief of Zeig, Tucker & Theisen, Publishers, and has worked as an editor in the behavioral sciences for 20 years. She was introduced to Bert Hellinger's family constellations in that capacity, but went on to organize workshops on the topic, eventually cofounding the Bert Hellinger Institute, USA, with systemic therapist Harald Hohnen. The Institute launched numerous trainings and helped to establish the work in the United States. Suzi Tucker teaches an ongoing Guided Learning in NYC and presents workshops regularly. (www.hellingerapproach.com)

Dan Booth Cohen, MBA, MA Psych, is a Constellation facilitator practicing in metropolitan Boston. He has had a diverse career as a small business owner, peace activist and counselor over the past 30 years. As a peace activist, he was a founding member of the City of Cambridge Peace Commission and co-Director of the Boston Children of War Program. He completed the Bert Hellinger Institute, USA training program in 2002 and regularly travels to Europe for additional training and supervision. He is currently a Ph.D. candidate doing research on the longitudinal outcomes of constellation work. (www.hiddensolution.com)

Jamy Faust and Peter Faust have been studying and practicing complementary healing for more than 15 years. They learned the constellation method from the Bert Hellinger Institute, USA, programs. **Peter Faust,** M.Ac., holds a master's degree in classical acupuncture and herbal medicine and is a leading facilitator in the Hero's Journey men's programs. **Jamy Faust,** M.A. has a master's degree in holistic counseling and psychology, and is a long-time practitioner of Japanese Shiatsu, Hawaiian Huna healing and Tibetan Buddhism. Both Jamy and Peter graduated from, and have held faculty positions at, the Barbara Brennan School of Healing. They maintain individual private practices, as well as leading constellation workshops. (www.hellingerboston.com)

Daniel P. Gates, MS, MFT, has been a licensed marriage and family therapist in the state of Connecticut for 18 years. He is currently in private practice. He holds masters degrees in special education and in marriage and family therapy, both from Southern Connecticut State University. He is a clinical member of the International Association of EMDR and an approved EMDR consultant. He has been training in family constellations with Edward Lynch for the last several years. He is the author of "Group Work with Juvenile Sex Offenders" published in *Voices from the Field: Group Work Responds* (1994).

Mary M. Gates, MSW, MDiv, is an Episcopal priest and a clinical social worker licensed in Connecticut. She is currently in private practice with adults, adolescents, and families, and previously managed an out-patient treatment program for adolescents and families. She is also a retreat leader. She holds an MSW degree from the University of Connecticut and a master of divinity degree from Yale University. She is currently training in family constellations with Dr. Lynch.

Michael I. Gurevich, MD, is a board certified psychiatrist with subspecialties in addiction psychiatry and holistic medicine. He has received extensive training in multiple alternative healing modalities: acupuncture, systemic family constellations, applied psycho-neurobiology, kinesiological testing, Eye Movement Desensitization and Reprocessing (EMDR), guided imagery, yoga, Chi Gong, and apitherapy. He is currently working in private practice in Glen Head, NY, where he combines holistic and allopathic treatment modalities.

Barbara Lynch, Ph.D., is Director of the Marriage and Family Therapy Program, Southern Connecticut Sate University, New Haven. She is coauthor, with her husband, of *Principles and Practices of Structural Family Therapy*. A couples therapist and clinical supervisor for over 30 years, she is also an international presenter in couples therapy and has published widely on the topic.

M. Jane Peterson is the founder of the Human Systems Institute. She started her professional career as an engineer and manager in a high tech firm. Jane has also been a professional ceramic artist. She has studied with a variety of cutting edge, systemic thinkers from Dr. Arnold Mindell of Process Oriented Psychology, to the Peruvian mystic and shaman Américo Yábar. Jane is a master practitioner of Neuro-linguistic Programming, a certified clinical hypnotherapist, and a certified professional coach. (www.human-systems-institute.com)

Dale Schusterman, D.C., DIBAK, is a chiropractic physician, practicing in Virginia since 1977. He is a graduate of the University of Michigan (1973) and a Diplomate in Applied Kinesiology (1986) from the International College of Applied Kinesiology. He is the author of *Sign Language of the Soul: A Handbook for Healing* and he teaches courses on these healing methods. Dr. Schusterman also facilitates family constellation workshops and trainings. (www.signlanguageofthesoul.com)

Andrea F. Stuck, Ph.D., LISW, is founder and owner of Stuck?, Inc., in Worthington, Ohio, which specializes in consulting with business organizations on organizational/systems change. In addition, she maintains a private psychotherapy practice serving individuals, couples, families, and adolescents. She consults across a variety of venues from business to one-on-one coaching to psychotherapy, blending family constellation work with other relevant modalities. (www.andystuck.com)

Mark Wolynn is a board-certified regression therapist, a medical hypnotherapist and a family systems therapist, who trains and supervises psychotherapists in the United States. Founder and Co-Director of the Bert Hellinger Institute of Western PA, he conducts family constellation workshops and trainings throughout the USA and in Latin America, as well as for the University of Pittsburgh's Graduate School of Social Work's Continuing Education Program. Mark Wolynn specializes in treating depression, anxiety, obsessive thoughts, fears, phobias, chronic pain and other medical conditions unresponsive to conventional treatment. (www.hellingerpa.com)